I will own th[em] [...] [...]
dead or alive [...] [...]
shortly.

Please send papers by first
mail as soon as possible as
it is quite necessary that we
should be after him at once —
Yours very truly
Jack Duncan
Detective

Dec. 4/77 Wrote to R. M.
Voucher, Co. Atty, Limestone Co.
for indictment &c.

BOUNTY HUNTER

by
Rick
Miller

THE
EARLY WEST

Creative Publishing Company
Box 9292, Ph. 409-775-6047
College Station, Texas 77840

Bounty Hunter

Miller, Rick, 1941—
    Bounty hunter.

    (The Early West)
    Bibliography: p. 235
    Includes index.
    1. Duncan, John Ripley, 1850-1911. 2. Hardin, John Wesley,
1853-1895. 3. Outlaws—Texas—History—19th century. 4. Frontier
and pioneer life—Texas. 5. Texas—History—1846-1950. 6. Detectives—Texas—Biography.
I. Title. II. Series: Early West series.
F391.D95M54   1988   976.4'061'0922   88-7168

ISBN 0-932702-41-4

Limited edition of 1000 copies

First Edition, First Printing

Dedication

Dedicated to

Paula

Bounty Hunter

Table of Contents

Bounty Hunter

6

Introduction

In one sense, there is a degree of irony in my introducing this first biography of Jack Duncan, detective-bounty hunter. Some years ago while researching William Henry Hutchinson and his involvement in the capture of John Wesley Hardin, I delved into newspapers and other records in an effort to learn more about Duncan, who was there with Hutchinson in capturing Hardin. He had captured my imagination almost as much as Hardin. Somewhere I had read that, prior to his becoming a special ranger in Texas, he had been a Chicago detective. This in itself was very interesting because there was such a difference in the two settings: a man seeking evil-doers in that populous city certainly must change his techniques and life-style to track down outlaws in Texas. Besides this seemingly drastic change of turf, there was a certain strange drama in the life of this man who grabbed onto fame by running down Wes Hardin, the deadliest gunfighter of Texas, and who would later suffer the ignominy of allowing himself to fall into the situation of being shot by a prostitute—soiled dove Hattie Washburn--with *his* own pistol on *her* turf! Perhaps this ascendancy to near greatness in capturing Hardin, then descending to scandal in the Washburn affair only underscores Duncan's humanness. At any rate, my interest in Duncan's career at that time was not diminished, although it never took any definite shape other than a meager file of newspaper articles and other worthwhile notes.

It was with enthusiasm that I encouraged Rick Miller to pursue his research in the life and career of Duncan. Perhaps, there was a mixture of reluctance to give him what I had gathered, yet at the same time I wanted his efforts to go far beyond what mine had: to result in an outstanding biography of this now-forgotten lawman. There are enough serious works devoted to those few westerners who are known to everyone—Hickok, Earp, Cassidy, Sundance—but unless serious work is done in researching the lesser known and now almost forgotten characters, it will be much too late for future historians to attempt to create a more complete panorama of the "Gunfighter's West." There were hundreds of individuals who lived a life with as much excitement as Kid Antrim or Doc Holliday. Many may remain only a name on a lawman's list; some occasionally will be saved from total oblivion by serious historians such as Rick Miller.

For a man who in his heyday was a celebrity, one who could boast of being the most successful detective in Texas, history has not been kind. Apparently, his one shining moment of bringing Hardin back to Texas in irons, with Ranger Armstrong, was extinguished with his own death. Possibly, it was a logical conclusion since everything happening from that August 23rd day onward would be anticlimactic. No other outlaw would ever hold a candle to Hardin. Not surprisingly, at Hardin's death in 1895, Duncan would again receive attention. A long interview was published in the *Dallas Daily Times Herald* in which Duncan revealed that ever since Hardin's release from prison, he had been kept informed of his movements.

It would be fascinating and interesting to know exactly how Duncan perceived his own role in the establishing of law and order in Texas. Although he referred to himself as a detective, he was also very, very conscious of the price on a wanted man's head. There is a strong negative connotation with the term "bounty hunter," as that man tracks down and captures or kills outlaws for whom a reward is offered, solely for the reward. The term "detective" does not place the stress on the monetary inducement involved. Duncan referred to himself as a detective, as did reporters who interviewed him (perhaps out of good taste). But the amount of the reward certainly was a strong factor in Duncan's decision as to which outlaws to pursue. In an 1895 interview, he was able to recite the names of the badmen he had captured and the amount of the reward he had earned for each—an impressive list which totaled over $12,000. Perhaps the question of Duncan's ridding Texas of outlaws for the sake of *justice* or merely for the rewards offered never consciously entered his mind. Without letters he may have written or other personal documents or statements, we may always be left to conjecture on how he perceived himself in this professional role.

This biography fills a great gap, as it provides the very first biography—in any form—of this particular lawman. Best of all, it is a serious and carefully researched work and is well written. I can happily state that Rick Miller's research went far beyond what I had once envisioned doing. Perhaps the word "exhaustive" is overused, but with the Duncan biography, it is proper and accurate. One man's life is never known totally to history, but the serious historian must do his best, and Rick Miller has done that. There may well be additional items concerning Duncan uncovered here and there, but what is certain is that any future historian who hopes to do anything with Duncan, Armstrong (who needs a biographer), Texas outlaws of the 19th Century or John Wesley Hardin must utilize *The Bounty Hunter* as an essential book.

Chuck Parsons
January, 1988

Preface

Without question, one of the most legendary and deadliest of frontier badmen was the notorious John Wesley Hardin. He was not an "outlaw" in the sense that most people think of it, such as was Jesse James or Billy the Kid, but, instead, just that—a *bad man.* Lawmen on his trail knew he was quick on the trigger and wouldn't hesitate to kill, but did not think of him in terms of a thief or rustler. Today, the image of the western gunfighter is distorted by years of media treatment. Hardin, however, was considered Texas' foremost desperado in his own time. Given the deadly reputation he had while alive, it is understandable that his pursuers would take every precaution to stack the deck in their favor before taking him on. Such a confrontation would not be a time for reckless bravado—such as that which cost Deputy Sheriff Charles Webb his life at Hardin's hands in Comanche, Texas.

Viewed in this perspective—that Hardin was hot-tempered, fast on the draw, and far too eager to spill blood—in a time when fierce loyalties and emotions overrode the strictures of the law, a decision by any lawman to go after this gunman and bring him before the bar of justice seems that much more remarkable. Yet Jack Duncan did that. Whatever his motive, reward or some sense of justice denied, Duncan entered Hardin's circle of loyal friends and relatives, unarmed against any reprisal by them should his identity be discovered except for his quick wits and ingenuity. And he did the job he was sent into the enemy camp to do. The fleeing killer was located and, in a few short days, was en route in chains to a Texas prison and, for all practical purposes, his days of terror were over.

Bounty Hunter

For his role in this frontier drama, Jack Duncan achieved immediate public attention as a skilled, able manhunter. However, beyond the oft-repeated tale of his deed in this event, Duncan has remained only an obscure actor in Hardin's legend. Today, little is known of the detective outside his association with the Rangers in tracking Hardin down. In truth, as might be suspected, Jack Duncan was a tough, resourceful, persistent man. He possessed a level of courage that enabled him to overcome not only the geographical and technological obstacles that lawmen of today can fully appreciate in getting his man, but also a physical handicap that certainly threatened his effectiveness. In the decade in which he was most active, 1877 to 1887, he made a name for himself as one of the best detectives in Texas, if not the Southwest.

Making his headquarters in early Dallas, Duncan rubbed shoulders with some of the most notorious men and women of that time—people who came to be singled out for exploits on both sides of the law, such as the Younger brothers, Doc Holliday, Longhair Jim Courtright, Belle Starr, and others. He developed his own network of informants and sources that allowed him to keep tabs on and track down those with a price on their heads, bringing to this task his own creative abilities and ingenuity to discover that information which would allow him to ferret out the quarry successfully. Duncan knew, as do today's detectives, that, for the most part, such information could come only from people close to the hunted fugitive or those who moved in the same circles. Thus, Duncan had to mingle in a milieu of gamblers, prostitutes, and cutthroats—a bawdy world of social outcasts who knew what was going on and who was doing it.

Despite being raised by pious, God-fearing parents, Duncan was comfortable in the saloons and sporting houses of early Dallas, and the life-style he adopted reflected that environment. He was a human, earthy man, but not a bad man. And like so many of the other prominent figures of the Old West—Hickok,

12

Earp, and others—his sterling qualities were occasionally offset by those human frailties and weaknesses that play a role in shaping and defining one's uniqueness as an individual. Duncan was certainly multi-dimensional, and the troubles and tragedies he encountered during his life's trek, coupled with the manner and courage with which he faced them, speak volumes about the man and what he was made of. The late 1870s and early 1880s was a primitive time in Texas, and prevailing conditions and attitudes, coupled with ineffective law enforcement, nurtured the John Wesley Hardins of that time and provided an environment in which they could flourish. Jack Duncan typifies the sort of man, be he detective, Ranger, or local lawman, who was so necessary to the taming of the frontier. He was, to borrow a trite phrase, a "man of his time," and he deserves greater recognition for his contribution.

This book has been written with two primary objectives. The first is simply to tell the story of Jack Duncan. For the casual reader interested only in that story or a simple entertainment, the frequent annotations may be ignored. They relate to the second objective, that of historical accuracy. Thus, the frequent annotations and any extended comments in the endnotes after each chapter are there for the benefit of serious "Old West Buffs" or other researchers interested in the sources from which I have drawn a fact or conclusion. Such comments were primarily intended to deal with areas of controversy which are not of sufficient importance to include in the text and which would have needlessly interrupted the telling of the story.

Basically, the book was written in chronological order, from antecedents to death. A major digression is taken in the second chapter in order to give some flavor of the environment of early Dallas in which Duncan moved after coming from Kentucky. Here, there was an opportunity to deal with many of the infamous characters who called Dallas home after the Civil War. Much of the information about their presence included in that chapter is printed for the first time and, although perhaps trivial in some cases, nevertheless helps in a small way to diminish some of the myths and reveal the truth. Hopefully, it will not prove distracting to the casual reader, and serious researchers will find it of assistance in filling in some of the blanks.

As in any research effort such as this, one can only work with available information, and some gaps cannot be filled. Of course, this is frustrating for a researcher who is eager to provide a definitive account of the life of someone like Jack Duncan. However, despite good intentions, there are some gaps in the recounting of his career, and future research will, I'm sure, ultimately uncover that information buried in some dusty record book or file that I didn't think about or locate. Among one of the major frustrations was the inability to locate one single likeness or photograph of Jack Duncan, which not even his descendants have ever seen. Another rather bizarre frustration was the unlikely coincidence that the particular collection of Dallas newspapers from which a microfilm record was made had many key articles dealing with Duncan's exploits neatly clipped out. Other sources of information helped overcome this somewhat, but no doubt some excellent firsthand accounts were lost.

This research effort would not have been possible without the help, cooperation, and encouragement of a large number of people. I am truly appreciative to the descendants of Jack Duncan's family who invited me into their homes and who, through their time and interest, made a major contribution to the telling of his story. His granddaughter, Frances Beebe of Houston, Texas, was most gracious in recalling the family stories she heard as a child, as well as in sharing family photographs. Her husband, Ward, who is himself a history buff, was quite helpful in giving me some direction in the style of this book. William B. Duncan, of North Richland Hills, Texas, spent a rainy day with me going over family stories that he heard from his father and his grandfather, George McAfee "Mack" Duncan, who was Jack's brother and probably closer to him than anyone else.

Dorothy Young, Mack Duncan's granddaughter, of Round Rock, Texas, also took a keen interest in the book and has been enthusiastic about its progress. Mrs. Joan Courtney, of Dallas, wife of Jack Duncan's late grandson, Frank Courtney, gave of her valuable time to answer my many questions. I owe a great deal to all of them.

A special debt of thanks is due two very prominent researchers of the frontier scene. Chuck Parsons, who has taken a special interest in John Wesley Hardin, not only agreed to write an introduction to this book, but has been most encouraging and has shared both information and photographs that he had accumulated in his own research. Chuck is one of the more capable and responsible researchers whose interest in accuracy parallels my own, and I am grateful for his input. A real pioneer in this field is Ed Bartholomew whose efforts at researching, writing, and publishing have made him most respected among buffs such as myself. A presentation he made in 1980 for the National Association and Center for Outlaw and Lawman History (NOLA) was one of the motivating factors that led me to try my hand at writing. His contribution to this book of information and ideas has been most helpful.

This book could not have come about without the able assistance and interest of the staff of the Texas/Dallas History and Archives Division of the Dallas Public Library. For many years, this professional and competent group has repeatedly guided me to sources of information I didn't know existed or expedited access to critical materials. Rather than leaving me to my own devices in figuring out how best to use their facilities, they took a sincere interest in the project and gave willingly of their time to locate new sources as well as "brainstorm" different ideas. I especially would like to thank Marcelle Hull, archival librarian, and Lucille Boykin, a local history specialist who has more feel for Dallas history than anyone I know. I am also appreciative of the interest and help of archivists Gary

Bounty Hunter

Jennings, Peter Kurilecz, and Gerald Saxon, all very able, competent, and committed.

A number of other people across the country also gave valuable assistance that deserves acknowledgment:

ALABAMA: A. J. Wright, Tuscaloosa; Lucy Farrow, Draughon Library, Auburn University; Genene E. Nelson, Jackie H. Pouncy, and Albert K. Craig, Jr., Alabama Department of Archives and History, Montgomery; the Mobile Public Library.

ARIZONA: Shirley Macias, Arizona Department of Library, Archives and Public Records, Phoenix.

ARKANSAS: Dr. Larry D. Ball, State University; the Fort Smith Public Library.

FLORIDA: Sandra Johnson, assistant curator, Pensacola Historical Museum; Ernie Lee Magaha, clerk of the Circuit and County Courts, Escambia County; Leora M. Sutton, historical researcher, Escambia County Circuit Court.

KANSAS: Larry Jochims, research historian, and Nancy Sherbert, Curator of Photographs, Kansas State Historical Society, Topeka.

KENTUCKY: The staff of the Brown-Pusey House, Elizabethtown; the Public Records Division, Kentucky Department for Libraries and Archives, Frankfort; Charles B. Castner, corporate communications, Seaboard System Railroad, Louisville; Paul F. Coates, director, micrographics/archives department, Jefferson County Circuit Court, Louisville; Mary Jean Kinsman, researcher, Jefferson County Office of Historic Preservation and Archives, Louisville; George M. Dexter, associate registrar, University of Kentucky, Lexington.

MISSOURI: Karen G. Quiring, State Historical Society of Missouri, Columbia; Mrs. Katherine Ismert, Kansas City.

NEW MEXICO: Lawrence Merchant, Carlsbad; Linda Blazer, assistant archivist, Rio Grande Historical Collections, New Mexico State University, Las Cruces; Elvis E. Fleming, volunteer

16

archivist, Chaves County Historical Society, Roswell; Sandra Esquibel, reference librarian, New Mexico State Library, Santa Fe.

OKLAHOMA: Christine M. Bittle, Oklahoma Historical Society, Oklahoma City.

TEXAS: Casey Greene, director, Library and Archives of the Dallas Historical Society; Dr. Larry D. Sall, assistant director for special collections, University of Texas at Dallas; Victoria Fornicola-Jones, administrative services officer for Dallas County; Raymond Bouska, manager of the Greenwood Cemetery Association, Dallas; Thelma B. Bradley, University Park; the offices of the Dallas County District and County Clerks; Alton B. Lynch, Grayson County district clerk; Jacqueline Vannoy, assistant library director, Sherman Public Library; the A. M. Aikin Regional Archives, Paris Junior College; the Paris Public Library; Dr. James H. Conrad, university archives, East Texas State University, Commerce; Dixie Webster, deputy district clerk, Cass County; Itoko McNully, library assistant, El Paso Public Library; Mrs. Virginia Ming, Texas Collection, Baylor University, Waco; the offices of the District and County Clerks, Marion County; M. A. Vaverek and Iris T. Schumann, archives-special collections, Southwest Texas State University, San Marcos; Bill O'Neal, Carthage; Nancy Merz, Carol M. Finney, Cynthia J. Beeman, and Donaly E. Brice, Texas State Archives, Austin; May Schmidt, Austin Public Library; William H. Richter, assistant archivist, Eugene C. Barker Texas History Center, Austin; Patricia Chadwell, Fort Worth Public Library; Charles W. Hughes, archivist, Texas Christian University, Fort Worth; Cecil McFarland, U. S. Army Corps of Engineers, Fort Worth; Carol Roark, assistant curator of photographs, Amon Carter Museum, Fort Worth; Texas and Southwestern Cattle Raisers Association, Fort Worth; and Barbara Rust, archivist, Federal Archives and Records Center, Fort Worth.

Bounty Hunter

Also, I appreciate the assistance of R. Michael McReynolds, Marion M. Johnson, and Richard C. Crawford of the Civil Archives Division, U. S. National Archives and Records Service, in fielding and responding to my inquiries; the National Society of the Daughters of the American Revolution, as well as the United Daughters of the Confederacy; and Timothy R. Crotty, Chief, Workforce Records Management Division, U. S. Office of Personnel Management, and Larry McGrath, National Personnel Records Center, General Services Administration, St. Louis, Missouri, for assistance in accessing the personnel folder of George M. Duncan.

Because of the diligence of a good friend, Dr. Nora Stafford, readers are spared a host of split infinitives and punctuation errors. Her expertise was indispensable, and I am in her debt.

Finally, absolutely, positively none of this book would have seen the light of day were it not for the loving indulgence of my wife, Paula, who, in addition to typing a final draft of the manuscript, kept everything else in our lives going in some form of rational order at those times I was 100 years away.

Rick Miller
Killeen, Texas

18

Preface

Katherine Ann Daughtery Duncan, mother of Jack Duncan, as she appeared in the early 1900's. (Courtesy of the Texas/Dallas History and Archives Division, Dallas Public Library).

Chapter 1

Kentucky Beginnings

John Wesley Hardin! Though he was but in his early twenties, it had been said that over two dozen men had fallen before his pistol. The stories of his deadly exploits, told and retold, formed the basis of a sort of legend that had grown up around him, making him to seem larger than life. That legend was a key reason why Hardin was the most wanted person in Texas, with a $4,000 bounty on his head. The legend also gave any right-thinking lawman pause to reflect at the idea of a possible confrontation with the gunman. After all, who wanted to add to Hardin's laurels by becoming his next victim?

But now, far from Texas, at a small railroad depot in Pensacola, Florida, the circle was drawing tighter, and the moment was at hand to bring him to bay. People moved about the station platform as they normally did; however, a close observer could detect several men here and there whose miens were more somber as they made every effort to blend in with the comings and goings around them. Interspersed among the crowd, each cautiously avoided a direct glance at the car in which the fugitive entered for fear of giving it all away—or worse, getting himself killed. Jack Duncan shared the apprehension, a gnawing, weak feeling in the pit of the stomach. He knew *who* the fugitive was, and the apprehension he felt was a conscious respect for his quarry that stemmed from what he knew of the truth behind Hardin's legend. The gunman's trail had led from Texas and the bloody Sutton-Taylor feud to this tranquil railroad sta-

Bounty Hunter

tion warmed by a balmy August sun. The hunters were only moments away from springing their hastily-concocted plan, but Hardin's reputation loomed, undermining their confidence that the prey could be successfully taken. Any mistake, no matter how slight, would mean instant death.

Duncan really had no time to reflect on how he had come to be at that depot, waiting outside that train, acutely aware of the heavy pistol beneath his coat. How could he know that what would happen minutes from now would catapult him into public prominence in his own time, as well as into a minor niche in history? It certainly was a long way from the tranquil Kentucky countryside and the young farmboy of only a few years before.

*   *   *   *   *   *

Hardin County had been a prominent part of North Central Kentucky since 1793, with its county seat located in Elizabethtown.[1] In those early days, pioneer settlers traversed the main road that led southwest from E-Town, as it came to be called, to the town of Leitchfield. In 1828, one of those pioneers, Nathaniel J. Duncan, purchased sixty-five acres of prime farmland on the north side of that road, some ten miles southwest of Elizabethtown, near the tiny communities of Stephensburg and Walker's Station. Five years later, his farm established, he purchased an additional 200 acres adjacent to his property.[2] By 1840, Duncan and his wife, Susan, had a family of three sons, including James Alexander Duncan, now thirteen years old.[3]

Nat Duncan helped in the periodic surveying of the Elizabethtown-Leitchfield Road,[4] continuing to build up his farm and add to his already extensive property holdings.[5] More children were born to his family, and his industriousness and labor paid off in a successful, abundant farm.

On November 28, 1846, as was the custom of the day, Nat Duncan and John Daugherty both gave consent for their children, James Duncan and Katherine Ann Daugherty, called Kitty, to marry. Less than two weeks later, James took Kitty as his bride on December 7,[6] the couple settling near their families at Stephensburg. John Daugherty, married to Elizabeth Hoover since 1826,[7] had been a soldier in the War of 1812 and had fought at the Battle of New Orleans.[8]

Early Stephensburg was a small farming community on the Elizabethtown-Leitchfield Road that came to include three churches, including a Presbyterian Church on the Old Camp Ground where farmers and their families would come from surrounding areas to stay for weeks while attending church meetings. The town also had several hotels, stores, and saloons. For the stagecoach from Elizabethtown, Stephensburg was the only stop for passengers until they reached Leitchfield.[9]

James and Kitty's first child, Marion N., was born on August 29, 1847, but lived only a short time, dying in October.[10] A second child, Simeon Winfield Scott Duncan, named after the prominent Mexican War commander, was born on October 22, 1848.[11] Early the next year, Nat Duncan made available large tracts of land to two of his sons, William and James. James purchased 137 acres on the south side of the road for $400.[12] Though neither James nor Kitty could read or write at this time,[13] they, like James's father, began to build a family farm. James continued to buy additional farmland as well as to build his livestock. By the early 1850's, he was paying taxes on 220 acres of land, one slave, nine cows, three horses, and one mule.[14]

John Riley Duncan was born in September, 1850.[15] Almost from the beginning, he was called Jack and, with few exceptions, he would retain this sobriquet for the rest of his life. A third brother, George McAfee Duncan, who was called Mack, was born on Aprial 1, 1854,[16] followed by a sister, Emma, in 1855 or 1856. A second daughter, Susan, named after James's mother, was born in 1859 and, in 1860, daughter Anna came along. By 1860, the Duncan farm had, in addition to these six children, two boarders, W. F. Daugherty, likely a relative of Kitty's, and school teacher M. F. Anderson.[17]

The Duncan farm in 1860 consisted of 240 acres, largely devoted to hay, wheat, and corn. The livestock consisted of ten horses, ten head of cattle, and twelve hogs. James Duncan was assessed taxes on the farm's production of two tons of hay, 250 bushels of wheat, and 2,000 bushels of corn.[18] Certainly, these were prosperous times, and James and Kitty Duncan could take a great deal of satisfaction in the manner in which they had been blessed.

But the countryside was now being caught up in the larger strife threatening to rend the country apart. Like its neighboring states, Kentucky was faced with the conflict over secessionism. Kentucky's State Guard, made up of local militias, was composed principally of membership with a distinctly Southern, pro-secession bias. James Duncan was a member of a local militia unit. However, those in the state who supported the Union held key legislative and governmental posts and thus controlled the reins of political influence. The anti-secessionists were able to reduce legislative funding for the State Guard in an effort to minimize its impact on the decision as to which way the state would go. With the opening shots at Fort Sumter in April, 1861, after Lincoln's election, when the federal government called for volunteers, Kentucky sought to resolve its dilemma by declaring itself neutral and refusing to provide any troops for either side. However, this did not diminish the partisan clamor on the part of both factions within the state. Various units of the pro-Confederate State Guard individually disbanded to go to other states and enlist in the Southern forces. A pro-union "Home Guard" was set up to counter the influence of the State Guard, thus sparking an aggressive recruiting campaign by both for manpower and arms. Of course, the passions were far too strong, and Kentucky's neutrality could not last. As the Union faction steadily increased its political and numerical strength, aided by Lincoln's government, Confederate forces were subsequently ordered from the state and, in September, Kentucky was officially aligned with the Union cause, even though it was a slave state.[19]

James Duncan regretfully left his family and enlisted in the Confederacy at Madison, Arkansas, on September 16, 1861. His unit was subsequently organized as the Eighth Regiment Mounted Infantry of the Confederate Kentucky Volunteers. What had been formerly Company B, 40th Regiment, of the Tennessee Infantry, was attached to the Eighth Regiment in October, 1862, becoming Company K. James Duncan was initially a Second Sergeant in Company K, but he became the First Sergeant and, on January 31, 1863, was elected a Junior Second Lieutenant.[20]

In the meantime, at home in Kentucky, Kitty had given birth to another son, Robert Lee Duncan, on December 18, 1862,[21] the name emphatically underscoring James's political sympathies. According to a story passed down in the Duncan family, when the war was imminent, James Duncan took his family, along with ample provisions, to stay with relatives in Savannah, Georgia. Then, taking his horse, a sword, and a pistol, he left to fight.[22] However, there is a distinct likelihood that Duncan's family remained in Kentucky since, during the course of the war, he and Kitty were periodically involved in several civil lawsuits and land transactions.[23]

On September 22, 1862, the Eighth Kentucky Regiment Infantry reorganized in Mississippi, having surrendered in February after fighting at Fort Donelson in Tennessee and being broken up, before Duncan joined it. Duncan assumed his post as First Sergeant of the newly-organized Company K. The regiment remained briefly in northern Mississippi, meeting Union forces in combat at Coffeyville in December, as well as in several other minor engagements. Assigned to a brigade in Confederate General John C. Pemberton's corps, the Eighth Regiment also was involved in bloody skirmishing at Champion Hills, Baker's Creek, Big Black Bridge, and Edwards Station in

Bounty Hunter

Mississippi, just prior to the fall of Vicksburg in July, 1863. In fighting at Jackson, Mississippi, Company K had already been reduced to fifteen men and, of that, eight were subsequently killed or wounded. James Duncan was one of those wounded.

Apparently because of his wounds, Duncan went on detached service as a Second Lieutenant and was hospitalized in Marion, Mississippi, continuing to receive his monthly salary of $80. By January, 1864, he was on "conscript service" in Mississippi, the next month becoming the acting adjutant in the Volunteer and Conscripts Bureau and Provost Marshal's Department, posted in Grenada, Mississippi. On July 25, 1864, he wrote a letter to his commander requesting continued assignment at the same position. However, the war had by now been seriously and permanently reversed against the Confederacy and, with general collapse following Lee's surrender in April, 1865, James Duncan signed his parole on May 13, 1865, at Meridian, Mississippi, and returned home to his family.[24] The fighting was over.

At home again in Hardin County, James and Kitty sought to take up their lives where they left off. Some of the property they owned was sold off near the small community of Glendale, which had formerly been known as Walker's Station after merchant Lewis B. Walker. There were only a small general store and a few residents making up the town; however, when the Louisville and Nashville Railroad came through, Glendale acquired a post office, with Walker as the first postmaster. A depot was built, and more people settled nearer the small crossroads town.[25] Some of the property in Glendale sold by Duncan was done so on the condition that it never be used for the purpose of conveying intoxicating beverages.[26] Such a provision was certainly consistent with the reputation of James and Kitty Duncan as maintaining strong religious beliefs. Those beliefs must have certainly been tested by the untimely death on June 26, 1866, of three-year-old Robert,[27] perhaps of a fever or some similar ailment which was frequently epidemic in those times.

For the three remaining Duncan boys, however, this was not necessarily a time for all work and no play. Mack Duncan later recalled a time when he, Sim, and Jack repeatedly climbed to the top of one of the many steep hills around Stephensburg and then ran down it, hollering at the top of their lungs, "Damn it, damn it, damn it!" as they raced to the bottom. It was great fun, at least until their father, who was nearby, heard them. Mack said that it was several years before any of them even thought about cursing again.[28]

Selling off more land, James Duncan apparently moved his family the short distance to Glendale in order to start up a dry goods store. In January, 1868, he gave Lewis Walker a note for $5,122.50 in return for considerable acreage in Glendale along the railroad line, anticipating rapid growth in the small town because of the railroad. However, Duncan's business was not successful. He found himself overextended and, in February, 1868, was forced to go into the U. S. District Court in Louisville and file a petition for bankruptcy. On March 20, 1868, attorney James Montgomery of Elizabethtown was appointed by the court as assignee of all of Duncan's property, except for that exempted by law. To the proud Duncan, this was not an acceptable state of affairs. By November of that year, he was able to return to court with a written agreement signed by his creditors, which included both his father and father-in-law, and the bankruptcy petition was withdrawn and his property reconveyed to him.[29] Now, James Duncan began to work on paying off his debts.

In 1868, James and Kitty's final child, a daughter, Mary Frances, was born to them.[30] Family stories have described Mary as being deaf. In the meantime, Sim had attended the University of Kentucky in Lexington, finishing his studies in 1868.[31] By 1870, James was still trying to keep his dry goods business going in Glendale, with Sim helping as a clerk, no doubt diligently working out the agreement with his creditors. Jack worked as a saddler in a small building on a lot they owned in Glendale. But things were still not going well for the family, and it was obvious that they could not keep it up for long.

Just when James Duncan decided to move from his homestead is unknown. Likely, the family's leaving would not be made a moment sooner than he had satisfied the last creditor. The brightest, most promising prospect for a new home and a new start was Texas—an open frontier that offered opportunities for a hardworking man to build a new life for himself and his family. The family began selling off its remaining property, Lewis Walker consenting to each sale because Duncan still owed him on notes for that property. Ready to move by October, 1870, and in a hurry to depart, the Duncans accepted promissory notes, which were also likely signed over to Walker. The Glendale lot with the small saddler's shop on it, apparently a gift to Jack by his father and his Aunt Eveline, wife of James's brother, William, was sold by Jack to Curtis Morrison for $200, fifty dollars in cash and a $150 promissory note. Since he was not yet 21, the deed had to be co-signed by his father and his aunt.[32] Gathering their belongings and giving their goodbyes to friends and relatives, the Duncans began the long trek to Texas.

Duncan family stories generally hold that James Duncan took his family by train to Memphis, Tennessee, from where they traveled by steamer down the Mississippi River and up the Red River, ultimately landing at Jefferson, Texas, in Marion County, not far from the border of Louisiana. Apparently staying in that area for a short time, the family then moved by wagon to Sherman, north of Dallas in Grayson County, almost to the Indian Territory.[33]

Another family story is that, while moving across some part of Texas by wagon, the Duncans encountered a group of cowboys with a herd of cattle. There were negotiations; a deal was struck; and James Duncan bought the cattle as a down payment on the family's new future. After resuming their journey, the

No. 462—

I, the undersigned, Prisoner of War, belonging to the Army of the Department of Alabama, Mississippi and East Louisiana, having been surrendered by Lt. Gen. R. Taylor, C. S. A., Commanding said Department, to Maj. Gen. E. R. S. Canby, U. S. A., Commanding Army and Division of West Mississippi, do hereby give my solemn PAROLE of HONOR that I will not hereafter serve in the Armies of the Confederate States, or in any military capacity whatever, against the United States of America, or render aid to the enemies of the latter, until properly exchanged in such manner as shall be mutually approved by the respective authorities. Done at Meridian, Miss.

this 13th day of May, 1865.

J. Duncan
2nd Lt. Co "K" 8th Ky. Regt.

Approved:

_____, Colonel C. S. A.,
Henry Bertram Col. 20th Wis. Vols. U. S. A.,   Com'rs.

The above named officer will not be disturbed by United States authorities, as long as he observes his parole, and the laws in force where he resides.

Henry Bertram

Col. 20th Wis. Vols., *Commissioner for the U. S.*

On May 13, 1865, James A. Duncan signed this Parole of Honor at Meridian, Mississippi, then returned home to his family in Kentucky. (Courtesy of the U. S. National Archives).

family ran into a posse searching for the cowboys who had stolen the cattle. While the story is not clear as to which parties were involved and when and where it occurred, there was supposedly some shooting, and Jack sustained a serious bullet wound across his abdomen that exposed his intestines. Mack was supposed to have placed him on a horse and jumped up behind him, putting his arms around his brother to help hold the wound as they rode in search of help. Subsequently, they located some community where Jack was sewn up. According

Bounty Hunter

to the story, the rustlers were tracked down and promptly dispatched to their eternal reward at the end of a rope.[34]

It is not definite when the Duncans finally moved south from Grayson County and settled in Dallas. For sure, Sim was there by mid-1871, employed as a bookkeeper for a mercantile firm, Clark & Bryan.[35] Very likely, the rest of the family was in Dallas at least by 1873, although there is no formal record of their presence until 1875. Sim may likely have preceded his family since, in the 1873-74 Dallas directory, he was boarding at the Commercial Hotel and there was no mention of any other family member.[36]

Nevertheless, James Duncan and his family had made the difficult trek to this new land and a new start. It was a far different land from anything they had known in Kentucky.

NOTES

1. Mrs. Thomas Durham Winstead, *Chronicles of Hardin County, Kentucky, 1766-1974* (Elizabethtown, Kentucky: Mrs. Thomas Durham Winstead, 1974), p. 5.

2. Deed Book, Hardin County, Kentucky, Vol. L, pp. 50-51; Vol. N, p. 195.

3. Sixth U. S. Census, 1840, Hardin County, Kentucky; *Dallas Morning News*, September 25, 1892.

4. County Court Orders, Hardin County, Kentucky, Book I, p. 206; Book L, p. 1.

5. Deed Book, Hardin County, Kentucky, Vol. V, pp. 65, 449; Vol. W, p. 183.

6. Marriage Register, Hardin County, Kentucky, Vol. B, No. 1500.

7. Mary Josephine Jones, *Marriages, Hardin County, Kentucky, 1820-1829* (Hartford, Kentucky: McDowell Publications, 1977), p. 18.

8. *Dallas Daily Times Herald*, June 3, 1912.

9. Daniel E. McClure, Jr., *Two Centuries in Elizabethtown and Hardin County, Kentucky* (Elizabethtown, Kentucky: The Hardin County Historical Society, 1979), p. 582.

10. James Allison Jones and Mary Josephine Jones, *Hardin County, Kentucky, Cemetery Inscriptions* (Owensboro, Kentucky: McDowell Publications, 1980), Vol. II, p. 118.

11. *Makers of Dallas* (Dallas, Texas: Dallas Newspaper Artists' Association, 1912), p. 201; Frank E. Johnson, *A History of Texas and Texans* (New York: The American Historical Society, 1914), Vol. V, p. 2538.

12. Deed Book, Hardin County, Kentucky, Vol. X, pp. 263, 299.

13. Seventh U. S. Census, 1850, Hardin County, Kentucky.

14. Tax Rolls, Hardin County, Kentucky, 1851-1852.

15. There is no official record of Jack Duncan's birth, and it can only be approximated. His obituary in 1911 stated that he was 61. A birth date of September, 1850, listed in the 1900 Census is consistent with the 1850 Census which, since it was taken prior to September, listed Sim as the only child. The 1860 Census listed Jack as 10 years old. Cemetery records in Dallas, taken from statements of family members at the time of his death, incorrectly give a date of birth of September 25, 1852, although the day and month might be correct. The 1870 Census also incorrectly listed him as 21 years old and the 1880 Census as 28.

16. Personnel Records of George M. Duncan, National Personnel Records Center, St. Louis, Missouri; Eighth U. S. Census, 1860, Hardin County, Kentucky; Twelfth U. S. Census, 1900, Dallas County, Texas; *Dallas Times Herald*, August 12, 1938; *Dallas Morning News*, August 13, 1938.

17. Eighth U. S. Census, 1860, Hardin County, Kentucky; Ninth U. S. Census, 1870, Hardin County, Kentucky.

18. Tax Rolls, Hardin County, Kentucky, 1860.

19. William C. Davis, *The Orphan Brigade* (Garden City, New York: Doubleday & Company, Inc., 1980), pp. 8-12; McClure, *Two Centuries*, p. 245.

20. Company Muster Rolls, U. S. National Archives and Records Service; *Confederate Kentucky Volunteers, War 1861-65*, Report of the Adjutant General of the State of Kentucky (Frankfort, Kentucky: The State Journal Co., 1915), p. 404.

21. Jones and Jones, *Cemetery Inscriptions*, Vol. II, p. 118.

22. Interview with William B. Duncan (grandson of George M. Duncan), North Richland Hills, Texas, November 26, 1982.

23. Circuit Court Order Book, Hardin County, Kentucky, Vol. 6, pp. 384 and 463; Deed Book, Hardin County, Kentucky, Vol. 7, p. 533.

24. Company Muster Rolls, Parole of Honor, and other documents, U. S. National Archives and Records Service; *Confederate Kentucky Volunteers*, pp. 406 and 408.

25. McClure, *Two Centuries*, p. 577.

26. Deed Book, Hardin County, Kentucky, Vol. 8, pp. 240 and 571.

27. Jones and Jones, *Cemetery Inscriptions*, Vol. II, p. 118.

28. Interview with William B. Duncan (grandson of George M. Duncan), North Richland Hills, Texas, November 26, 1982.

29. Deed Book, Hardin County, Kentucky, Vol. 9, pp. 78 and 536; Vol. 11, p. 276.

30. Ninth U. S. Census, 1870, Hardin County, Kentucky; *Dallas Morning News*, September 27, 1940.

31. *Makers of Dallas*, p. 201; Johnson, *Texas and Texans*, p. 2538; *Dallas Daily Times Herald*, October 27, 1916.

32. Deed Book, Hardin County, Kentucky, Vol. 11, p. 277; Vol. 12, pp. 110, 297, and 459.

33. Johnson, *Texas and Texans*, p. 2538; *Dallas Morning News*, October 27, 1916; January 3, 1935; and September 27, 1940. No records could be located in Marion or Grayson Counties to verify the Duncans' presence.

34. Interview with William B. Duncan (grandson of George M. Duncan), North Richland Hills, Texas, November 26, 1982.

35. Johnson, *Texas and Texans*, pp. 2538 and 2539. In the 1872 Dallas County tax rolls, S. W. S. Duncan is listed as having $125 worth of miscellaneous property for tax purposes, but no other family members are mentioned until 1875.

36. Dallas City Directory, 1873-1874.

Chapter 2

Early Dallas

The area of North Central Texas that was to become Dallas was settled by John Neely Bryan of Tennessee in 1841, and it was he who subsequently oversaw the creation of a community there. Located on a high bluff overlooking the Trinity River, the new settlement soon attracted farmers and merchants and slowly began to flourish. By 1856, there was a sufficient population to justify formal organization, and the city of Dallas was incorporated. Primarily a farming area, Dallas during the Civil War served as a central area for the organization of a number of Confederate military units as well as a key distribution point for grains and crops to support Southern forces. After the war, as throughout the rest of the state, Dallas fell under the hated Reconstruction Act and, from 1867 through 1874, reluctantly faced the bitter fact of military control.

By 1870, there were close to 3,000 people living in the raw new town with its dirt streets and over 13,000 in Dallas County.[1] However, these numbers were periodically swollen by people moving through town, on their way to the opening west. In addition to settlers, there were other transients, such as soldiers, buffalo hunters, and cowboys. The Shawnee cattle trail had coursed through the town in the late 1860's, introducing an even more wild and woolly frontier flavor until a quarantine against Texas longhorn cattle suffering a contagious fever forced South Texas cattlemen to find alternate routes to railheads in Kansas. However, at the start of the 1870's, Dallas had some eighteen stores, two hotels, four small grocery stores, and a number of other businesses.[2] Of course, the town also had its district for coarser pursuits, calculated to extract money from the pockets of young cowboys. Just off the courthouse square, in the southwestern part of the small town, there were numerous saloons, gambling halls, and whorehouses that attracted a raucous crowd, countering the influence of Dallas's four churches in other parts of town.[3] A trip along Dallas's dusty streets would present a potpourri of wagons, carriages, horses, mules, pigs, and assorted two-legged animals, all busily moving this way and that in a jumble of energy and industry.

Very early after his arrival, Sim Duncan became the first of his family to gain a public reputation in Dallas. With only four stagecoach lines serving the town, community leaders knew that Dallas's ultimate survival would require better transportation facilities. Already, by 1871, the Houston & Texas Central Railroad was pushing its line northward to Dallas from Houston through Corsicana, induced by a gift of free right-of-way voted by the town. The H. & T. C. line would allow goods and passengers to be more quickly routed to and through Dallas, avoiding the more cumbersome approach of slow barge shipments from New Orleans to Jefferson, in East Texas, then across land by wagon, as the Duncans had traveled.[4]

Even though a railroad was at last scheduled to come to Dallas, however, town leaders were also aware of the even greater advantage the city would enjoy as a transportation center if it were a terminal point on the planned southern continental route as well. In March, 1871, the Memphis, El Paso, and Pacific Railroad had been authorized by Congress to begin laying track where construction on the continental line had reached Shreveport, Louisiana, and Marshall, Texas, and continue that construction on to San Diego, California, following the 32nd Parallel. Unfortunately for Dallas, this line lay south of the city some fifty miles when it crossed the H. & T. C. line, taking it through Corsicana instead to that town's great delight. Dallas leaders

A view of a muddy Elm Street in Dallas, Texas, in 1873---about the time the Duncan family moved to Dallas. (Courtesy of the Texas/Dallas History and Archives Division, Dallas Public Library).

well knew that any direct attempt at state legislation to alter the planned route to go through Dallas would fail as a result of vigorous opposition by the towns of Tyler and Corsicana, who obviously stood to reap the benefits of the line. It was time for some quick thinking.

Immediately to the south of Dallas, a little area known as Browder Springs provided the city with clear, sparkling water. Few outside of the area had ever heard of Browder Springs. Sim Duncan and employer W. J. Clark put their heads together and came up with a scheme to divert the line to Dallas. Working closely with Dallas's state legislator, John W. Lane, the two were able to tack a small, innocuous rider onto a bill that the Texas Legislature was desirous of passing which gave public lands as subsidy to the railroads. The tiny rider gave the railroad reasonable latitude in construction from Longview, in East

Texas, but required that the railroad line cross the H. & T. C. line within one mile of Browder Springs. The bill and its rider were passed without objection in November, 1871, and the legislature promptly adjourned. By the time Corsicana and others discovered where Browder Springs was and what had happened to their future, it was too late and Dallas was assured of what became the Texas and Pacific Railroad line and an important role in the commerce and trade of the American Southwest.[5]

On July 16, 1872, the first Houston and Texas Central train arrived in Dallas. Sim Duncan, along with young lawyer Robert Seay and friend Tom Marsalis, hired a hack and rode to the new depot one mile east of town to join the large crowd welcoming the train. After the perfunctory speechmaking, there was a barbecue of buffalo steaks provided by cattleman Charles Goodnight.[6]

However, despite the yearning of community leaders that Dallas have respectability as a leading city, this was still the turbulent post-Civil War era, and Dallas attracted its share of a wide variety of opportunists who couldn't care less about its future. The passions of the war had abated only slightly, Reconstruction notwithstanding, and, given the rowdy frontier enthusiasm of the times, it was not unusual that a number of undesirables would find their way to the still primitive Dallas scene. Also, those freebooters who had once served the Confederate cause could count on some degree of sympathy and refuge, regardless of their depredations elsewhere. In the mid-1800's, Dallas hosted a number of unique individuals who would go on to achieve considerable notoriety in the annals of western outlawry. Their presence and activities highlight the lusty frontier environment so prevalent at the time and in which young Jack Duncan was baptized into the life he would follow.

John Shirley had moved his family from Missouri to Texas during the war, including his daughter, Myra Maybelle, who would later be better known as Belle Starr. The Shirley family settled in Dallas County in the small town of Scyene, some ten miles southeast of Dallas. As early as 1864, Shirley had seven slaves and had begun to accumulate livestock for his farming operation. He had acquired 484 acres of farmland by 1868, as well as three lots in the town of Scyene.[7] In November, 1866, Myra had married former Confederate guerrilla Jim Reed in Collin County, north of Dallas, giving birth in September, 1868, to a daughter, Rosie Lee, Myra Reed's "pearl."[8] She would also have a son by Jim Reed.

During the war, elements of Quantrill's guerrillas, including one of his lieutenants, Thomas Coleman Younger, better known as Cole, had pierced North Central Texas.[9] Cole and his brothers, who, along with Frank and Jesse James and other outlaws, would carve a place for themselves in the history of the Old West, found Dallas an attractive place to settle. As early as 1859, there had been a Younger living in Dallas County,[10] although whether this involved any relatives of the Younger brothers themselves is unknown.

Perhaps on the advice of their friend John Shirley, the Youngers decided to move to Texas from Missouri in 1868, settling in Scyene. Brothers Cole, Jim, and John Younger prepared a home for their mother and sister, anxious to have a place where they could be free of harassment by Missouri military authorities—as well as a place of respite from robberies carried out with the James boys.[11] Periodically in the first part of 1869, the Younger brothers openly visited Dallas, registering in their own names in either the City Hotel or the Crutchfield House. Often there were others registering with them from Scyene or Missouri who could very well have been outlaw associates.[12] The 1870 census listed the family of "farmer" J. H. Younger as including Thomas, 26; James, 22; Robert, 16; Bettie, 13; and Bersha, 50.[13] Cole even later asserted that Jim and Bob helped take the "scholastic census" of Dallas County in 1870.[14]

On January 15, 1871, John Younger, who worked as a store clerk, was in a saloon, probably in Scyene, drinking with friends of his, all of them in a boisterous mood. Shakily leveling his pistol, he attempted to shoot the pipe out of the mouth of a man named Russell. Understandably frightened, Russell ran from the building, his footsteps accentuated by random gunshots from the gleeful Younger. Russell complained to Dallas County Sheriff Jeremiah M. Brown and a warrant was sworn out for John Younger's arrest.[15] Sheriff Brown, better known in Dallas as Jere, had been appointed Dallas's city marshal in November, 1865, by provisional Governor A. J. Hamilton, then became deputy sheriff. When a new Texas constitution was passed in 1866, he became sheriff, but was removed in 1867 by the incoming military reconstruction government. He worked as a photographer in Dallas until he was again elected sheriff in November, 1869, under an even newer Texas constitution.

Jere Brown assigned execution of the warrant for Younger to a deputy, Charles H. Nichols. Nichols, a former Confederate colonel who had served under General Jo Shelby, as had Cole Younger,[16] had settled in Dallas with his wife and three children.[17] On Monday morning, January 16, 1871, the deputy rounded up some help, including James McMahon, and rode in the cold to Scyene. When they arrived, Nichols assigned one or more guards to watch the stable where John Younger's horse was kept, as well as that of Tom Porter, a "friend recently arrived from Missouri,"[18] whose true name was Thompson McDaniels.[19]

Leaving McMahon in a nearby store, Nichols located John Younger in the middle of a meal and informed him of the warrant for his arrest. Younger asked to finish his meal and Nichols consented, instructing him to report to the store. Declining an invitation to join in the meal, Nichols rejoined McMahon at the store where they waited, warming themselves by a stove. After a hasty consultation, Younger and McDaniels, neither of whom had been disarmed by Nichols, went to the stable and discovered that it was guarded. Sharing some whiskey, the two then walked down to the store where the lawmen waited.

Upon entering the store, Younger and his companion opened fire, one round hitting McMahon in the chest and instantly killing him. Nichols received a fatal wound but was able to return the fire, hitting Younger in the arm. Younger and McDaniels then took Nichols' horse and another and fled north. Nichols lingered, then died four days later on Friday, January 20, the first lawman to be killed in Dallas County.[20] The two gunmen escaped, only briefly encountering a pursuing posse and exchanging gunfire as they tried to cross the Red River.[21] John Younger and "Tom Porter" were indicted for murder in Dallas County on June 1, 1871,[22] but were never arrested. John Younger was subsequently shot to death by detectives in Missouri in 1874.

Despite this act of wanton bloodshed, however, the remaining Younger brothers apparently continued to be welcome in the Dallas community. Cole had been in Louisiana on cattle business at the time of the shooting, thus was not blamed, although he contended that John had been innocent of any wrongdoing. In various letters to friends in Dallas published years later, Cole stated that he, Jim, and Bob were frequently called on by Sheriff Brown, Deputy Nichols, and subsequently Sheriff James Barkley to help make arrests and even to take convicts to the state penitentiary in Huntsville. He wrote that, in 1870 and 1871, Jim was actually a deputy sheriff himself, also stating that Jim and Bob were both on the city police force in mid-1872, when the railroad came to Dallas, "to help put down the rough characters that had overrun the place."[23] As a matter of record, Jim Younger was briefly one of nine Dallas policemen under Marshal Tom Flynn early in 1873.[24] Cole said that Jim and Bob sang with a Baptist Church choir in 1871 and and 1872, adding that Bob never took one drink of whiskey while he was in Texas.[25] Although the tax rolls of Dallas County do not show that the Youngers ever owned any land, in 1871 Cole was assessed for five horses and Jim for two.[26]

Brother Jim wasn't totally law-abiding, however, as, shortly after he became a Dallas policeman, he was indicted in February, 1873, for robbery, along with fellow officer J. J. L. Hollander. Hollander was found guilty and sentenced to serve five years, but then was granted a new trial.[27] Jim Younger and his brothers quickly left Texas, never to return. The three brothers were later captured in Minnesota, after an ill-fated bank robbery attempt at Northfield with the James boys in 1876. However, they continued to correspond from prison with such wartime friends as Col. E. G. Bower, a local judge. Their long prison ordeal in Minnesota made the brothers a popular topic in Dallas, especially because of the fervent efforts of two of their sisters to gain clemency for them, a Mrs. Jones in Denison, and Mrs. A. B. (Henrietta) Rawlins, who lived in the small Oak Cliff community across the Trinity River from Dallas.[28]

Another associate of the Youngers, Frank James, also made occasional appearances in Dallas in the early days. He once recalled that he was arrested in Dallas for "a tear" and was fined fourteen dollars. Another time, he had visited Dallas "with his men" and they were forced to flee out the back door of a variety theater when the police came in the front.[29] After the death of his brother, Jesse, and after he had been absolved of his crimes, Frank moved to Dallas in 1887 and lived there as a respectable citizen, although frequently traveling, until 1893. While in Dallas, he worked for Sanger Brothers, a prominent clothing store, as a salesman. During that period, he once had his horse stolen; he served on a murder trial jury; and his son, Robert, won a year's scholarship to a Missouri military academy as a result of votes in a newspaper coupon contest in Dallas.[30]

In the meantime, things had happened in the life of Myra Reed, John Shirley's daughter. In August, 1874, her husband, Jim, was shot to death by a lawman near Paris, Texas. Reed had been widely sought as the leader of a gang suspected of holding up the San Antonio and Austin mail coach on April 7, 1874, as well as robbing Watt Grayson, an old Creek Indian, in the In-

A disputed photograph of Cole Younger (left) and Jim Younger as they appeared prior to joining Quantrill's raiders. (Courtesy of Mrs. Katherine Ismert and the Historical Society of Missouri).

dian Territory the previous November.[31] After Reed's death, the manhunt continued for members of his gang, although at least one of them wasn't too worried about it. Cal Carter, in a rather cavalier manner, casually rode into Dallas on August 13, 1874, enjoyed a leisurely drink in a saloon, then began slowly riding out of town again. City Marshal Junius Peak, a twice-wounded Confederate veteran and former deputy sheriff, was alerted to the wanted man's presence in town and hastily jumped on the first available horse, hurrying to intercept the outlaw. Looking over his shoulder and spotting the pursuing Peak, Carter put spurs to his mount and, despite a valiant effort by the lawman, who unfortunately had not chosen the fleetest of animals, quickly outdistanced his pursuer.[32] Conditions were still sufficiently primitive in the Dallas of the 1870's to permit such a flaunting of the law.

After Jim Reed's death, his widow remained in Scyene with her two children, reportedly operating a stable which occasion-

Bounty Hunter

ally dealt in stolen horses. Her brothers, Edwin and Mansfield, had been in trouble with the law in Dallas in 1866, and even her father had been arrested. Another brother, Cravens, better known as Shug, was also occasionally in trouble.[33] Apparently, she did not remain inactive and conducted herself in a manner calculated to thoroughly alarm her neighbors, even writing threatening letters. Concerned about the number of desperadoes wending their way in and out of Scyene, the murder of Nichols and other offenses, not to mention Mrs. Reed's impudent threats, Scyene society took some decisive steps. In addition to mounting a vigilante effort to arrest outlaws, but without the lynchings usually found accompanying such ventures, on March 29, 1875, a committee of ten of Scyene's leaders composed and sent a letter to Texas Governor Richard Coke complaining about Myra Reed and asking for help. Among the group appointing the committee was Amon McCommas, Sr., whose granddaughter, Rosa, had been seduced by Jim Reed and abandoned at San Marcos, Texas, when he and his men robbed the San Antonio stage. Rosa has often been mistaken by writers as Belle Starr. The petition lamented Scyene's lawless state:

> For several years past the town of Scyene, Dallas Co., Texas, and vicinity, has been noted as a place of resort for horse thieves, desperadoes and other bad characters—certain parties having located themselves here as a place of rendezvous for such characters, thus giving aid and comfort to thieving and marauding bands infesting all parts of the state. Here is the home of the widow and family of James Reed, the San Antonio mail robber, his widow being no less celebrated in such exploits than her notorious paramour. Here the robber and outlaw himself made his home and sought refuge while resting from his daring and infamous robberies and murders. Here Porter and the Younger Brothers, whose names have since become synonymous of infamy throughout the length and breadth of the land, for a time rested secure. Here was murdered Colonel Nichols, a deputy sheriff of this county, and Mr. McMahon, one of his posse, while attempting to arrest Porter and John Younger. Here, for a time, was the headquarters of the notorious desperado Hays, alias Parker, who shot off Judge Hart's arm, and murdered in cold blood James Loving, a peaceable citizen of Dallas County. Here the robber and desperado, Wilder,

42

who now lies in prison at Ft. Smith, rested while he concocted his infamous plans.

For such characters the latch string of the home of this family has ever hung out; and as courier, and if need be coworker of the band, she (Mrs. Reed) has done them good service. Donning often male attire, she has ridden hundreds of miles to apprise them of pending danger.

Quite recently she has threatened to burn out any one who proposed to interfere with her nefarious plans, and states, in a threatening letter to one of our citizens, that she has twenty-five men who will do her bidding and annihilate Scyene, if necessary.

Thus have they conducted themselves until they have become a terror to the citizens of the county at large, and the citizens of Scyene have been driven to the necessity of organizing and banding themselves together to aid each other in protecting their lives and property, and to aid the officers of the law in arresting and bringing to justice all offenders against the law, and by their vigilance to obtain and convey to the proper authorities all infractions of the law, as well as to collect and present the evidence in such cases, thus aiding to bring to the bar of justice the parties who have so long preyed upon us.

In doing this, the citizens are desirous of being assured that they are doing nothing contrary to the laws of the state and that they have the sympathy of the officials of the state in what they consider a laudable undertaking.

With this view we, the undersigned, have been selected as a committee to confer with Your Excellency and ask your aid and advice. We have been led to adopt this course from a feeling sense of the responsibility resting upon us as good citizens and law-abiding men, having in view not only the good of the county, but of the whole state.

In Your Excellency's message to the Fourteenth Legislature, on pp. 15 to 18 inclusive, we have noticed certain recommendations in regards to such means as you deem most expedient to preserve the peace and quietude as well as the dignity of our state, which meets with our approbation. And, while we do not ask either pay or subsistence from the state, except in such actual expenditures as may be incurred in pursuing thieves and desperadoes for their capture and arrest, we desire the approbation of the executive of the state in our proceedings.

We propose to act only as law-abiding men and good citizens, and to go only where the laws of the land will protect us, and in no wise to take the law into our own hands.

Since our organization we have arrested and turned over to the proper authorities some half a dozen or more offenders, two of whom are charged with horse stealing.

Bounty Hunter

> We forward you herewith the certificate of our county officials, certifying to our standing as citizens of Dallas County, and ask that you take the matter into consideration and give us an early answer.[34]

Governor Coke, certainly sympathetic to the community's plight but hampered by limited state resources, responded with a very noncommittal reply, reminding the group of the importance of staying within the law. A change in priorities from Indians to outlaws for the state police was still a few years away.

Despite the disappointing response of the governor, those who opposed Mrs. Reed's presence in their midst kept up the pressure. On April 28, 1875, the Dallas County grand jury indicted Myra Reed for an arson allegedly set some four years earlier to the store of a Nannie Alexander. On May 1, District Judge Barksdale set her bail at a stiff $2,500, no doubt reflecting the close attention being paid to her case by prominent voters in Scyene.[35] A Dallas newpaper reporter was moved to comment:

> There are at present 48 prisoners confined in the county jail, one of whom is a woman, charged with setting a house on fire some four years ago. In answer to an inquirer, the reporter will say that he certainly thinks the amount of bail—$2,500—in connection of the circumstances, excessive. Her attorneys will move for a reduction this morning.[36]

The record does not disclose whether or not the bond was ever reduced; however, there is a good chance that she remained in the county jail for a considerable period of time.

As if she didn't have enough problems at this point, on August 12, 1875, Myra Reed and Mike McCommas were indicted for theft of a gelding, and, if she was out of jail at that time, she was quickly behind bars again.[37] She was still in jail in November, which prompted an anonymous letter to Sheriff Barkley:

44

John Younger, who killed Deputy Sheriff Charles Nichols. (Courtesy of the State Historical Society of Missouri at Columbia).

Dear Sir—you ought to treat that lady you have in jail right. I tell you this for your own good. If you don't, it will be hard for you; you will come up missing one of these fine days if you mistreat her. Remember that there is lots of Jim Reed's friends left yet—don't you never forget it. But as long as you treat her right you will be treated right, and if you please, see that she is treated as a lady as long as she stays in there. I will see you on the road probably one day, and we will have a good talk over it. I remain still a friend.[38]

The two cases were continued until, on June 17, 1876, the county attorney announced that he would not prosecute the horse theft case, and she and McCommas stood acquitted of that charge. Apparently, important state witnesses could not be located or brought to Dallas in time, one of them being Sul Ross, a noted Texas Ranger.[39] On June 20, Myra Reed stood trial for arson, pleading not guilty. After the jury heard the evidence, foreman Joseph A. Harris delivered their verdict of not guilty and she was finally free.[40] After this ordeal, it is little wonder that a weary, ill Myra Reed would write her Reed in-laws in August, on a piece of Sheriff Barkley's stationery, telling of her father's death and her intention to sell the farm.[41] Faced only with continued harassment, there was no future for her in Dallas County, and it was time to go elsewhere. She soon left Dallas, only to return occasionally for visits, but never in a manner that caused a community to rise up against her. Her fame as Belle Starr would come in the Indian Territory, not in Texas, where her path would later cross that of Jack Duncan.

The Youngers and the Reeds had been prominent on the Dallas scene even before the coming of the railroad in 1872. But with that event, the floodgates now opened to every opportunist imaginable. As one observer at the time noted: "The merchants, professional men, gamblers and floaters who had followed the terminus all the way to the north moved from Corsicana to Dallas in a body. Up to that time the town had been confined to the courthouse square. The newcomers bought on the road now known as Elm Street . . . and began to set up their portable houses which in sections they had brought from Corsicana. Almost overnight they built a new town."[42] Indeed, there was a widespread influx of gamblers, prostitutes, and thieves, all anxious to cash in on the new prosperity at each opening railroad terminal. One such newcomer, gradually moving westward because of a nagging, persistent tubercular cough, was Dr. John Henry Holliday, later to be known as Doc Holliday and to stand with the Earp brothers at the infamous O. K. Corral gunfight in Tombstone, Arizona.

In November, 1872, Dallas dentist J. A. Seegar thanked his customers of the last five years and announced the move of his office to a new one over Cochran's Drugstore.[43] Within the next year, Seegar took on John Holliday as a partner. In October, 1873, the two dentists won small cash premiums at Dallas's State Fair for displaying the best false teeth.[44] Born in Griffin, Georgia, on August 15, 1851, Holliday had graduated on

*"Doc" Holliday,
better known as a
gunfighter, once
practiced dentistry in
Dallas. (Courtesy of the
Arizona Department of
Library, Archives,
and Public Records,
Phoenix).*

March 1, 1872, from the Pennsylvania College of Dental Surgery in Philadelphia, briefly practicing in Atlanta before moving on to Dallas.[45] The harmony between Seegar and his new partner proved shortlived, and in March, 1874, they made a public announcement:

> Upon mutual consent the firm of Seegar and Holliday have disolved (sic). J. H. Holliday will be responsible for the two debts against the firm. J. A. Seegar will remain at the old office, over Cochran's Drug Store, Elm Street. J. H. Holliday's office is over the Dallas County Bank, corner of Main and Lamar streets.[46]

No doubt, the nightlife of the tubercular Holliday did not sit well with the conservative Seegar, who prided himself on a quiet, peaceful dental practice. He had little room for a partner who spent much of his time at the gaming tables and whorehouses, reeking of whiskey—not to mention the adverse effects of Holliday's persistent cough as he peered into a patient's mouth. During 1874, Doc paid $2.80 in poll and county taxes.[47] Doc's extracurricular activities caught up with him when, on May 12, 1874, he was arrested and indicted for gaming.[48] On Saturday, December 26, 1874, he and saloon keeper Charles Austin were arrested for exchanging shots at each other, although without injury.[49] Doc was indicted for assault to murder on January 18, 1875, while Austin was only charged with carrying a pistol.[50] The following April, Doc pleaded guilty to the gaming charge and a jury, headed up by foreman H. McDowell, assessed a fine of ten dollars.[51] Although the disposition of Holliday's assault charge is unknown, the pistol charge against Austin was dismissed on May 4, 1875.[52] Writers have generally held that this embarrassing incident led to the quick departure of Holliday from Dallas,[53] but there are indications that, if he did leave, he returned. On January 8, 1877, Dr. Holliday's name appeared three times in indictments, most likely for gaming, and the cases were transferred to a justice of the peace to handle.[54] Another entry, the following September, indicated that Doc may have been nabbed again by the local police during a sweep of local gamblers.[55] Beyond this, there is no further mention of Doc Holliday in Dallas and he apparently left without leaving a single corpse behind. Nevertheless, his presence and activities are indicative of an atmosphere in Dallas that continued to attract gamblers, prostitutes, and others eager to make easy money.

This was the side of Dallas that Jack Duncan soon became familiar with. For a young Kentucky farm boy with little worldly experience outside the labors of a farm, this new world with its cacophony of flashy sights, raucous noises, and fast-living people, who ventured far beyond the bounds set for him by his God-fearing parents, must have proven an irresistable temptation. Like any young man, he repeatedly tested the traces that confined him to the life he knew in Kentucky, rubbing shoulders with people of the ilk of the Younger brothers, Myra Reed, Doc Holliday, and similar notorious characters. No doubt such exposure would induce an adventurous spirit to sample some of the new life style.

By March, 1872, Sim Duncan had resigned as a bookkeeper and contracted to survey the town, after which he went into the abstract and land business. He and W. F. Cummins formed a partnership as general land agents, setting up an office on Dallas's Commerce Street, on the south side of the county square.[56] By 1875, the Duncan family had definitely established itself in Dallas. Sim, in addition to serving as city engineer, was also the county surveyor and had an office in the county courthouse. The family, including Sim, lived at No. 14 Cora Street. Both James and his son, Jack were working as butchers, James being assessed in 1875 for taxes on two horses.[57] Although there is no record of what type of work Mack Duncan was doing, it is apparent he was working at something as he was indicted along with many other good citizens in September for failure to pay his occupation tax.[58]

Given Jack Duncan's increasing exposure to some of the sporting life in Dallas, the monotony of a butcher's routine must have palled on him somewhat. Despite the rudiments of his upbringing, the combination of a young man's curiosity for adventure and Dallas's rowdy frontier atmosphere make it easier to understand his decision to try a new calling. On about September 27, 1876, Jack Duncan became the newest member of the small Dallas police force under City Marshal William F. Morton.[59] No doubt, this decision raised some consternation on the part of James and Kitty Duncan. Just in August, Dallas had been shocked when one of its policemen, John Carter, had been brutally clubbed in an effort to rescue his prisoner and had almost died.[60]

The Dallas police force at this time fluctuated between ten and eleven officers, depending on town finances, to provide protection for over 10,000 citizens. Marshal Morton, the son of a North Carolina physician and Baptist minister, had been the captain of an Arkansas Confederate regiment, twice wounded and once captured. After farming in Mississippi and running a grocery in Jackson County, Texas, he had brought his wife and three children to Dallas in 1873, initially working for a lumber company. Morton joined the police force under City Marshal June Peak in April, 1874, although still looking for better employment prospects in the druggist business. In August, 1875, he was shot and seriously wounded while trying to arrest a wanted murderer. Recovering, Morton ran against Peak for the marshal's job in April, 1876, and won the election. A calm, competent man, Morton had ably assisted Sheriff William Marion Moon in talking a mob out of lynching the men suspected of having beaten Policeman Carter.

Duncan went to work for fifty dollars a month, which he received for performing his duties twelve hours a day, seven days a week. He had to purchase his own uniform, which consisted of a dark blue sack coat and a black felt slouch hat.[61] Officers were assigned to patrol certain beats on foot, usually in pairs, and were expected to deal firmly and aggressively with the drunks, vagrants, gamblers, prostitutes, thieves, and other types of lawbreakers who routinely came to police attention. There was no training in the law and a new officer had to be guided by the advice and counsel of Marshal Morton and older, more experienced officers. The headquarters for the force was the city jail, or calaboose, a two-story ramshackle building of ancient vintage. A room downstairs was utilized for confining the ever-present drunks, while women and prisoners used on city work gangs in the streets were kept upstairs. The calaboose was badly ventilated and, in the heat of a Texas summer, conditions for prisoners were miserable at best.[62]

Duncan set about the task of learning how to enforce the law as a city policeman and very early received a valuable lesson. After barely two weeks on the job, on October 14, 1876, at about four o'clock in the afternoon, Duncan attempted the arrest of some miscreant he had encountered. The suspect resisted arrest vigorously, but Duncan finally managed to throw

John T. Carter, long-time "Keeper of the Calaboose" as he appeared in 1885. (Author's Collection).

him to the ground. Suddenly, the downed prisoner delivered a vicious kick to Duncan's abdomen that was so severe, he fell to the ground unconscious. For a short time, the attending doctor was uncertain whether or not he would recover; however, he did recover and was soon back on duty.[63]

A week later, on October 21, Duncan assisted Marshal Morton and Policeman James C. Arnold in the arrest of Duff Hammett, who was wanted for murdering Hammett's brother-in-law. Arnold, who was originally from Georgia, would himself become city marshal in 1881 and be chief of police in Dallas until his death in 1898. On the same day as Hammett's arrest, Duncan and Policeman W. L. Dunn also arrested two suspected pickpockets.[64]

In August, 1873, in Ellsworth, Kansas, Sheriff C. B. Whitney had been shot to death by a shotgun in the hands of a drunken Billy Thompson, brother of the notorious Texas gunman, Ben Thompson, who held off officers until Billy could escape. A requisition for Billy's arrest was sent to Texas and, in

Bounty Hunter

November, 1876, Texas Ranger Captain J. C. Sparks, along with two guards, arrested Billy and, in Austin, put him on a train northbound for Kansas. Sparks felt that there might be an attempt to rescue Thompson and, after the train left Corsicana bound for Dallas, he grew increasingly suspicious of a number of men on the train. At one stop, he telegraphed Austin, directing that Dallas Sheriff Moon be notified to gather and stand by with a sufficient force of men to accompany them through the Indian Territory. Once in Dallas, Thompson was lodged in the county jail overnight while Sparks successfully defeated a bid in Justice Court to have him arrested for kidnapping Thompson. On the 21st, Sheriff Moon had a force of deputies, as well as city policemen, perhaps including Jack Duncan, and members of the local militia, standing by as security against a possible rescue attempt. With Thompson safely aboard the train, Moon and several deputies then accompanied Sparks and his men to Salina, Kansas, before returning.[65]

Dallas was stunned in December, 1876, when a city policeman, Robert Duft, was arrested as an accomplice, along with a local private detective, T. C. Speiden, and Speiden's two sons, in the attempted burglary of a bank. Pinkerton detectives had intercepted correspondence from Speiden to a Chicago burglar and slipped in an undercover operative posing as the burglar. Along with Sheriff Moon's help, the detectives trapped them in the act. Subsequently, charges were dropped against Duft, who had acted as a lookout.[66]

As 1876 drew to a close, Jack Duncan had learned a number of important lessons about the policing business. He had gained insight as to the type of people he dealt with and the world in which they dwelt—how to talk to them and acquire important information, as well as techniques for moving about comfortably in such circles. He also had the opportunity to develop and hone important investigative skills. It would be these skills, coupled with his unique ability to anticipate and outwit his quarry, that would gain him success in getting his man. As

52

Duncan began using this ingenuity to detect fleeing fugitives and solve otherwise baffling crimes, he stood out from the mainstream of policemen around him, and some of his exploits began to be passed on by an attentive press. His name would soon attract the attention of state officials who saw an important role for him in the hunt for a more dangerous quarry than the small-time thieves of Dallas.

NOTES

1. Darwin Payne, *Dallas: An Illustrated History* (Woodland Hills, California: Windsor Publications, Inc., 1982), p. 61.

2. Payne, *Dallas*, p. 61.

3. A. C. Greene, *Dallas: The Deciding Years* (Austin, Texas: The Encino Press, 1973), p. 20.

4. Payne, *Dallas*, pp. 64 and 65.

5. Johnson, *Texas and Texans*, p. 2539; Payne, *Dallas*, p. 66; John William Rogers, *The Lusty Texans of Dallas* (New York: E. P. Dutton and Company, Inc., 1951), pp. 123 and 124.

6. Rogers, *Lusty Texans*, pp. 117 and 118.

7. Tax Rolls, Dallas County, Texas, 1864-1868; Deed Record, Dallas County, Texas, Vol. J., p. 643; Vol. R, p. 33.

8. Glenn Shirley, *Belle Starr and Her Times* (Norman, Oklahoma: University of Oklahoma Press, 1982), pp. 72 and 73.

9. Carl W. Breihan, *Younger Brothers* (San Antonio, Texas: The Naylor Co., 1961), p. 184.

10. Tax Rolls, Dallas County, Texas, 1859. William H. Younger owned one acre in Dallas County, at least into the mid-1860's. See also Minute Book, Dallas Board of Aldermen, 1866, where he is called up for road duty.

11. A. C. Appler, *The Younger Brothers* (New York: Frederick Fell, Inc., 1955—reprint of 1892 edition), pp. 20, 44; J. W. Buel, *The Border Outlaws* (Baltimore, Maryland: I. & M. Ottenheimer, n.d.), p. 151.

12. *Dallas Herald*, January 23, 1869, through June 19, 1869.

13. Ninth U. S. Census, 1870, Dallas County, Texas.

14. Letter to E. G. Bower from Cole Younger, dated February 14, 1898, as quoted in *Dallas Morning News*, February 20, 1898.

15. *Dallas Herald*, February 4, 1871; *Dallas Daily Times Herald*, December 8, 1893; Cole Younger, *The Story of Cole Younger* (Houston, Texas: Frontier Press of Texas, 1955—reprint of 1903 edition), p. 67; Breihan, *Younger Brothers*, p. 61; Appler, *Younger Brothers*, p. 158.

16. Shirley, *Belle Starr*, p. 91.

17. Ninth U. S. Census, 1870, Dallas County, Texas.

18. *Dallas Herald*, February 4, 1871; *Dallas Daily Times Herald*, December 8, 1893.

19. Younger, *Cole Younger*, p. 67.

20. *Dallas Herald*, February 4, 1871; *Dallas Daily Times Herald*, December 8, 1893.

21. Appler, *Younger Brothers*, p. 159; *Dallas Herald*, March 18, 1871.

22. *Dallas Daily Times Herald*, December 8, 1893.

23. Younger, *Cole Younger*, p. 58; Letter to E. G. Bower from Cole Younger, dated February 14, 1898, as quoted in *Dallas Morning News*, February 20, 1898.

24. *Dallas Herald*, January 4, 1873.

25. Younger, *Cole Younger*, p. 58; Letter to E. G. Bower from Cole Younger, dated February 14, 1898, as quoted in *Dallas Morning News*, February 20, 1898.

26. Tax Rolls, Dallas County, Texas, 1871.

27. Criminal District Court Minutes, 1874-1875, Dallas County, Texas, p. 10 (*State of Texas v. James Younger and J. J. L. Hollander*, cause no. 1397); Criminal Docket, District Court, 1874, Dallas County, Texas, p. 12 (*State of Texas v. James Younger and J. L. L. Hollander*, cause no. 1397); *Dallas Weekly Herald*, March 1, 1873.

28. *Dallas Morning News*, July 15, 1897; see also W. C. Bronaugh, *The Youngers' Fight for Freedom* (Columbia, Missouri: E. W. Stephens Publishing Co., 1906).

29. *Dallas Daily Times Herald*, March 11, 1887.

30. *Dallas Daily Times Herald*, November 7, 1887; September 10, 1891; and June 6, 1892.

31. Shirley, *Belle Starr*, pp. 100, 118-121; *Dallas Daily Herald*, August 11, 1874.

32. *Dallas Daily Herald*, August 14, 1874.

33. Minutes, 14th District Court, Dallas County, Texas, Vol. D, pp. 105, 146 and 147; Vol. E, p. 381; Vol. H-2, p. 492; Vol. O, p. 86.

34. *Dallas Daily Herald*, April 15, 1875; Shirley, *Belle Starr*, pp. 111-113.

35. Minutes, 14th District Court, Dallas County, Texas, Vol. I, pp. 54, 60 (*State of Texas v. Myra Reed*, cause no. 2873); Rogers, *Lusty Texans*, p. 152.

36. *Dallas Daily Herald*, May 4, 1875.

37. Minutes, 14th District Court, Dallas County Texas, Vol. I, p. 110 (*State of Texas v. Mike McCommas and Myra Reed*, cause no. 2965).

38. *Dallas Daily Herald*, November 10, 1875.

39. Minutes, 14th District Court, Dallas County, Texas, Vol. I, pp. 209, 257 and 258, 265 (*State of Texas v. Mike McCommas and Myra Reed*, cause no. 2965).

40. Minutes, 14th District Court, Dallas County, Texas, Vol. I, p. 267 (*State of Texas v. Myra Reed*, cause no. 2873). This documentation finally puts to rest the oft-repeated myth that Belle Starr charmed a deputy into helping her escape and eloping to the Indian Territory.

41. Shirley, *Belle Starr*, pp. 130 and 131.

42. Rogers, *Lusty Texans*, pp. 118 and 119.

43. *Norton's Union Intelligencer* (Dallas), November 23, 1872.

44. *Dallas Herald*, October 11, 1873.

45. Albert S. Pendleton, Jr., and Susan McKey Thomas, *In Search of the Hollidays* (Valdosta, Georgia: Little River Press, 1973), p. 35 and Appendix p. 19; Letter to author from Mrs. Susan McKey Thomas, Valdosta, Georgia, October 11, 1983.

46. *Dallas Daily Commercial*, March 2, 1874.

47. Tax Rolls, Dallas County, Texas, 1874.

48. Minutes, Criminal District Court, 1874-1875, Dallas County, Texas, p. 209 (*State of Texas v. Dr. Holliday*, cause no. 2236).

49. *Dallas Daily Herald*, December 27, 1874.

50. Minutes, Criminal District Court, 1874-1875, Dallas County, Texas, p. 486 (*State of Texas v. J. H. Holliday*, cause no 2643); p. 482 (*State of Texas v. Charles Austin*, cause no. 2636).

51. Minutes, 14th District Court, Dallas County, Texas, Vol. I, p. 5 (*State of Texas v. Dr. Holliday*, cause no 2236).

52. Minutes, 14th District Court, Dallas County, Texas, Vol. I, p. 65 (*State of Texas v. Charles Austin*, cause no. 2636).

53. Pendleton and Thomas, *Search*, p. 38; Pat Jahns, *The Frontier World of Doc Holliday* (New York: Hastings House, Publishers, 1957), p. 49; John Myers Myers, *Doc Holliday* (Lincoln, Nebraska: University of Nebraska Press, 1955), pp. 40, 43.

54. Minutes, 14th District Court, Dallas County, Texas, Vol. J, p. 80 (*State of Texas v. Dr. Holliday*, unknown cause no.).

55. Minutes, 14th District Court, Dallas County, Texas, Vol. J, p. 467 (*State of Texas v. McCune J. Holliday* (sic), unknown cause no.).

56. Johnson, *Texas and Texans*, p. 2539; Dallas City Directory, 1873-1874, p. 40.

57. *Makers of Dallas*, p. 201; Dallas City Directory, 1875; Tax Rolls, Dallas County, Texas, 1875.

58. Minutes, 14th District Court, Dallas County, Texas, Vol. I, p. 142 (*State of Texas v. G. Mc. Duncan*, cause no. 3050).

59. Treasurer's Ledger, City of Dallas, Texas, Vol. C, p. 66.

60. *Dallas Weekly Herald*, August 26, 1876.

61. Minutes, Board of Aldermen, Dallas, Texas, May 9, 1876.

62. *Dallas Daily Herald*, June 10, 1877.

63. *Dallas Daily Herald*, October 15, 1876.

64. *Dallas Daily Herald*, October 21 and 22, 1876.

65. Floyd B. Streeter, *Ben Thompson: Man With a Gun* (New York: Frederick Fell, Inc., Publishers, 1957), pp. 111 and 112; *Dallas Daily Herald*, November 21 and 22, 1876.

66. *Dallas Weekly Herald*, December 16, 1876.

THE EARLY WEST

Chapter 3

The Policeman

Officer Jack Duncan continued his duties as a Dallas policeman until he resigned in July, 1877. As before, those duties remained typically mundane: encountering and arresting drunks and petty thieves, quieting nightly disturbances, checking closed businesses for burglars, and insuring that all street lamps were burning. To review Duncan's brief ten-month career as a policeman is to see the variety of activities encompassed in a policeman's daily routine, no one day exactly like another. The unpredictable cropped up when least expected and no officer could afford to be lulled into a feeling of being in a routine lest he be injured or even killed. He had to stay on his toes.

In January, 1877, some local boys found a four-year-old named Bessie wandering alone in town. They delivered the child to the Duncan residence where Jack took charge of her. Taking her by the hand, he visited the offices of the *Dallas Herald* so that notice of her being found could be printed and her parents would know where to retrieve her.[1]

In addition to making arrests and keeping the peace, a policeman had to appear in court to give evidence, just as an officer does today. On the evening of February 22, 1877, Duncan and policeman John W. Spencer, along with a Mr. Davenport of Dallas's Exchange Bank, accompanied Deputy U. S. Marshal Purnell by train to Austin to testify in the trial of a counterfeiter named Webb. The party returned to Dallas on the 27th.[2]

Bounty Hunter

Periodically, usually after some public concern had been voiced about crime, the marshal would order a "sweep" of vagrants in the street, the theory being that idle men had a proclivity for stealing and other crimes. It was not unusual at such times to see thirty or forty such undesirables being marched openly from the calaboose to the justice court, where most would plead guilty and, since they couldn't afford a stiff fine, be put to work cleaning the streets of Dallas.[3] Duncan, like the other officers, made his share of such arrests, such prisoners for the most part being regular habitues of the city prison.

During February, 1877, an out-of-town cattleman named Kennedy was visiting Dallas, staying at the Rawlings House hotel on the east side of town. While visiting the hotel's outdoor privy one Saturday evening, he was knocked unconscious, and his attacker took $800 in cash and $1,500 in drafts and notes. Two black boys nearby found the cattleman's pocketbook but surrendered it to a man who happened by and claimed it. On Wednesday, February 28, four days after the incident, an East Dallas shoemaker turned the pocketbook over to Marshal Morton, insisting that when he claimed it from the boys, there was no money in it and that he had claimed it in the hope that whoever lost it would advertise a reward. The boys, however, insisted to the marshal that there had been money in the purse. Suspecting a flim-flam, Morton obtained a search warrant, and he and Duncan thoroughly examined the man's shop. They could not find any money or clues as to its whereabouts. A telegram was sent to Kennedy about the search, the police knowing full well, though, that he could not identify his assailant. Reluctantly, the shoemaker was released and the crime went unsolved.[4]

Duncan's developing skills as a detective first bore fruition in March, 1877. A month or so earlier, the chief of police in Louisville, Kentucky, had sent out a notice accompanied by a photograph of a young man who had fled the state, suspected of embezzling funds from the Louisville and Nashville Railroad.

Duncan saw the photograph and something clicked in his mind. After a day or so of checking among various of his sources, he determined that the Kentucky fugitive, L. C. Eustick, was the same young man who had recently visited Dallas under the name of Frank Morton and had left. Duncan wrote to Kentucky and, on February 22, Kentucky Governor James B. McCreary issued a requisition to the Texas governor, R. B. Hubbard, for Eustick's apprehension.[5] Governor Hubbard signed the requisition and, by the first week of March, it was in Duncan's hands. With Marshal Morton's permission, he swapped his police uniform for plain clothes and launched his pursuit.

Believing that the fugitive had gone to Houston, Duncan took the train to that city. However, Eustick was not there, nor was he at another nearby town where information had indicated he might be found. Slowly backtracking from town to town along the International Railroad line, the policeman finally stopped off in Dickinson where he discovered that "Morton" had left town owing a board bill but had then sent a letter to his landlord asking that he forward his trunk to Troup, in East Texas near Tyler, promising to forward the money he owed. With the letter in hand, Duncan eagerly took the next train for Troup. No sooner had he stepped off the railroad car than he spotted his man in the station crowd. Not wanting to alarm Eustick nor have to resort to physical action if he could help it, Duncan approached the crowd as if in an official railroad capacity and announced, "Mr. Dickinson is on the train and wants to see Mr. Eustick." Off guard, the young man waved his hand: "That's me!" Eustick boarded the train, closely followed by Duncan, who immediately slapped handcuffs on his surprised prisoner. The two returned to Dallas on March 6, and Eustick was lodged in the calaboose.[6] Despite efforts by his friends to free him on a writ of habeas corpus, Eustick was returned to Kentucky authorities on March 10. It was subsequently learned that after Eustick was returned to Kentucky, despite Duncan's efforts, he was released on a bond of over $1,000, and he then fled again.[7]

Bounty Hunter

In the meantime, it was back to police business as usual. On March 7, the day after Duncan returned to Dallas with Eustick, the police were notified that a white man had entered the residence of a black woman and grabbed ten dollars. Duncan and his partner, Policeman Edwards, spotted the suspect and began pursuit on foot, chasing him along the Dallas and Wichita Railroad track. Losing the fleeing man in a heavy thicket, the two officers returned to town, only to encounter a belligerent drunk who doffed his coat in order to do combat with the blue-coated policemen. He lost.[8] In another situation a day or so later, the frigid March air drove "Irish Jimmy," a calaboose regular who didn't relish the idea of sleeping outdoors, to take calculated measures. He "stationed himself by the Senate (saloon) and began a tirade on the political depravity of the age." As soon as his audience had reached an appreciable size and the drunk began to explain things in even greater intellectual depth, Duncan and Edwards came along and granted his wish for a warm night's lodging.[9]

The typical petty thief in Dallas, when he couldn't find cash, would steal something that he could convert to cash, such as in a pawnshop or across the bar in a saloon. Another routine duty for policemen was keeping an eye out for stolen property, and they regularly inspected for such items. Toward the middle of March, as an example, Duncan and Edwards were trying to run down the whereabouts of a number of gold watches that had recently been reported as stolen. A stolen watch they had not been looking for was recovered from Jim McIntyre, a black comedian in a Dallas variety theater. The man from whom he had purchased the watch, however, had already left town. The marshal, in such cases, would not go after such a thief unless there was some assurance of a reward or that his or an officer's expenses would be paid.[10] The approximately $1.66 per day that the marshal and his men earned didn't stretch very far. The city's board of aldermen was usually not willing to fund the pursuit of petty thieves, and such matters were generally dropped, as in this case.

When celebrants at a local saloon began having too much fun, it would frequently spill out onto Dallas's dusty streets. It would then be up to any policemen in the vicinity to get things back under control. Such was the case on March 17, 1877, when "two countrymen imbibed too much cistern water, and it flew to their heads. They cavorted about the square in a lively and energetic manner, and conducted themselves in a manner prejudicial to the peace and dignity of the city of Dallas. Officers Edwards, Duncan, Arnold, Waller and Spencer rounded them up and put them in the Hotel de Crossbar."[11] Such was the routine for the small police force each night.

However, things quite frequently took a serious turn, often involving matters of life and death. On March 27, 1877, for example, Marshal Morton received word that a man by the name of Atkinson, who had been arrested a number of times for vagrancy and told to leave town, had sneaked back in. Morton dispatched Duncan and Edwards to find him. As the two officers neared the St. Louis House, three rapidly fired pistol shots echoed through the darkness. Running in the direction of the shots, they spotted a black man running and gave chase, but it turned out that he had run only because he thought the officers were after him. Resuming their search, the officers located Atkinson in a small shack with a local "lewd woman" and lodged him in the calaboose charged with vagrancy. They could find no pistol after a vigorous search, but were convinced he had done the shooting.[12] On another occasion, Duncan put a black woman in jail for attempting to take her life with an overdose of morphine.[13] Such suicides were quite frequent in Dallas, especially among prostitutes who found themselves desperate to escape a life of depravity at the bottom rung of the human social order. Drugs such as laudanum, or opium, and morphine were freely available. Unfortunately, in those times, to avoid such tragedies, the only solution available to the police was to put such people in jail for making attempts on their own lives.

There were many occasions when physical demands were placed on policemen. At Main and Lamar Streets, on the courthouse square, two black men got into an argument on the evening of April 9, 1877. One of them picked up a rock and threw it at the other, missing his target and almost striking a woman passing nearby. Duncan, who had observed what happened, quickly came up and arrested one man and, starting his prisoner toward the calaboose, directed the other to follow him. Instead, the second man, not wholly desirous of spending the night in the stinking calaboose, jumped into an express wagon pulled by a single horse that he had parked nearby and started off down the street. Duncan called for him to halt, but the man liberally applied his whip to the horse and made his break. Duncan released his prisoner and started in pursuit on foot. Cheered on by a gathering crowd, he caught up with the wagon and climbed into the rear of the vehicle. At this point, the fleeing driver decided to abandon ship and jumped overboard, followed closely by Duncan, leaving the horse to ramble on through the city streets as he wished. Seizing the man, Duncan soon brought him under control and marched him to a waiting cell. After catching his breath, Duncan then went in search of the first man he had taken into custody, who had predictably not continued on to the calaboose voluntarily when Duncan went after his companion. Looking along Elm Street, he finally spotted the man. But the black man also spotted Duncan and, after he pulled off his shoes, the chase was on again. Unfortunately for Duncan, after he had run the man to the southern city limits, he lost sight of the fugitive and had to retire. As the newspaper observed, "to be a good runner is an advantage sometimes to the police."[14]

The volume of police activity predictably picked up with the coming of spring. In April, Marshal Morton, in a spurt of morality, announced that, henceforth, each applicant for a position on the police force would have to sign an oath swearing total abstinence from the "use of spiritous liquors" so long as he was a policeman. The *Dallas Daily Herald* approved, commenting that "no man who drinks to any degree can serve the people faithfully as a policeman."[15] One can well imagine the sideward glances the present officers on the force, including Duncan, gave each other. Duncan had cultivated a taste for whiskey now and then, as did most of the other officers, often while on duty, and they were likely relieved that the marshal's order was not retroactive. The reasons behind such a policy are not known, although saloon owners didn't mind having an officer dropping in every now and then to keep the peace and often encouraged such visits with free drinks. The marshal's policy, as might be expected, did not prove very successful.

On April 7, Duncan, along with officers Jim Arnold and Henry C. Waller, broke up a fight between two men on the east side of the Courthouse square. A man carrying a shotgun was passing by and, seeing the gathered crowd, ran over to see what was going on. Suspecting that the man might be trying to rescue their prisoners, the three officers alertly drew down on the unsuspecting man but, to his great relief, let him go on his way once he had explained.[16] On April 14, Arnold and Duncan had to arrest a belligerent John Bowman in a Main Street saloon after he became upset about a watch he claimed he had pawned there.[17]

The police force in Dallas was overseen by a Police Board consisting of the mayor and two aldermen appointed by the mayor. Each year, the members of the force were reviewed by the board for reappointment, usually following the recommendations of the marshal. Duncan survived this review and was reappointed to the force on April 16, 1877, along with ten others.[18] There had been pressure from the newspapers to increase the size of the force, but city finances, as usual, were much too limited.

The local newspapers consistently filled the role of community conscience when it came to the police. For example, when an 1877 Texas Supreme Court decision criticized the liberal use of clubs by policemen on resisting prisoners, the *Daily Herald* reprinted the court's opinion in its entirety. "As several instances have occurred in this city when policemen have used their locusts, we publish this for their special guidance."[19] The fact that none of the officers had received any training in the law or their duties and how to carry them out probably did not worry the officers themselves, but it often worried the newspapers and others. In an effort to improve the quality of cases brought before him by policemen, former marshal June Peak, who had been recently elected to the new position of city recorder and who tried offenders of municipal ordinances arrested by the police, gathered the entire police force in his office and lectured them on obeying the law themselves in carrying out their duties. He urged them to become familiar with the city's ordinances, noting that some of the officers had never even seen a copy.[20] Quite likely, many people were arrested for behavior that constituted a personal affront to an officer who thought such actions ought to be against the law, whether or not they actually were.

On April 25, 1877, two strangers entered the Mint Saloon and sat down near a billiard table where a man was playing by himself. One of the strangers, a small, cross-eyed man with a white hat, called to Harry Watters, the barkeeper, who was eating his lunch.

"If you want to see me, come here," Watters replied, thinking that the other man, who was slumping against his companion, was only drunk. The small man then said that his companion was cut, lifting up the man's shirt to expose his bloody wounds. The man playing billiards went after a doctor, and the small man led his wounded friend to the door, where he fell to the sidewalk. Two doctors came on the run and examined the man's four knife wounds, his intestines protruding from one of the savage cuts. The man in the white hat had run

Longtime Dallas Police Chief James Carter "Jim" Arnold, as he appeared in 1885. (Author's Collection).

away as soon as his companion had fallen. As the victim lapsed into unconsciousness, Officer Pat Sheehan recalled that he had seen him with three others earlier in the evening and in an intoxicated state. Duncan and Edwards, one of the officers who had not been reappointed by the police board, quickly developed some information identifying a man named Moffitt as the person committing the stabbing. They boarded an eastbound train to the White Rock Bottoms not far from Dallas and soon located the suspect. Moffitt, who claimed self-defense, was lodged in the calaboose as a result of the diligence of the two men.[21]

But, in spite of the good police work, an officer could not rest on his laurels. The very next evening, Duncan and Edwards assisted Officer Ed Cornwell in subduing and arresting two drunk women.[22] Two nights later, on Sunday, April 29, passersby along Main Street, near the Crutchfield House, watched as a German, Henry Holesworth, chased another man down the street. Suddenly, the man turned and struck Holesworth with a rock. Stunned, Holesworth fell to the ground, and the man leaped on him, stabbing him seven times, then fleeing. Holesworth got up and staggered to a nearby shack where he lived with a black woman, saying over and over, "I am dead! I am dead!" Duncan and Jim Arnold went to work running down information from their sources in the black neighborhood, their attention soon focusing on a man named Jim Gilland. The officers subsequently arrested Gilland and brought him before Holesworth, who identified him as his assailant. Gilland claimed self-defense, contending that Holesworth meant to harm him. He was later released without charges being filed by Holesworth, who subsequently died of his wounds.[23]

With the arrival of May, Marshal Morton shifted the duties of his officers, those on the day watch being placed on night duty and vice versa. This rotation was a tactic to try to prevent possible corruption. An officer who remained assigned to the same time period might be inclined to accept bribes regularly for looking the other way, such as when a saloon owner wanted to stay open past the legal closing time or when gambling was going on. The *Daily Herald* also suggested that the practice of city policemen acting as "special detectives" outside the city limits was diluting enforcement efforts inside the city and should be stopped. This ultimately led to the board of aldermen passing a resolution that the marshal, except when in actual pursuit of violators, be required to remain within the city limits. The city fathers also asked the county sheriff to cease the practice of deputizing the marshal in cases outside the city.[24]

The month of May also brought the onset of staggering heat, resulting in police officers sweltering beneath the heavy coats that constituted their regular uniform. There were appeals for a summer uniform, and the police board finally approved. Duncan and the other officers went to a local clothier, E. M. Kahn and Brothers, and each purchased a light grey suit for fifteen dollars.[25]

On Sunday evening, May 20, 1877, a man named Wilkinson and a friend went to the St. Louis House, Wilkinson flashing a roll of some $700. In the morning, Wilkinson found he was missing $350. He reported his loss to Duncan, who promptly began an investigation. The officer soon determined that the money had been slipped from the victim's pocket by a black woman named Maggie Mitchell, who then gave it to her sister, who had slipped it through a knothole in a fence behind the boarding house to a third woman. Duncan arrested all three and recovered $175.

But Wilkinson was apparently not one to learn from experience. That same evening, desiring to retire early, Wilkinson gave his remaining money to a black companion named Claib to keep for him. Claib possessed a few character flaws, however, and visited a nearby saloon. Sight of the roll of money he carried quickly attracted a friendly crowd around him. A friend of Wilkinson's who knew about Claib having the money saw the crowd and immediately got Wilkinson. By the time they relocated Claib, however, he had only ten dollars left, the rest of the money having been spent or stolen from him.[26] Neither Duncan nor any officer could be of much help this time.

During the previous January, the board of aldermen had passed an ordinance regulating the serious problem of dogs running loose. The very thought of an outbreak of rabies in these frontier times was enough to cause widespread panic in the community. An annual one-dollar dog tax was imposed, and all dogs were required to have a collar and to be muzzled, if running loose. If a stray dog was not muzzled, it was to be impounded and, if not claimed within twenty-four hours, to be killed. Further, a policeman or any other person had the right to shoot or kill any rabid dog "or any dog in the streets which shall manifest a disposition to bite." Marshal Morton began a concentrated enforcement of the ordinance in late spring of the year.[27] Thus, in addition to drunks and thieves, the officers now had to chase down dogs.

In late May, Duncan and Edwards captured a dog which had bitten a child in the face and had eluded capture. They took the animal to the Trinity River bottom, shot him, and left him for dead. The dog survived, however, and crawled home, and remained there until his wound healed. Venturing out, the dog again bit another child. This time, Marshal Morton personally took the animal to the calaboose and killed it.[28] By June 9, Morton could report over 300 dogs destroyed for the year, twenty-one killed only the previous afternoon. One of those dogs was named Beasly and had apparently proven quite elusive to the pursuing Duncan. The *Herald* reported that Beasly's howl would no longer be heard on the street and "Jack Duncan is inconsolable."[29]

Despite the distractions of chasing down stray dogs, other police work was not being neglected. One close call Duncan had was only briefly reported:

> Last night about 9:00 o'clock, a number of pistol shots were heard in the vicinity of the cemetery. Officer Duncan went over in that direction to find, if he could, who did the shooting. In the graveyard he found a darky whom he suspected, and proceeded to search him, when the Negro pulled a pistol, and firing at Duncan, broke away. Duncan returned the fire with two shots, and at the present writing is still in pursuit of the darky, assisted by several deputy sheriffs.[30]

The suspect was not subsequently reported to be located and Duncan, unharmed, could only return to his duties. Through June, Duncan followed through in his routine activities with the usual success. He made arrests for the theft of a ten-dollar bill, assisted in the jailing of a drunk woman at the Central Railroad depot, and confirmed that a Chicago bank note was counterfeit.[31]

By this time, after ten months, the daily duties of a Dallas policeman may have become too routine for Duncan. Fifty dollars a month was not much compensation for the risks of the job, not to mention the disagreeable people and situations encountered nearly every day. Also, the uniformed policeman was much too visible, often resulting in restrictions placed on him by a politically-oriented marshal. Duncan was likely quite receptive to an opportunity to do what he liked best—catch crooks—but for more money.

The name of John Wesley Hardin was by now well-known to anyone in Texas who read a newspaper. His reputation as a gunfighter was enhanced by stories that he had killed twenty-six men. His deadly exploits had begun in the early turbulent days of Reconstruction immediately after the Civil War, when the Union Army took over the reins of Texas government, and trite as it may sound, he truly became a legend in his own time. The association of this hot-headed, remorseless killer with the Taylor faction in the bloody Sutton-Taylor feud in Gonzales and DeWitt Counties in 1873 and 1874 gave him the opportunity to increase the number of notches on his pistol.[32] In a report to Texas Reconstruction Governor Edmund J. Davis, the state adjutant general, who oversaw the state police force, described a "strong band of thieves and murderers, headed by John Hardin," that was terrorizing Gonzales County. A reward had been offered for Hardin by both Texas and Missouri, and efforts to apprehend him had been futile. The adjutant general wrote:

> The sheriff of Gonzales County informs me that he has made no effort to arrest any of these parties; that the citizens will not answer his summons, and that the outlaws would be released, even if caught and placed in Gonzales jail. I have made several efforts to arrest Hardin and his companions, but owing to the police force having received no pay for several months, it is impossible to move them in sufficient strength to capture the outlaws.[33]

Hardin, the son of a Methodist preacher and lawyer, had been born in Bonham, Texas, on May 26, 1853, and subsequently raised in Trinity County in southeastern Texas. According to Hardin's autobiography, his first killing came at the age of sixteen when he was attacked by a black man with a club. This led to the cold-blooded ambush of three members of a "Yankee" patrol sent to find him. Briefly teaching school in

Bounty Hunter

Navarro County in 1869 at the age of sixteen, he continued to have confrontations with pursuing federal troops which, according to him, resulted in more deaths. His parents settled in Comanche County where his brother, Joe, practiced law. At one point, Hardin went on a cattle drive to Abilene, Kansas, where he allegedly "got the drop" on City Marshal Wild Bill Hickok. Back in Texas, trouble and death seemed to follow him wherever he went. After marrying Jane Bowen, he was seriously wounded in one escapade and jailed, but escaped, at which time he was drawn to join his friends with the Taylor faction. By this time, there is little wonder why Hardin could be termed the "worst bad man" in Texas and the Rangers believed him to be "the champion desperado of the world."[34] Many believed he had killed over forty men. He was now a top priority target for the Texas Rangers, and a confrontation was inevitable.

On May 26, 1874, in the town of Comanche, Deputy Sheriff Charles Webb of Brown County was shot to death by Hardin and others on the public square near Jack Wright's saloon. Earlier, a witness had seen Hardin and his close friend, Jim Taylor, crying after a long conversation behind Carnes and Wilson's saloon, no doubt such emotions being induced by copious amounts of liquor consumed during and after some races held that same day. After recovering, Hardin treated his friends to drinks and spotted Webb walking toward Wright's saloon. Several weeks earlier, Webb had arrested the son of an old woman acquaintance of Hardin's, allegedly mistreating her in some fashion. Seeing the deputy, Hardin, Taylor, and Bud Dixon, all now well-liquored, confronted the lawman, and Hardin goaded him. As the conversation between Hardin and Webb wound to its inevitable conclusion, Webb took a step back, saying, "No, Goddamn you, I'm not afraid of you!" and hastily drew his pistol. The weapon discharged prematurely as it cleared his holster, before he could point it at any of the three before him. As Webb's pistol went off harmlessly, three pistols barked in simultaneous response, and the deputy fell dead, bullets having

John Wesley Hardin in Abilene, Kansas, in 1871. (Courtesy of Southwest Texas State University, San Marcos, Texas).

pierced his head, abdomen, and hand.[35] Hardin would continue to insist until his death that Webb tried to back-shoot him and that he killed the deputy in self-defense.[36] However, he and Taylor were indicted for murder on October 31, 1874.[37] Webb's tragic death excited the community, grown weary of the bloody conflict, and Hardin, faced with the prospect of death at the hands of a lynch mob should he be caught, gathered his family to flee the state.

Thus, throughout Texas, Hardin's name was a notorious one. Even though he disappeared from sight after the Webb shooting, he nevertheless remained present in the minds of Rangers and other lawmen. An incident in Dallas is illustrative of the impact of Hardin's name at the time and how touchy lawmen could get at the prospect of a showdown with him.

At about 4:30 p. m., Saturday, November 6, 1875, a local carpenter named Eugene McGee approached Dallas County

Bounty Hunter

Sheriff Jim Barkley and asked for a warrant for Hardin. The surprised lawman denied his request, as he did a request for a photograph of Hardin. The sheriff also denied McGee's request for permission to carry a pistol, which was against state law. Without explaining his requests, McGee said he didn't give a damn for all the officers in existence and that he thought he could arrest Hardin, but didn't say anything to the sheriff about Hardin's whereabouts. The sheriff likely dismissed him as suffering from the "jim-jams."

Since City Marshal June Peak was out of town in pursuit of a robbery suspect, McGee approached Deputy Marshal Morton at 7:30 that evening, telling him that Hardin had slipped into Dallas. In response to Morton's urgent questions, McGee claimed to know the gunman intimately, stating that he had conversed and shook hands with his outlaw friend just moments before. Morton asked him if he might not be mistaken, but McGee assured him that he knew Hardin as well as anyone and that the desperado was at that very moment in bed with a woman on Wood Street. Convinced of McGee's sincerity, Morton had him go to the Lamar Hotel and wait for him. The deputy marshal then went to the calaboose and rounded up officers James F. Hamel, John T. Carter, and John W. Spencer, the latter already somewhat weary from having disarmed two dangerous drunks earlier that same day.

The four officers rendezvoused with McGee at the hotel where he again assured them that he could not be mistaken. McGee volunteered to go into the house first, since Hardin would not suspect him, and then get the drop on him. Morton stationed his officers around the house to prevent escape, he and Spencer near a back window to the room where Hardin and the woman were supposed to be. As McGee prepared to enter the front door, Spencer joined him in the front of the house. In the dark, a man carrying a Navy Colt six-shooter confronted McGee at the door, and Spencer ordered the man to halt and throw up his hands. The man said nothing, but Spencer could

*A photograph
of Dallas policeman
John W. Spencer
taken in 1885.
(Author's Collection).*

see his silhouette advancing, and he again called from the dark for the man to halt. The shadowy figure seemed to make a threatening motion with his pistol, and Spencer, only too aware of Hardin's reputation, fired at the man, as did McGee. The man crashed to the floor, and the officers rushed in, turning the body over cautiously for examination. "Good God!" exclaimed Spencer. "It's not John Wesley Hardin!" McGee countered, "I know the man to be John Wesley Hardin and I am responsible for the killing."

The next day, an inquest was held in which it came out that McGee had been staying with the woman on Wood Street, Mrs. Annie Sullivan, and that she had kicked him out in favor of the dead man, named Monroe, whom she had met at the Central depot. In December, 1875, McGee was indicted for murder. Although McGee was subsequently found not guilty, it is curious to note that one of the witnesses subpoenaed to testify

Bounty Hunter

Texas Ranger Captain J. Lee Hall, as he appeared in an 1873 edition of Scribner's Magazine. *(Courtesy of Chuck Parsons).*

on behalf of the defendant was Mrs. Myra Reed—although what her role in the incident was—is unknown.[38] Nevertheless, the incident was underscored by the fact that, but for the injection of Hardin's name, a man might not have so easily died.

Though Hardin had left Texas, the newspapers continued to report periodically some new exploit concerning him, such as a threat to burn the town of Comanche or the death of a man named Beard in Kaufman County who was supposed to be a member of Hardin's "gang."[39] The depredations by many outlaws in the early 1870's, in addition to Hardin's, were finally sufficient to induce the Texas Legislature to authorize the reorganization of the Texas Rangers in 1874 to replace the hated state police force of Reconstruction. Governor Richard Coke organized a Frontier Battalion to cope with the ongoing Indian problem and a Special Force under Captain L. H. McNelly, which was assigned to deal with the many bands of rustlers and

John Barclay Armstrong, Texas Ranger, who helped capture John Wesley Hardin. (Courtesy of John M. Bennett and Chuck Parsons).

outlaws terrorizing the state.[40] McNelly was succeeded as commander of the Special Force by J. Lee Hall in January, 1877.

Hall, easily identified by his brilliant hair and known as Red, was born in North Carolina in 1849 and came to Texas when he was twenty years old. Initially teaching school in Grayson County in North Texas, he became the city marshal of Sherman, then a deputy sheriff in Denison in 1873, and served as a sergeant-at-arms for the State Legislature before he was appointed a second lieutenant under McNelly in the Texas Rangers in August, 1876.[41] Here he met Sergeant John Barclay Armstrong, known as "McNelly's Bulldog," who had come to Texas from Tennessee in 1871, at the age of twenty-one, and joined the Rangers the following year. Armstrong was made a lieutenant when Hall took command of the Special Force.[42]

The Rangers were sent into DeWitt County to put an end to the Sutton-Taylor feud and all of its resulting bloodshed. At one point, a truce had been worked out, but another killing sparked the violence anew. William H. Steele, the state adjutant general, at the behest of Governor Coke, ordered Captain Hall to arrest indiscriminately members of either faction, which the Rangers promptly did. Steele also told Hall that he wished he would take steps to arrest Hardin, not only because of the $4,000 reward now being offered for the gunman, but also because he wanted all the leaders of the violence brought to justice.[43]

In May, 1877, while performing duties at Goliad, Texas, Armstrong carelessly handled his pistol, and it discharged accidentally, the ball entering his groin and striking his hipbone. By the end of June, however, though limping with the aid of a cane, he was sufficiently recovered to resume his duties.[44] In an incident similar to the Eugene McGee incident in Dallas in 1875, Armstrong received word that Hardin was in a saloon and laid plans with a local officer to take him alive. Armstrong approached the stranger, offered to buy him a drink, and, as the local officer grabbed the man's arm, the Ranger thrust his cocked six-shooter into the man's stomach. Embarrassed to find out the man was not Hardin, Armstrong became intrigued with the idea of tracking down the real outlaw and asked for that assignment, which was granted.[45]

Hall and Armstrong knew that the only way to locate Hardin would be by penetrating the close circle of friends and relatives around Hardin. Someone who was not known to any of Hardin's crowd was needed—someone who had the skill and daring to carry off an undercover role and who could withstand the close scrutiny he would most certainly undergo. It was a dangerous mission and Red Hall cast around Texas for the man who could do the job.

NOTES

1. *Dallas Daily Herald*, January 25, 1877.

2. *Dallas Daily Herald*, February 23 and 28, 1877.

3. *Dallas Weekly Herald*, February 3, 1877.

4. *Dallas Daily Herald*, March 1, 1877.

5. Executive Journal, 1875-1877, Papers of Kentucky Governor James B. McCreary, February 22, 1877.

6. *Dallas Weekly Herald*, March 10, 1877.

7. *Dallas Daily Herald*, March 8-11, 23, 1877.

8. *Dallas Daily Herald*, March 8, 1877.

9. *Dallas Daily Herald*, March 10, 1877.

10. *Dallas Daily Herald*, March 17, 1877.

11. *Dallas Daily Herald*, March 18, 1877.

12. *Dallas Daily Herald*, March 28, 1877.

13. *Dallas Daily Herald*, April 3, 1877.

14. *Dallas Daily Herald*, April 10, 1877.

15. *Dallas Daily Herald*, April 10, 1877.

16. *Dallas Daily Herald*, April 8, 1877.

17. *Dallas Daily Herald*, April 15, 1877.

18. *Dallas Daily Herald*, April 17, 1877.

19. *Dallas Daily Herald*, April 22, 1877.

20. *Dallas Daily Herald*, May 26, 1877.

21. *Dallas Daily Herald*, April 25 and 26, 1877.

22. *Dallas Daily Herald*, April 27, 1877.

23. *Dallas Daily Herald*, May 1 and 2, 1877.

24. *Dallas Daily Herald*, May 3, 1877; Minutes, Board of Aldermen, City of Dallas, Texas, May 15, 1877.

25. *Dallas Daily Herald*, May 13-20, 1877; Ledger Book, E. M. Kahn & Co. (Dallas Public Library), May 19, 1877, p. 168.

26. *Dallas Daily Herald*, May 22, 1877.

27. Minutes, Board of Aldermen, City of Dallas, Texas, January 26, 1877; *Dallas Weekly Herald*, June 2, 1877.

28. *Dallas Daily Herald*, May 23, 1877.

29. *Dallas Daily Herald*, June 9, 1877.

30. *Dallas Daily Herald*, June 13, 1877.

31. *Dallas Daily Herald*, June 17, 1877; June 28 and 29, 1877.

32. For excellent accounts of the Sutton-Taylor feud and Hardin's role in it, see Robert C. Sutton, Jr., *The Sutton-Taylor Feud* (Quanah, Texas: Nortex Press, 1974), and C. L. Sonnichson, *I'll Die Before I Run* (New York: The Devin-Adair Co., 1962).

Bounty Hunter

33. Report of State Adjutant General, 1873, pp. 122 and 123.

34. James D. Horan, *The Authentic Wild West: The Gunfighters* (New York: Crown Publishers, Inc., 1976), p. 155; John Wesley Hardin, *The Life of John Wesley Hardin*, reprint ed. (Norman, Oklahoma: University of Oklahoma Press, 1961), pp. 13-88; George Hendricks, *The Badman of the West* (San Antonio, Texas: The Naylor Co., 1970), p. 13; James B. Gillett, *Six Years With the Texas Rangers* (New Haven, Connecticut: Yale University Press, 1925), p. 85.

35. *John W. Hardin v. The State of Texas*, 4 Texas Court of Appeals Reports 355 (1878). For the most accurate account of Webb's shooting, see Thomas Ripley, *They Died With Their Boots On* (New York: Pocket Books, Inc., 1949).

36. Hardin, *Life*, pp. 92 and 93.

37. *Hardin v. State of Texas*, 4 Texas Court of Appeals Reports at 360 (1878).

38. *Dallas Daily Herald*, November 7 and 9, 1875; Minutes, 14th District Court, Dallas County, Texas, Vol. I, p. 197; Vol. J, p. 78; Vol. K, pp. 540 and 541 (*State of Texas v. Eugene McGee*, cause no. 3126).

39. *Dallas Weekly Herald*, June 2 and 9, 1877.

40. Wayne Gard, *Frontier Justice* (Norman, Oklahoma: University of Oklahoma Press, 1949), p. 224; Joseph G. Rosa, *The Gunfighter: Man or Myth?* (Norman, Oklahoma: University of Oklahoma Press, 1969), p. 56.

41. Dora Neill Raymond, *Captain Lee Hall of Texas* (Norman, Oklahoma: University of Oklahoma Press, 1940), pp. 3-13; Texas Ranger Muster Rolls, Texas State Archives.

42. Raymond, *Lee Hall*, p. 49; Johnson, *Texas and Texans*, Vol. III, p. 1358; Ripley, *Died With Their Boots On*, p. 175; Walter Prescott Webb, *The Texas Rangers*, 2nd ed. (Austin, Texas: University of Texas Press, 1965), p. 294.

43. *San Antonio Daily Express*, September 12, 1895.

44. Report from Lt. J. L. Hall, Adjutant General Records, May 31, 1877; June 29, 1877, Texas State Archives.

45. Lewis Nordyke, *Wes Hardin, Texas Gunman* (London: John Long Limited, 1958), p. 160; Webb, *Texas Rangers*, p. 298; Rosa, *Gunfighter*, p. 57.

THE EARLY WEST

78

Chapter 4

Get Wes Hardin!

Upon leaving Texas in the summer of 1874 and catching up with his family—whom he had sent ahead—in New Orleans, Hardin, using the alias Walker, finally landed in Cedar Keys, Florida. After briefly mulling over the idea of fleeing to England, Hardin moved his family to Gainesville, Florida, changed his alias to John H. Swain, and bought a grocery and liquor business.[1] Still, trouble followed. Three days after opening for business, he was deputized to help the city marshal keep a mob from lynching a black prisoner. In the resulting confrontation, Hardin ended up shooting a man. The prisoner, subsequently released, was later arrested again for raping a white woman, and Hardin admitted that he assisted another mob in torching the jail and burning the man to death.

Early in 1875, he again moved his family, this time eighteen miles away to Micanopy. Hardin, alias Swain, operated a bar and traded horses briefly, then moved his family again to Jacksonville, Florida, where a son was born and he subsequently went into the butcher and liquor business. Because of rumors of detectives lurking around, the family moved in the summer of 1876 to Pollard, Alabama, just north of the Florida state line, where they lived with Neil McMillan, a deputy sheriff, who was Jane Hardin's uncle.

In August of 1876, Hardin attempted to take his family to the New Orleans area, but, because of a yellow fever quarantine, sent them back to Pollard. He and a friend, Gus Kennedy, then went to Mobile, Alabama, where they were jailed for disorderly conduct arising from an argument about politics, during which scuffle at least one local policeman was wounded. Returning to Pollard, Hardin went into the logging business with Sheppard Hardy. At this time, Brown Bowen, Hardin's brother-in-law, who was also fleeing a murder indictment in Texas, came to Pollard with his family and joined him.[2]

Meanwhile, in Texas, the Rangers continued to search for Hardin. Recognizing that Hardin's whereabouts could probably be determined only from one of the outlaw's friends or relatives, Hall placed several detectives on the Ranger payroll, keeping their identities secret, even from other Rangers, for fear they would be compromised. One detective was assigned to find out where the wanted gunman was, but failed.[3] Finally, Jack Duncan's name came to Hall's attention as a resourceful and shrewd investigator, a relentless manhunter who had a good record for getting his man.[4] Duncan appeared to be the one man who could carry out the dangerous mission he had in mind.

Hall went through Dallas in March, 1877, ostensibly on his way to visit relatives and friends in Sherman.[5] He was later quoted as saying he personally contacted Duncan in Dallas at some point in time and went over his plan, the detective then agreeing to accept the job.[6] The trip through Dallas in March may have been when that contact occurred. However, Duncan remained in Dallas and continued his duties as a policeman. In mid-July, Duncan, accompanied by fellow officers Spencer and Dunn, went to Austin to testify again as a witness in a counterfeiting case. Immediately upon his return to Dallas on July 19, Duncan submitted his resignation to Marshal Morton, effective at once, and that evening reportedly left for San Antonio where he was to "enter into other duties."[7] There could have been several discussions between Duncan and the Rangers prior to the Austin trip, or he could have been initially contacted in Austin. Nevertheless, he was enlisted in the Special State Troops under Hall as a Ranger private on July 15, 1877,[8] four days prior to the date of his resignation in Dallas. No doubt, Duncan was induced to make this move by the tempting $4,000 reward offered by the state in 1873 for Hardin, but the challenge presented to his skill and ability as a detective must also have been a factor. Assigned to work with Lieutenant Armstrong, the twenty-six year old Duncan prepared for his task.

According to Hall's recollections, just prior to hiring Duncan, he had received information from DeWitt County Deputy Sheriff Dick Hudson, a member of the Sutton faction, that Hardin was supposed to be somewhere in Florida, using the name Swain.[9] In order to determine if this was true and exactly where he was, it was planned that Duncan, in disguise, would approach and become friendly with friends and relatives of Hardin and his wife. Someone in Gonzales County was bound to be in contact with the fugitive killer. Of course, Duncan, Hall, and Armstrong all knew that if there was even a hint that Duncan was not who or what he claimed to be, his life was forfeit.

Adopting the alias of Williams, Duncan went into Gonzales County, initially working as a laborer on several farms.[10] Over a period of days, he began cultivating the friendship of a number of people in the area, including Neal Bowen, Hardin's father-in-law. Duncan passed himself off as sympathetic to the Taylor faction and as having experienced some trouble with the law himself. Bowen operated a small grocery, and Duncan patiently built a relationship with the older man, visiting him on a regular basis. Within a very short time after Duncan had first appeared in the area, Neal Bowen took him into his house as a boarder. Indicating an intention to be a merchant, "Williams" discussed with Bowen the possibility of renting a storehouse on Bowen's property. Before anything was decided in the matter, Duncan had learned somehow that a wagon on Bowen's property was not Bowen's and, suspecting it belonged to Hardin, expressed an interest in buying it. The cautious Bowen told him that he could not sell it because it belonged to someone else. Duncan casually urged him to write the owner to see what he would take for it, careful not to push the matter and risk possible suspicion as to his motives or identity.

At some point about this time, it is possible, though unlikely, that Duncan returned to Dallas. If he did, he was said to have encountered a close acquaintance or perhaps a relative of Hardin's who was not aware of his true identity. Playing his role, Duncan was supposed to have asked the acquaintance if he had ever heard of Hardin, telling him further, "I wish he would kill all of Comanche and I'd help him do it!" Such a statement, of course, would have served to further strengthen his acceptance by Hardin's crowd. Whether this incident actually happened is subject to a great deal of question, especially given the risk involved in briefly absenting himself from such a dangerous undercover role to a town where he was well known.[11]

Shortly after Duncan expressed an interest in buying the wagon, he observed Bowen receive a letter and watched as his placed it in a trunk. At the first opportunity, he slipped into the room and retrieved it. The letter, written in response to an earlier one from Bowen to his daughter, Jane Hardin, had been penned instead by his son, Brown. Though the younger Bowen worded the letter guardedly, he could not resist slipping in the phrase, "My sister joins me in sending love to all." Jane Hardin was at that time in bed recovering from the birth of her third child on July 15. This was the evidence that Duncan was looking for to prove Neal Bowen was in correspondence with the Hardins, fully aware that Hardin would be with his family. Now he needed to know exactly where they were.

Several days later, Bowen and Duncan went into the tiny town of Cuero in neighboring DeWitt County where Bowen intended to buy some supplies. According to Hall, Bowen had too much to drink, no doubt encouraged by "Williams," who also reminded Bowen to write a letter to determine the asking price for the wagon. At some point, Bowen had written a letter and

Get Wes Hardin!

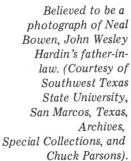

Believed to be a photograph of Neal Bowen, John Wesley Hardin's father-in-law. (Courtesy of Southwest Texas State University, San Marcos, Texas, Archives, Special Collections, and Chuck Parsons).

Duncan gave him an envelope in which to mail it—after carefully marking that envelope. Duly depositing the letter in the local post office, Bowen then went off to get his supplies. As soon as he was out of sight, Duncan approached the postmaster and told him that he had just deposited a letter, but that he was afraid he had misdirected it and wanted to check to see if the address was correct and perhaps to add a line or two. The marked envelope enabled him to spot the right letter quickly and he noted that it was addressed to Mr. J. H. Swain, Pollard, Alabama, in care of Neil McMillan. Scanning the contents of the letter, Duncan had no doubt now that he had established the whereabouts of John Wesley Hardin.[12]

Duncan wasted no time in alerting the waiting Armstrong by a prearranged code: "Come get your horse." On August 15, 1877, Lieutenant Armstrong, still limping from his wound, and several Rangers rode boldly into Hardin territory and arrested "Williams," boasting of their capture of "one of Hardin's gang." Manacled, Duncan was placed in a wagon and taken to the railroad depot in Cuero. The lawmen then put their prisoner on the train for Austin, where they arrived on August 17.[13] The local newspaper reported Armstrong's presence in the city, noting his recovery and that he was staying at the Avenue Hotel.[14]

Once in Austin, Armstrong requested State Adjutant General William Steele to cause warrants to be issued for Hardin, one in Hardin's true name and one in that of his alias, Swain, and to send them on to him at Montgomery, Alabama. One warrant was to be transmitted by regular mail and, just in case, the other was to go by express.[15] Not waiting for the warrants, eager to nab their man, Armstrong and Duncan then left Austin by train on August 18, 1877.[16] Lee Hall, now a Ranger captain, had planned to accompany his lieutenant and Duncan on the trip, but was unable to get to Austin in time. He had not anticipated that Duncan would be able to work up the information so soon and was tied up on another job.[17]

Armstong and Duncan arrived in Montgomery, Alabama, on the evening of August 20. It had been decided that Armstrong would wait there for the requisition papers from the adjutant general, while Duncan would go ahead to scout out the area. Armstrong telegraphed General Steele to that effect.[18] Dressed in well-used clothing to disguise himself as a transient, Duncan went on to Pollard, just north of the Alabama-Florida line. He looked up Neil McMillan to inquire about a fictitious brother of his somewhere in the county. During the course of the conversation, Duncan casually mentioned Swain's name, and McMillan told him that Swain lived in Whiting, a tiny community a short distance south of Pollard. Duncan then walked to Whiting where he struck up a conversation with a merchant named Brown. As they talked, Duncan was able to elicit the information that Swain was at Pensacola, Florida, on a gambling trip. Quickly going to the telegraph operator at the small depot in Whiting, Duncan hurriedly got off a telegram to Armstrong in Montgomery that Swain was in Pensacola and for him to take the first available train and meet him in Whiting.

At this point, the quest for Hardin took a bizarre turn. The telegraph operator, after sending Duncan's telegram, nervously asked the detective to step back into his private office. He told Duncan that the superintendent of the Pensacola Railroad, William D. Chipley, was quite anxious to see both Swain and Brown Bowen gone from the area as they had made threats against him.[19]

There is some dispute as to how Chipley came to be threatened by either Hardin or Bowen. Swain, Bowen, Shep Hardy, and Chipley were apparently well-acquainted and gambled together often. Hardin contended many years later that Bowen, while drunk, had gotten into a "row" with Chipley. Bowen was supposed to have gotten the worst of the encounter and, in threatening Chipley, revealed Swain's true identity.[20] As to the contention that Hardin himself threatened Chipley, an Atlanta newspaper reported that on August 20, 1877, in Pensacola, Swain had gotten drunk and chased a black man through the combination train station and hotel. As Chipley was going into his office, Swain asked him, "Why didn't you stop that nigger for me?" Chipley replied, "I have nothing to do with your nigger." At this, Swain pointed his pistol at the superintendent and threatened to shoot him. Before the hammer could fall, Chipley alertly thrust his hand between it and the cylinder, jerked the pistol away with some damage to his hand, and buffaloed the intoxicated Mr. Swain over the head several times with it. As a crowd gathered, Swain swore to kill him and left.[21]

Nevertheless, regardless of who assaulted him, Chipley apparently had ample motivation to want to see both men out of his life. Armstrong, still without the necessary papers from Texas, joined Duncan the next morning, August 23, in Whiting and had the telegraph operator send a message to Chipley in Pensacola. After a brief long distance conversation by wire, Chipley agreed to provide a special engine and car to bring the two to Pensacola, some forty-four miles to the south. Several hours later, the engine and boxcar arrived in Whiting, accompanied by Chipley, a judge of the court in Pensacola, and Escambia County, Florida, Sheriff William H. Hutchinson.[22]

Bounty Hunter

Texas Adjutant General William H. Steele. (Courtesy of Barker Texas History Center, University of Texas at Austin).

The two Texas Rangers told them that they were there to arrest John Swain, without mentioning who he really was. Armstrong was asked if he also wanted Brown Bowen and, upon receiving an affirmative answer, the three from Pensacola agreed to assist the Rangers. In the meantime, the Whiting telegraph operator, by contacting a friend in Pensacola, was able to learn that Swain and a number of his friends were then at the hotel there.[23]

Boarding the special train, the five started for Pensacola. Forced to sit on wooden benches while the train labored along the rough road,[24] they ignored their discomfort and discussed a number of plans for the arrests. Duncan and Armstrong tried to learn as much as they could about the locale in which the trap would be set.

As soon as they arrived, the Rangers learned that John Swain had sent some groceries ahead by train to his family in Pollard and had purchased a ticket for the evening train. Brown Bowen was not with Swain's party.[25] There was not much time to waste in developing a plan to take the gunman by surprise. Secluding themselves in Superintendent Chipley's office, the

*Brown Bowen (right)
with Thomas Caffall.
(Courtesy of
Southwest Texas State
University, San Marcos,
Texas, Archives-Special
Collections and
Chuck Parsons).*

five men discussed the manner in which the arrest would be carried out. Sheriff Hutchinson voted to take Swain in the most direct manner on the street but was overruled by Armstrong, who decided the least dangerous approach was to try to take the outlaw on the train.

Since Swain was scheduled to leave Pensacola for Whiting on that afternoon's train, Hutchinson had very little time to round up and deputize a group of men to assist in the capture. Among that group of local citizens were Martin Sullivan and perhaps John E. Callaghan, County Constable Joseph Commyns, E. R. Payne, John Bard, William McKinney, M. L. Davis, and Richard L. Campbell.[26] The deputies were to be posted around the depot to prevent escape in case Hardin managed to get away from his captors on the train.

What actually happened on that balmy afternoon is subject to some radically different accounts, a number of facts being hotly disputed afterwards by all of the participants. The exact truth will probably never be known, and the best that can be done is to piece together the various accounts for what *most likely* happened.[27]

Bounty Hunter

William D. Chipley, superintendent of the Pensacola Railroad. (Courtesy of Chuck Parsons).

Late that afternoon, Hardin, accompanied by Shep Hardy, Neal Campbell, Jim Mann, and perhaps several others, boarded the train for Whiting. The men went into the smoking car where Hardin could enjoy the pipe he had just taken up. Armstrong, still bothered by the limp from his gunshot wound, stationed himself in the express or baggage car next to the smoker, while Duncan remained outside the train on the opposite side from the depot. The engineer and conductor, standing by at their posts, had already been instructed to move the train out with all possible speed once the bell cord was pulled as a signal.

Hardin took a seat at the forward end of the car, his back to the forward door. According to one report, he and the other men had stored their shotguns they were carrying in the luggage racks above their seats. Lighting his pipe, Hardin leaned back and relaxed, his arms stretched across the back of the seat. As was customary, Sheriff Hutchinson and a deputy sauntered through the car, looking for possible undesirables or wanted persons they might encounter, and perhaps briefly greeted Mr. Swain and his companions. Another deputy, A. J. Perdue,

Get Wes Hardin!

*Escambia County
Sheriff William Henry
Hutchinson, circa 1900.
(Courtesy of L. L.
Bruington
and Chuck Parsons).*

walked through the smoker after them, stopping to talk to Swain about possibly staying over in Pensacola so the deputy could try to win back some money he had lost to Swain. After Swain declined, commenting about business before pleasure, they engaged in small talk for a few more seconds, then Perdue left. The stage was set and the actors were in their places. The signal was given.

Hutchinson, Perdue, and perhaps the other deputy suddenly re-entered the smoker from behind Hardin, and the sheriff grabbed him. Simultaneously, Armstrong came into the car from the other end, a pistol in his hand, followed closely by Chipley and perhaps one other person, John Callaghan. Hardin, caught totally off his guard, began to fight like a man possessed, screaming and kicking, and he, the sheriff, and Perdue, who was clinging for dear life to one of Hardin's legs, tumbled to the aisle floor. Jim Mann, rising from his seat opposite that of Hardin, panicked and drew a pistol, then moved to escape through a car window on the depot side of the train, perhaps firing while inside the car or as he jumped out the window to the station platform.

Bounty Hunter

Gunshots exploded inside the car, and, as Mann began to run along the station platform, more shots rang out from the waiting deputies, and he fell, riddled. The local judge who had accompanied Chipley and Hutchinson to meet with Armstrong and Duncan in Whiting grabbed Mann as he sank to the platform, a dead man. On the train, other passengers, frightened by the sudden violence, sought refuge under their seats.

Hardin continued to thrash, kick, and scream, his captors doing their best to get him under control and manacled. The gunsmoke, echoing gunfire, and curses of struggling men accentuated the confused scene. Armstrong limped down the aisle and fiercely clubbed Hardin across the head with his pistol. The blow had the desired effect, rendering the gunman unconscious for a few moments, although Armstrong was almost convinced the blow was hard enough to kill him. Duncan had come into the car right behind Hutchinson and his deputy. A search of the prisoner revealed a pistol concealed inside Hardin's trousers with a suspender strap through the trigger guard which Hardin, no doubt, had been trying to reach.[28] The lawmen quickly handcuffed their prisoner and tied him to his seat. Armstrong pulled the bell cord, and the train began to gather steam, quickly leaving the Pensacola station.[29] The two other men who had accompanied Hardin, Campbell and Hardy, remained under close guard, being quite subdued after witnessing the brief, violent struggle.

Though Armstrong and Duncan did not have the necessary warrants to arrest Hardin outside of Texas, it was a "legal nicety" that they would worry about later. Hardin had proven too elusive and dangerous in the past to allow a "paperwork problem" to stand in the way of his apprehension. When he regained consciousness, Hardin cursed his captors, swearing that his true name was Swain and that they were kidnapping him.

After the train had gotten far enough away from Pensacola and there was little likelihood of a rescue attempt, the engineer was signaled to stop, and Hardy and Campbell were allowed to

The Pensacola, Florida, train station as it appeared in the 1870's. (Courtesy of the Pensacola Historical Society).

get off, there being no charges against them. At this time, Armstrong informed Hutchinson and Perdue who "Mr. Swain" really was, offering them $500 for their assistance. Excited at this news, Hutchinson and Callaghan left the train to return to Pensacola, but Perdue remained to help in the attempt to arrest Brown Bowen, aided by some other men gathered up along the road by Chipley. Shortly before the train reached Whiting, it stopped again, and Duncan, Perdue, and several others got off to see if they could locate Bowen. Armstrong took Hardin on to wait at the little town, no doubt fully prepared to stand off any effort to take his prisoner from him. Bowen could not be located, and Hardin's captors reassembled at Whiting, where Hardin was allowed to send some money to his wife and Armstrong sent a telegram to Adjutant General Steele:

91

Bounty Hunter

Arrested John Wesley Hardin, Pensacola, Fla., this p.m. He had four men with him. Had some lively shooting. Hardin fought desperately. Closed in and took him by main strength. Hurried aboard the train then started for this place. We are waiting for a train to get away on. This is Hardin's home and his friends are trying to rally men to release him. Have some good citizens with [me] & will make it interesting. J. B. Armstrong, Lt., State Troops.[30]

Guessing that, by now, friends of Hardin in Pensacola had gotten the word to friends in Pollard, the journey by train was resumed and Armstrong had it speed through that station without stopping to avoid any possible rescue attempt. Hardin was taken to Montgomery, the trio arriving early on the morning of August 24, where he was placed in jail. Duncan and Armstrong went to a hotel for a brief but well-deserved rest.

Later that morning, the two Rangers took their prisoner before Justice of the Peace John B. Fuller. Armstrong had already wired General Steele advising him that the Alabama governor had not received any of the requisition papers from Texas and asking him, "What is the matter?"[31] Based on telegrams in response confirming that requisitions had been sent, Judge Fuller heard testimony from Armstrong and Duncan and ordered Hardin back to jail until the hearing could be continued on Wednesday, August 29, by which time it was hoped the papers would have finally arrived from Texas. The Rangers worried that a five-day delay would likely give Hardin's friends time to organize a rescue attempt. In the meantime, Hardin, still insisting that he was John Swain and that he had been kidnapped, hired a local Montgomery attorney, J. W. Watts. Watts had his client brought before City Court Judge John A. Minnis on a writ of habeas corpus. A. A. Wiley appeared to argue the prosecution's side.[32] A panicky Armstrong, sensing that all of his and Duncan's efforts were being jeopardized by legal manuevering, sent another telegram to General Steele:

Hardin taken out on writ of habeas corpus. Case continued to Wednesday. Send another requisition by men or express. Am afraid it will miscarry as did the first. Answer.[33]

Watts argued before Judge Minnis that Swain should be released because the Rangers did not have sufficient legal process to justify his being held. Wiley responded by reading the telegrams from Texas stating that a requisition was on the way. He put Duncan on the stand to identify Swain as John Wesley Hardin, the man he and Lieutenant Armstrong had come after. Hardin did not testify. Reviewing previous decisions of the Alabama Supreme Court dealing with similar problems, Judge Minnis ordered Hardin back into jail pending further orders of the court,[34] thus giving Wiley a form of continuance during which time it was hoped the legal hassle would be rendered moot by the arrival of the Texas papers. Armstrong then sent two telegrams to Texas. One was to General Steele:

If requisitions don't come tonight Gov. Houston will issue a warrant on Gov. Hubbard's telegram so I can leave here at six tomorrow evening. Have arranged to have Bowen captured.

To Governor Hubbard, Armstrong wired:

Please telegraph the Governor of Alabama that you have forwarded requisition for John Wesley Hardin alias John Swain. They are trying to release him on writ of habeas corpus.[35]

Finally that evening, the requisition papers arrived in Montgomery. The next morning, Saturday, concerned that there might have been a rescue effort organized during the forced delay, Armstrong boarded the train alone while Duncan spirited Hardin out of the city in a hack, driving to a small station nearby where, without interference, they rejoined Armstrong on the train for Decatur, Alabama, where they would change trains for Memphis, Tennessee.[36] Before they left

Bounty Hunter

the small station, Armstrong wired General Steele that the papers were okay and that they were on the way.[37]

Arriving at Decatur and having a little time before taking the train to Memphis, the Rangers checked into a hotel with their prisoner and sent for a meal to be brought to the room. Hardin was by now beginning to cease claiming that he was John Swain and even signed his true name to the hotel register.[38] However, he had not given up the idea of escape. As he later wrote:

> I knew my only hope now was to escape. My guards were kind to me, but they were not most vigilant. By promising to be quiet I had caused them to relax somewhat, and they appeared anxious to treat me kindly, but they knew their life depended on how they used me. When we got to a little town, I think it was Decatur, we had to stop and change cars for Memphis. They took me to an hotel, got a room, and sent for our meals. Jack and Armstrong were now getting intimate with me, and when dinner came I suggested the necessity of removing my cuffs and they agreed to do so. Armstrong unlocked the jewelry and started to turn around, exposing his six shooter to me, when Jack jerked him around and pulled his pistol at the same time. "Look out," he said, "John will kill us and escape." Of course, I laughed at him and ridiculed the idea. It was really the very chance I was looking for, but Jack had taken the play away just before it got ripe. I intended to jerk Armstrong's pistol, kill Jack Duncan or make him throw up his hands. I could have made him unlock my shackles, or get the key from his dead body and do it myself. I could then have easily made my escape. That time never came again.[39]

While in Decatur, Hardin was allowed to write his wife in Whiting. On stationary from the local law firm of J. S. Clark and David P. Lewis, the manacled Hardin hastily scribbled his version of what had happened, curiously signing the name of Swain:

> Marian McMillan I hope you will consider Janes circumstances and Help Her all you can
> My Dear Wife and children this is the first time that I have had an opportunity of writing you a letter Since I was arrested in pensacolia. Jane they Had me foul yes very foul I was Sitting in the Smoking car

94

Get Wes Hardin!

Neal C & poor (Jimmie M) By my Side with my arms Strached on the Side when they came in. 4 men grabed me one by each arm and one by each Leg so the Strached me locking and quick. But poor Jimmie he Broke to run out of the cars and was Shot dead by some of the crowd on the out Side. Jane I am in good Hands now they treat me Better than you have any Idea and assure that I will not Be mobed and that when I get ther that the Governor will Protect me from a mob and that I will hav the Law Jane Be in cheer and dont take trouble to Heart But look to the Bright Side Jane I have not murded any Body Nor robed any one But what I have done in Texas was to Save my Life Jane time will Bring me out. Jane I got a rit of Habas corpus yesterday But fail to get out my trial was set for tuesday but a requisition come for John Wesley Hardin last night So they Say & Swore that I was the man J. W. Hardin that Killed Web of Comanchie Texas So they Had to give me up Jane be cautious in writing me for they will examine your Letters before I seen them [illegible] Direct your letters to Austin texas to J H Swain. Jane they can Never Hang me nor penitenchry me for Live by Law times are not like they was when we left Texas Mob Law is played out Jane I expect that it is a Good thing they caught me the way they did for they Had 40 men withe the Shariffe and Deputie of pensacola So you see I would have been a corps Now instead of Being a prisner if they Had not Streached me as they did Jane I had no Show to get my pistol if I Had I would Have Been Killed my Hands were caught the first pass Jane I am in Good Hopes yet—write to me at austin Texas Jane Brown's Bad conduct caused me to get caught in Pensicolia and all so his Last Letter to Texas Stating that his sister Joines Him in Sending Love to all the Detective was Boarding at N B When the Letter come an watched them put the Letter away and then Stole the Letter out N. B. thought thought the man Mr. Williams to Be a merchant wanting to rent the Store Hous But His name is John Dunkan a State Detective of Texas Jane B. is the cause of my arrest. Jane go to your F as Soon as possible and then You can come to See me if You wish do not Give up where there is a will there is a way Remember 1874 & 1872 So Good By my Dear Wife (You Hav ever Been True) remember me to the children and also to all my friends and do the Best You can Tell you connection your cicumstances So Good By Dearest one.

J. H. Swain[40]

Duncan would later recall that Hardin proved to be a difficult prisoner, continuing to kick and curse, and generally refusing to cooperate. Hardin's language throughout the first part of the journey led to a number of lady passengers seeking another car in which to ride. Getting off at stops for meals, Hardin would sulk and refuse to reboard the train. Armstrong and Duncan would have to physically drag him back onto the train, Duncan carrying the brunt of that effort because of Armstrong's wound.[41]

By now, the word of Hardin's capture had been picked up by the national press, and almost all major newspapers had reported it. Arriving in Memphis on August 26, the three were greeted by a large crowd curious to see the celebrated Texas gunman. Missing a train connection, Hardin was placed in the local jail overnight, where a squad of policemen had to control the crowd. Somehow, he was able to lay his hands on a pocketknife, but a jailer saw it and told the two Rangers the next morning when they came to pick him up. For some reason, they didn't take it from him then, but, wending their way through the throng of people, boarded the train and left Memphis, headed for Little Rock, Arkansas. As the train entered Arkansas, Duncan saw the knife in Hardin's sleeve and, taking it from him, tossed it out the open train window. At this, the fierce, rebellious killer gave up his attempts at resistance and broke down and cried. After he had fled Texas, his brother, Joe, and other friends had been lynched by a mob because of who they were, and Hardin had the greatest fear that such would also be his fate. Armstrong and Duncan told him to behave himself and also assured him that he would be all right, even promising to give him a pistol to defend himself with should there be an attempt to lynch him, but adding that he would be protected from any mobs. From this point on, Hardin regained his composure, and he and his captors got along well for the remainder of the trip.[42]

Crowds continued to throng at each of the train stations along the route back to Texas, all eager to catch a glimpse of Hardin. Some even boarded the train to ride from one station to another, hoping to see him. Fearful that a lynch mob might have been planned, the two officers took their prisoner to a sleeper car. W. E. Atmore, a passenger agent for the Memphis & Little Rock Railroad, was on the train and assisted them in getting accommodations to isolate Hardin from the other passengers.[43] A fellow Texan, G. W. Haley, had boarded the train at Memphis and had an opportunity to discuss the capture with the two Rangers before he left the train near Waco.[44]

The Rangers and their prisoner encountered crowds at Little Rock, as well as at Texarkana, where special guards were required to keep the crowds back.[45] At 5:30 p.m., August 27, while stopped in Longview, Texas, Duncan sent a telegram to his brother, Sim, in Dallas:

> We are here with Hardin, all safe. Will be in Austin tomorrow morning.
>
> Jack Duncan[46]

Anticipating the crowds that would be waiting for the train at Austin the next day, Armstrong arranged for the train to be stopped before it got to the city. Hardin was quickly shuffled into a closed hack with curtains over the windows, then driven to the Travis County jail, accompanied by a squad of heavily-armed Rangers. When they arrived at the jail, another crowd was encountered and proved so large that Hardin had to be bodily lifted and carried over their heads into the safety of the jailhouse.[47] John Wesley Hardin had been returned to Texas to stand trial for his crimes. Weary, both Armstrong and Duncan checked into the Avenue Hotel,[48] their mission over.

Although Armstrong and Duncan had safely returned Hardin to Texas, events in Florida and Alabama related to his capture were not yet over. On August 26, the Sunday after the arrest, Jane Hardin went up to Montgomery from Pollard and granted a reporter an interview. Fearing that her husband would never reach Austin alive, she boasted "of being able to shoot and manage a horse as well as most men, and [said] things will be made extremely lively for Armstrong and Duncan, the detectives, and also for some others who had a hand in the capture of Hardin."[49] Mrs. Hardin did not have sufficient funds to take her three children back to Texas and remained in Alabama for some time.

The elusive Brown Bowen was finally arrested on September 17 near Pensacola, possibly by Superintendent Chipley, who turned him over to Florida officials for return to Texas.[50] Bowen was subsequently found guilty of murder and sentenced to hang, despite his unflagging insistence that Hardin was the actual killer. Hardin, apologizing to his wife as he made his brother-in-law a scapegoat for his own capture, for which he bore Bowen great enmity, stoutly denied it. Brown Bowen was "launched into eternity" by the hangman on May 17, 1878.[51]

In Florida, events took a rather strange turn. The Escambia County grand jury, on October 4, 1877, returned a true bill of indictment against Martin H. Sullivan, one of the deputies present at the depot, for an assault with the intent to cause the death of James W. Mann.[52] According to one researcher, although the outcome of the case against Sullivan is not on record, the case was still pending in June, 1878, when the court refused a plea to abate the indictment because of improper selection of the grand jury. Apparently Sullivan survived this legal problem as he subsequently became co-owner of a successful lumber company and died in 1911.[53]

Two days after Sullivan was indicted, the grand jury also indicted Sheriff Hutchinson for kidnapping Hardin "with intent to cause him to be sent out of the State of Florida against his will."[54] No doubt, the fact that the two Texas lawmen had carried no legal process with them when Hardin was hustled out of the state pricked the legal conscience of local officials, prompting this action. However, despite returning the indictment against the respected sheriff, the grand jury also took the unusual step of asking Florida Governor George Drew to pardon the sheriff. "While our oath obliges us to bring this matter before the court, we recommend that Sheriff Hutchinson's official

Get Wes Hardin!

The Travis County Jail in Austin, Texas, in the 1870's. (Courtesy of the Austin-Travis County Collection, Austin, Texas, and Chuck Parsons).

status be not affected by it, as his act, though illegal, relieved the community of a desperate and dangerous character."[55] Apparently Hutchinson's actions were subsequently excused, as he was re-elected sheriff in 1880.[56]

In Texas, Hardin remained in jail in Austin. On September 19, 1877, under heavy Texas Ranger guard, he was taken back to Comanche to stand trial for the murder of Deputy Sheriff Charles Webb. After a brief trial, he was found guilty of second degree murder and sentenced to spend twenty-five years in the penitentiary at Huntsville.[57] He had escaped the rope that he feared so much, but his reign as "Texas' worst desperado" was over. In denying Hardin's appeal of his conviction, the Texas Court of Appeals noted his reputation:

> Though yet a young man, the appellant, John Wesley Hardin, has succeeded in achieving a remarkable and widespread reputation for sanguinary deeds. For years during the era of civil disorganization which succeeded the war between the states, he and his "gang"

99

Jane Bowen Hardin at the age of 18, when she married John Wesley Hardin. (Courtesy of Southwest Texas State University, San Marcos, Texas, Archives-Special Collections).

100

Get Wes Hardin!

were the terror of whole communities in different sections of western Texas, and the law long proved impotent to arrest their career, or afford protection to those who had incurred their easily-earned animosity.

The appellate court, refuting each of Hardin's legal arguments, most of a technical nature, summed up its outrage, and likely that of most law-abiding Texans, as to Hardin's crime:

> It only remains for us to pass upon the sufficiency of the evidence; and when we consider it as it appears in this record, we can but conclude that the life of the deceased—"a quiet, peaceable man, and a brave and efficient officer," who was an entire stranger to defendant and the other two murderers who aided and assisted him in killing— was taken without provocation, in cold blood, with premeditation, and in pursuance of a diabolical conspiracy, concocted and agreed upon several days prior to the homicide. Under all the circumstances as detailed in the evidence before us, defendant could have had no other motive in beginning and urging on the difficulty with deceased than that of killing, or having him killed by his confederates, the two dastardly and inhuman assassins who aided him in the accomplishment of the foul deed.
> We see no error for which the case should be reversed, and the judgment is, therefore, in all things affirmed.[58]

After Hardin's case was finally disposed of, Duncan, in addition to his salary, was authorized to be paid $32 "for commutation of rations and forage from August 15, to August 31, 1877, at $2 per day."[59]

NOTES

1. *Galveston Daily News*, August 31, 1877; Hardin, *Life*, p. 110.

2. Hardin, *Life*, pp. 110-114; A. J. Wright, "A Gunfighter's Southern Vacation," *Quarterly of the National Association and Center for Outlaw and Lawman History*, VII:3 (Autumn, 1982), 12-14; Chuck Parsons, *The Capture of John Wesley Hardin* (College Station, Texas: Creative Publishing Co., 1978), pp. 7-16; Norman B. Wiltsey, "40 Times a Killer," *Frontier Times*, 38:1 (January, 1964), 68; Ripley, *Died With Their Boots On*, pp. 169-173.

Bounty Hunter

3. *San Antonio Daily Express,* September 12, 1895; N. A. Jennings, *A Texas Ranger* (Dallas, Texas: Southwest Press, 1930), p. 309.

4. Ripley, *Died With Their Boots On,* p. 176.

5. *Dallas Daily Herald,* March 17, 1877.

6. *San Antonio Daily Express,* September 12, 1895.

7. *Dallas Daily Herald,* July 20, 1877.

8. Texas Ranger Muster Rolls, Texas State Archives.

9. *San Antonio Daily Express,* September 12, 1895.

10. *Dallas Morning News,* August 22, 1895; *Dallas Daily Times Herald,* February 19, 1894; Letter from Hardin to his wife, August 25, 1877, as quoted in Parsons, *Capture,* p. 65.

11. Letter to Hardin from "Doc J. An," October 13, 1877, John Wesley Hardin Collection, Southwest Texas State University, San Marcos, Archives-Special Collections; see also Parsons, *Capture,* pp. 22 and 33, 66 and 67. The letter was sent to Hardin after he was in jail and postmarked from Navarro County. A portion of it includes this statement:

> I knew that man that arrested you he lives in dallas they had him chained down in Comanche when I left for one of your gang as they called him I thought they would hang him I saw him in Dallas about three months ago he asked me if I ever heard of you and said he wish you would kill all of comanche and he would help you do it he is Jack Duncan Jack Ducan Duncan

Parsons suggests that "Doc J. An" was named Anderson, since the writer referred to Hardin as "Cousin" and Hardin did have a relative by the name of Dr. Jim Anderson in Navarro County (letter to author from Chuck Parsons, May 20, 1986). The accuracy of this letter, in my opinion, is questionable without more facts. See Footnote 13.

12. Letter from Hardin to his wife, August 25, 1877, as quoted in Parsons, *Capture,* p. 65; Nordyke, *Wes Hardin,* pp. 160 and 161; *San Antonio Daily Express,* September 12, 1895; Hardin, *Life,* pp. 114 and 115; Raymond, *Lee Hall,* p. 130; Wright, "Gunfighter's Southern Vacation," p. 13.

13. Hardin, *Life,* p. 115; Wiltsey, "40 Times a Killer," p. 69; Letter to Hardin from "Doc J. An," October 13, 1877, John Wesley Hardin Collection, Southwest Texas State University, San Marcos, Archives-Special Collections; Nordyke, *Wes Hardin,* p. 161; *Austin Daily Democratic Statesman,* August 16, 1877. "Doc J. An," in his letter to Hardin after the gunman's capture, stated that he saw Duncan in chains in Comanche when the Rangers arrested him (see Footnote 11), from which Parsons, in *Capture,* p. 32, concludes that the lawmen took Duncan from Gonzales to Comanche in order to better screen his true identity. I have a problem with this and feel that "Doc J. An" was incorrect for some rea-

son. Comanche is in Central Texas, over 200 miles from Cuero. Armstrong was reported in Cuero on August 15, 1877, and was in Austin by the 17th, making a trip from Gonzales to Comanche and then back to Austin quite unlikely. Since the Rangers were anxious to arrest Hardin before his trail was lost again, such a detour would have meant critical delay and the idea defies the urgency of the moment. Further, the rationale for such a side trip seems a little thin and the manner in which it would likely have been carried out would have done more to create rather than allay suspicion.

14. *Austin Daily Democratic Statesman*, August 18 and 19, 1877.

15. Webb, *Texas Rangers*, p. 299.

16. *Austin Daily Democratic Statesman*, August 25 and 29, 1877.

17. Report, September 1, 1877, Adjutant General Records, Texas State Archives.

18. Telegram, August 21, 1877, Adjutant General Records, Texas State Archives.

19. *Dallas Morning News*, August 22, 1895; September 11, 1895.

20. Hardin, *Life*, p. 115

21. *Atlanta* (Georgia) *Daily Constitution*, September 1, 1877. Parsons, in *Capture*, pp. 36-40, concludes that it was Hardin who was actually beaten by Chipley, primarily because the incident reflects Hardin's well-known racial prejudice, his predilection for gambling, the violence induced by intoxication, and because, in blaming Brown Bowen for his capture, Hardin could rewrite history to enhance his own image and avoid any blame for his own capture. The *Montgomery* (Alabama) *Advertiser*, August 25, 1877, reported that Chipley's assailant, rumored to be "one of the Hardin gang," made two attempts to shoot him before he was disarmed and punished. The *Mobile* (Alabama) *Daily Register*, September 22, 1877, in reporting briefly on the September 17 arrest of "one of Hardin's supposed confederates," likely Brown Bowen, stated that he was the same man who had attacked Chipley several weeks before.

22. *Dallas Morning News*, September 11, 1895. There is some difference of opinion as to exactly when Sheriff Hutchinson became involved. The *News* reprinted a verbatim letter from Duncan in response to a claim by Hutchinson for credit in the arrest of Hardin. Duncan stated that the Sheriff came to Whiting with Chipley. In an interview in the *News* two weeks earlier, on August 22, 1895, he was quoted as saying that the sheriff was not contacted until he and Armstrong arrived in Pensacola. I am inclined to believe the September 11 statement, which was clearly intended to clarify and which was a verbatim letter to the newspaper, not an interview subject to a reporter's liberties in interpretation. Even Hutchinson, in a letter printed by the *News* on September 6, 1895, stated that he went to the state line to meet Armstrong and Duncan.

Bounty Hunter

23. *Dallas Morning News*, September 11, 1895.

24. *Dallas Morning News*, August 22, 1895.

25. Hardin, *Life*, p. 116; Nordyke, *Wes Hardin*, p. 162.

26. Wright, "Gunfighter's Southern Vacation," p. 15; True Bill of Indictment, Circuit Court, Escambia County, Florida, October 4, 1877 (*State of Florida v. Martin H. Sullivan*, record no. 1877-5945-Ca-01). These men were listed as witnesses in the assault case filed against Sullivan for shooting Jim Mann.

27. For a full discussion of all versions of Hardin's capture, see Parsons, *Capture*, pp. 44-45.

28. T. U. Taylor, "New Light on John Wesley Hardin," *Frontier Times*, 2:11 (August 25, 1925), 16.

29. This account of Hardin's capture is derived primarily from contemporary news stories and documents, as well as accounts by the participants both at the time and some eighteen years later on the occasion of Hardin's death, not to mention Hardin's own autobiography. Most writers have taken their version from one or more of the following sources:

> *Montgomery* (Alabama) *Advertiser*, August 25, 1877.
> *Austin Daily Democratic Statesman*, August 29, 1877.
> *Atlanta* (Georgia) *Daily Constitution*, September 1, 1877.
> *Dallas Morning News*, August 22, 1895; September 6, 1895; September 11, 1895.
> Hardin, *Life*, pp. 116-120.

Parsons, in *Capture*, pp. 52-56, discusses a contemporary account from the *Pensacola* (Florida) *Gazette*, as reprinted in the *Tallahassee* (Florida) *Weekly Floridian*, September 11, 1877, which stated that Hutchinson and Perdue accomplished Hardin's capture singlehandedly without *any* involvement by Armstrong and Duncan. Hutchinson later sought a greater share of the reward for Hardin, contending that he deserved the major credit for his arrest. In addition to the above, see also Wiltsey, "40 Times a Killer," p. 69; Ripley, *Died With Their Boots On*, pp. 179-183; Webb, *Texas Rangers*, p. 299 (who gave Armstrong credit for making the arrest by himself); Nordyke, *Wes Hardin*, pp. 162 and 163; and Wright, "Gunfighter's Southern Vacation," p. 15.

30. Telegram, August 23, 1877, Adjutant General Records, Texas State Archives.

31. Telegram, August 24, 1877, Adjutant General Records, Texas State Archives.

32. *Montgomery* (Alabama) *Advertiser*, August 25, 1877; Wright, "Gunfighter's Southern Vacation," p. 16.

33. Telegram, August 24, 1877, Adjutant General Records, Texas State Archives.

34. *Montgomery* (Alabama) *Advertiser*, August 25, 1877.

35. Telegrams, August 24, 1877, Adjutant General Records, Texas State Archives.

36. Hardin, *Life*, p. 121.

37. Telegram, August 25, 1877, Adjutant General Records, Texas State Archives.

38. Hardin, *Life*, p. 121; Wright, "Gunfighter's Southern Vacation," p. 16.

39. Hardin, *Life*, p. 121.

40. Letter from Hardin to his wife, August 25, 1877, as quoted in Parsons, *Capture*, pp. 60-65.

41. *Dallas Morning News*, August 22, 1895.

42. *Dallas Morning News*, August 22, 1895; Hardin, *Life*, p. 122.

43. *Dallas Morning News*, August 22, 1895; *Austin Daily Democratic Stateman*, August 29, 1877.

44. *Waco* (Texas) *Daily Examiner*, August 29, 1877.

45. Mollie Moore Godbold, "Comanche and the Hardin Gang," *Southwestern Historical Quarterly*, LXVII (July, 1963), 260.

46. *Dallas Daily Herald*, August 28, 1877.

47. Hardin, *Life*, p. 122; Godbold, "Hardin Gang," p. 260.

48. *Austin Daily Democratic Statesman*, August 29 and 30, 1877.

49. *Montgomery* (Alabama) *Advertiser*, August 28, 1877.

50. *Mobile* (Alabama) *Daily Register*, September 22, 1877; Wright, "Gunfighter's Southern Vacation," p. 17.

51. Wright, "Gunfighter's Southern Vacation," p. 17; Parsons, *Capture*, p. 36. See also Chuck Parsons, "The Death of Brown Bowen," *Real West*, 19:148 (November, 1976), pp. 32-34 *et seq.*

52. True Bill of Indictment, Circuit Court, Escambia County, Florida, October 4, 1877 (*State of Florida v. William H. Hutchinson*, record no. 1877-5945-Ca-01).

53. Wright, "Gunfighter's Southern Vacation," p. 17.

54. True Bill of Indictment, Cicuit Court, Escambia County, Florida, October 6, 1877 (*State of Florida v. William H. Hutchinson*, record no. 1877-5918-Ca-01).

55. *Montgomery* (Alabama) *Advertiser*, October 12, 1877, quoting the *Pensacola* (Florida) *Herald*, as quoted in Wright, "Gunfighter's Southern Vacation," p. 17.

56. Wright, "Gunfighter's Southern Vacation," p.17.

57. Wright, "Gunfighter's Southern Vacation," p. 17; Hardin, *Life*, pp. 124 and 125; Parsons, *Capture*, p. 83.

58. *John W. Hardin v. The State of Texas*, 4 Texas Court of Appeals Reports at 356, 360 (1878).

59. Voucher, Adjutant General Records, Texas State Archives (Courtesy Chuck Parsons).

Chapter 5

The Gunshot

John Wesley Hardin was behind bars, and Jack Duncan was an instant celebrity. Newspapers around the country reported one version or another of the daring arrest, with the most prominent mention being given to Duncan's role. An Austin man visiting in Houston told a local reporter that Duncan was "an old Chicago detective," in addition to spinning a garbled version of how Duncan established Hardin's whereabouts.[1] Varying accounts had Duncan spending as much as seven months in his undercover role before he got his information. The *Dallas Daily Herald*, in referring to a *Chicago Times* story on the capture, declared that the item placed Duncan alongside the famous Pinkerton as a detective.[2] In Austin, the local newspaper commented: "This is one of the most important arrests yet accomplished in Texas, and Lieutenant Armstrong and Detective Duncan have made enviable reputations for themselves and rendered great service to the state." Even Hardin was quoted as saying, "The officers treated me kindly, and they deserve the greatest praise for capturing me alive."[3]

However, not all of the news accounts were totally favorable. In Fort Worth, ever the rival of bustling Dallas thirty miles away, one editorial comment scoffed at the accolades for the detective:

> The *Dallas Mail* claims that Hardin was arrested by Jack Duncan, recently of the police force of that city. The telegram from Whiting,

Alabama, announcing the capture is signed J. B. Armstrong, and says "I did it." Considering the propensity of the Dallas press for claiming credit for all the good done under the sun, we are inclined to doubt the *Mail's* assertion.[4]

Clearly, Duncan's reputation as a bona fide hero and skilled detective was firmly established. The capture of the legendary Hardin was a deed that ignited the public imagination and, when Duncan returned briefly to Dallas on the morning of August 30, he was met by a large number of people eager to congratulate him and to hear more details on the arrest.[5] The fact that he and Armstrong were entitled to the $4,000 reward for Hardin, which had been prominently mentioned in news accounts, also was a major topic of discussion.

In Florida, Sheriff Hutchinson, reading accounts of the arrest with only bare mention of his role, not to mention the large reward offered by Texas for Hardin, reflected on the $500 he had been paid by Armstrong and Duncan. On September 1, 1877, he sent a telegram to the editor of the *Dallas Daily Herald:* "I captured and forwarded John Wesley Hardin, the noted Texas outlaw. Please telegraph me amount of authoritative rewards offered. W. H. Hutchinson, Sheriff of Escambia Co., Fla."[6] At the same time, the *Herald* commented on an article in the *Pensacola Gazette* which gave the entire credit for Hardin's arrest to Hutchinson and Perdue: "How true all this is, we do not undertake to say, only we know the arrest would never have been made but for the energy and intelligence of the Texas officer, who tracked the blood-stained desperado to his lair in the swamps of Florida."[7]

Hutchinson left Pensacola on September 6, 1877, for Austin to make his claim for a larger share of the reward. However, at Whiting, he received a telegram from his attorney and, for whatever reason, turned back.[8] Since Armstrong and Duncan apparently had already been paid the reward, the *Herald* generally reflected the official view: "The whole matter rests with the gentlemen who brought Hardin home and delivered him within

Bounty Hunter

the doors of the Austin jail according to the terms of the law. If they divide all right, if not, the state cannot help it."[9] For now, this ended the question of credit for Hardin's arrest.

Duncan was still a Texas Ranger and, despite the public attention, life had to get back to normal and he had to go back to work. Unfortunately, there are very few records that deal with his activities with the Rangers after Hardin's capture. Apparently, one of his first assignments by Captain Hall was to check up on the activities of a discharged Ranger named Wright to confirm if the man "was drinking and doing no good."[10] On September 6, 1877, Duncan was staying at the Avenue Hotel in Austin, perhaps ready for a new assignment.[11] The only other mention in Ranger records is a telegram to Adjutant General Steele on October 14, 1877:

> Thompsons is at Miletts Ranch in Shackleford Co. Will take five men to arrest him. What shall I do?
>
> Jack Duncan.[12]

Probably referring to an outlaw named Green Thompson, for whom Duncan later insisted he received a reward, the answer he received to this telegram is unknown. Also unknown is the reason why Duncan left Ranger service, mustering out of Hall's Special State Troops on November 15, 1877.[13] In an interview over sixteen years later, Duncan asserted that the question of how much credit either he or Hall should receive for Hardin's capture induced a quarrel which led to his leaving.[14] Whether or not this was the real reason will never be known. Perhaps Duncan liked the public attention he received and became frustrated with the routine of investigative work for the Rangers. Add to this the low pay a Texas Ranger received, compared to the high rewards offered for various wanted fugitives, and Duncan's actual motivation for returning to civilian life may be more apparent. An enterprising, skillful detective, on his own and unburdened by the restrictions and confinement of Ranger service, could do quite well for himself. Thus, perhaps he decided to capitalize on his newly-acquired reputation and seek his fortune as a private detective.

Duncan returned to Dallas, no doubt to attend Sim's wedding on November 27, 1877, to Emma McPherson at the home of former sheriff James Barkley.[15] Duncan wasted no time in making his presence known, becoming involved in an incident which, though unimportant, nevertheless was quite representative of his personality and the feistiness that characterized him throughout his life. As the *Dallas Daily Herald* reported on December 5, 1877:

> While a Negro boy bootblack was polishing Jack Duncan's boots yesterday, on Main Street, a Negro man came up and began abusing the boy. Duncan told him to go away and wait til the "shine" was over, if he had anything to say to the boy. Whereupon the colored individual became indignant and began abusing Jack. He had fairly commenced when a well-directed blow, dealt by Duncan, knocked the darky off the pavement into the gutter. It was some time before he could pick himself up.[16]

By the 28th of November, 1877, Duncan had begun his work with the arrest of Ed Higgins, a young man he believed had stolen a horse. When Higgins was searched at the calaboose, officers found a "thousand ticket," a ticket sold by the railroad which was good for one thousand miles of travel, and this one still had fifty miles left on it. Another such ticket was also taken from him and both were turned over to the Texas Pacific Railroad to determine if they were stolen. Higgins claimed he had bought the first ticket from a man in Plano, just north of Dallas, and that the second had been sent to him by his mother from Crab Orchard, Kentucky. Higgins was kept in the calaboose for over eight days, during which he repeatedly demanded to be brought to trial. The first ticket proved to be stolen but, since there·was insufficient proof that he was the one who stole it, Higgins was told that he was free to go on December 6. But now, Higgins refused to leave the calaboose, declaring his intention to sue the police for false imprisonment.

Bounty Hunter

He finally left the jail, however, and his suit was subsequently dismissed in January, 1878.[17]

When Duncan took up his new trade in Dallas, brother Sim was secretary of the Texas Copper Mining & Manufacturing Company, located on Elm Street. The president of the company was James W. Throckmorton, a former Texas governor who had been removed from office by the federal military as "an impediment to the reconstruction." Using his brother's stationery on December 3, 1877, the new detective wrote to Texas Governor R. B. Hubbard requesting a requisition for the arrest of Mitch Cotton, a black man wanted for the 1871 murder of Sheriff Applewhite of Limestone County. Now believed to be in Louisiana, Cotton was one of several defendants indicted for the lawman's death, and witnesses said that Cotton fired the first shot. One defendant was sentenced to life imprisonment and another was spared the gallows because of his tender years. Stressing urgency, Duncan wrote: "I think I will soon be able to bring him dead or alive to Austin very shortly. . .Please send papers by mail as soon as possible as it is quite necessary that we should be after him at once. Yours very truly, Jack Duncan, Detective." The requisition was issued, however, Cotton was not immediately captured.[18] Duncan looked for other business.

Jack Duncan's movements in Dallas were not among the community leaders and society members who sought to introduce elements of culture in this still crude frontier town, desirous of elevating Dallas in comparison with older cities in the East. Duncan was comfortable with people of more common pursuits, and part of his success as a detective was his ability to mingle freely in the saloons and red-light areas, among the thieves, gamblers, and *demimonde* who were his key sources of information. He enjoyed the crude conviviality of the crowded, loud, and smoky saloon, the frequent faro or poker game, and the occasional uninhibited hellraising brought about through overindulgence in this particular life-style. He had shaken off some of the moral values taught by his parents during his childhood in Kentucky. Duncan's career as a detective would be interspersed with occasional visits to the calaboose himself for trangressing various laws. One of the first of these arrests came in 1878 when, on January 4, he was indicted for a misdemeanor charge of aggravated assault, perhaps growing out of his reported fight in December. To compound this, on January 11, he was indicted, along with gamblers Charles and Frank Austin, for gaming, the cases to be tried in the court of a Justice of the Peace.[19] The details of the latter offense are unknown, but as to the aggravated assault charge, Duncan pleaded guilty in county court on February 4 and was assessed a fine of twenty-five dollars.[20]

The influence of prevailing Victorian standards among the better class of citizens notwithstanding, Dallas, as did most other frontier communities, tolerated its share of brothels, periodically trumpeting a sense of moral indignation and having its police force conduct wholesale arrests of prostitutes and their keepers. Mollie Cross had maintained one of Dallas's better-known sporting houses since at least 1875 at the corner of Commerce and Ervay Streets. She, too, was periodically arrested, as were the "inmates" of her establishment, and fined for "keeping a disorderly house," the polite phrase of the times, in an amount generally between $100 and $150. In October, 1877, Marshal Morton had initiated another one of the periodic "crackdowns" on prostitution, leading to a new indictment for Mollie Cross, as well as others. Also indicted on December 22 for vagrancy and prostitution was one of Mollie's girls, Hattie Washburn, who went by the alias of Bates.[21] Hattie and Jack Duncan were good friends at this time, the detective very frequently visiting her at Mollie's house. In fact, he had even approached his old friends on the police force and asked if they might not overlook Hattie in their frequent sweeps of the whorehouses. In spite of that, however, she was not spared a trip to jail in December.

Late on Saturday evening, February 9, 1878, Duncan, in the

Bounty Hunter

company of two companions, Billy Eels and a man named Rookstein, came in out of the cold night air to warm themselves in Mollie's parlor. Hattie asked him to come up to her room with her, and, at first, Duncan declined. He changed his mind, however, and, at about half past midnight on Sunday morning, he, Eels, Hattie, and another girl named Mabel, who was quite drunk, went up to Hattie's room. Once in the room, Duncan took off his overcoat and his gunbelt and holster and tossed them on the bed. Hattie asked him to have a drink, offering him a quart bottle of whiskey from her bureau. The four shared a drink. Hattie and Duncan lay across the bed, and she asked him if he intended to stay all night. Duncan responded that he would not if it meant leaving Billy Eels alone; if Eels went home, he would stay. He offered his pistol to Eels to take with him, telling him that he was going to stay all night if Eels was leaving, but Eels declined the offer and Duncan laid the gun back on the bed.

Eels, deciding to leave in a few moments, sat by the stove in the room warming himself while Duncan and Hattie resumed their hushed conversation on the bed. Presently, Duncan stood up and said that he was going home after all. He put his overcoat back on and walked to the bureau in order to light a cigar with the lamp. He looked at himself in the mirror and casually brushed back his black hair. Hattie, sitting on the bed, upset by something he had said, lifted up Duncan's gunbelt and holster with her left hand, took out the large-caliber Colt revolver with the other, and pointed it directly at Duncan. The weapon exploded in her hand, smoke filling the room, and the ball slammed through his right shoulder and burrowed into his right lung.

Stunned, but still standing, Duncan turned to face Hattie on the bed, sitting there amid the thick smell and smoke of the gunshot, the pistol still in her hand. "Hattie, you've shot me," was all he could think to say. Every night for the past six nights, Duncan had experienced the same dream that he had been fatal-

The Gunshot

*An 1885 photograph
of Dallas policeman
Pat Sheedan.
(Author' Collection).*

ly shot. The image of that dream flashed through his mind again when the big slug hit him.

Hattie was amazed that he was still standing. "You are not hit?"

Duncan opened up his vest and shirt and the blood from the wound gushed onto his clothes and the floor. Mollie Cross, awakened by the shot, and another prostitute named Walley came rushing into the room.

"Jack, if I have killed you, I'll kill myself," stammered Hattie, still not aware exactly of what she had done or why. Duncan forced a laugh, intently eyeing the pistol still in her hand. When Mollie Cross ran in, he said, "Mollie, she's shot me."

Regaining some sense of composure and still angry, Hattie spit out, "Jack, I told you I'd kill you and I've done it." She repeated this several times, still cradling the smoking pistol. Hoping to put her off guard, Duncan replied, "Hattie, I'm not hurt." Then, in spite of the pain and loss of blood, he wrenched the pistol away from her and gave it to Mollie. Eels was sent to fetch a doctor. At this point, Hattie became hysterical and clung to Duncan in spite of his wound. She had to be forcibly taken from the room. Duncan said several times that he was all right and not hurt much and, without waiting, decided to walk to the doctor's residence.

William T. Duncan, a cousin, upon hearing about the shooting, went to Mollie Cross's place and, talking with Hattie, said, "I suppose it was an accident." Still hysterical, Hattie responded, "No, I tried to kill him. He brought it all on himself." The two walked over to the residence of Doctor Allen where she continued to cry and "take on" over Duncan as the physician tried to ascertain the seriousness of the wound and treat it.

Concluding his examination, Doctor Allen allowed Duncan to be taken by carriage to Sim's home on Main Street. Mortified at the circumstances behind the shooting, the embarrassed and shocked Duncan family ministered to him. Jack told brother Sim that Hattie had shot him intentionally, but later stated that he had only said that because he was afraid that if he didn't, Sim would have put him out of the house. His family was furious with him for frequenting such places as that operated by Mollie Cross, continuing their disapproval of the life-style that he had adopted.

That evening, on a complaint sworn out by William Duncan, Hattie Washburn was arrested by police officers Jim Arnold and John Spencer and lodged in the calaboose. The officials wanted to await the outcome of Duncan's wound before formal charges would be preferred. From Sim's home, Jack was subsequently removed to that of his parents, no one sure whether he would live or die.

By February 22, 1878, however, less than two weeks after being shot, Duncan had recovered sufficiently to testify in Hattie's examining trial before Justice of the Peace McLure. Attorney Robert Cowart handled the prosecution's side of the case while W. L. Crawford defended Hattie. After testimony by

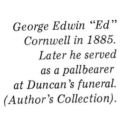

*George Edwin "Ed"
Cornwell in 1885.
Later he served
as a pallbearer
at Duncan's funeral.
(Author's Collection).*

Eels, Mollie Cross, and William Duncan, Jack Duncan told the
court that the shooting was an accident and that he had never
heard Hattie say that she would kill him. He said that they had
been and still were very good friends and that he knew she did
not shoot him intentionally. In commenting on the attitude of
his own family, he sadly observed that "he was done with his
home folks forever, for it was all spite in the family." After
hearing the testimony, and despite Duncan's contention that
it was an accident, Judge McLure placed Hattie under a $1000
bond and, since she was unable to post that amount, she was
remanded to the custody of Sheriff William M. Moon and
placed in the county jail.[22]

Duncan's recovery was slow, and the doctor was not able to
locate and remove the slug. Some of Hattie's relatives had come
to Dallas from Marshall and Shreveport to see what they could
do for her.[23] On Saturday, March 2, she was finally released on
bond, Jack Duncan and a man named Dudley Crawford going
her bail.[24] Four days later, she was indicted by the Dallas

County grand jury for assault to kill,[25] and, perhaps reflecting some sense of moral indignation at the whole sordid affair, Duncan was also indicted two days after her for carrying a pistol, his case to be tried in a justice court.[26]

The excitement generated in Dallas by Duncan's embarrassment was immediately overshadowed by the first train robbery ever committed in Texas. On the evening of February 22, 1878, the same day as Hattie's examining trial, Sam Bass and his men held up a train at Allen Station, some twenty-four miles north of Dallas. This holdup was the first of four such robberies in the Dallas area within the next sixty days that Bass and his gang pulled, thoroughly alarming the railroads and the community in general. The robbery at Allen brought Lee Hall and several of his men to scour the area, and Governor Hubbard offered a $500 reward for each of the six men thought to be involved. That reward was matched by the Texas Express Company and the Houston and Texas Central Railroad, upping the amount to $1,500 per robber.[27]

No doubt, a healthy Jack Duncan would have been quickly on the trail, induced by such rewards. But his wound was far too serious. Even the local press lamented: "If Jack Duncan were only well now, it wouldn't take long to bag the rest of the train robbers. Hurry up Jack, and get after 'em."[28] Duncan did continue to improve and apparently was soon able to get around fairly well, although not quite up to the rigors of a horseback pursuit in the field after train robbers.

By April, 1878, Duncan was apparently feeling well enough to be falling back into some of the old mischief. On the evening of April 22, Special Officer John E. Hess took his station in front of the Tivoli Beerhall on Main Street. Such officers were specially commissioned by the city's police board, giving them power of arrest, so that business establishments such as saloons could hire them to help keep the peace on the premises. On this occasion, Hess was in a boisterous mood, perhaps a little influenced by his employer's business specialty, and, helped by a few friends, accosted passers-by and acquaintances and forced them into the saloon to stand a round of beer. There were soon complaints to the police, and Policeman Pat Sheehan, a former British soldier in India who had also served in the Union Army during the Civil War, appeared on the scene. When Sheehan began to place Hess under arrest for creating a loud and unnecessary noise, Hess's friends got into the act, and Sheehan had to call officers Jim Arnold and Henry Waller to his aid. In the mayor's court the next morning, Hess's case was continued, as was that of Jack Duncan for using indecent language. The subsequent outcome of these cases is unknown; however, the proximity and nature of the charges suggest Duncan's involvement in the Tivoli incident.[29] A year later, Hess would be appointed as a regular policeman and would serve on the force for over two years.

During 1878, Jack Duncan was apparently not very active professionally, probably because of the severity of his wound. In June, 1878, his brother, Mack, was indicted for carrying a pistol,[30] and Jack's old friends Mollie Cross and Hattie "Bates" were among those indicted after another sweep of disorderly houses.[31] Duncan's father worked for a man named C. S. Bell, still maintaining the family residence on a lot James Duncan owned on the south side of Main Street, between South Harwood and Cabell Streets. Sim, elected as city engineer in April, 1878, and continuing his business as an abstractor of land titles, officed on the southwest corner of Commerce and Houston Streets, he and wife Emma living at 1227 Main Street.[32] On January 14, 1879, Jack Duncan was again indicted for carrying a pistol.[33] As to the assault case pending against Hattie Washburn, it was dismissed in May, 1879, most likely because Duncan remained reluctant to pursue the case or testify against her.[34] She disappeared from Dallas shortly thereafter.

With the advent of 1879, Duncan was apparently sufficiently improved to take up the trail again after wanted men. In January, he reportedly nabbed Mitch Cotton, for whom he had

Bounty Hunter

sought a requisition from the Texas governor in December, 1877. Cotton was reported as arrested by Duncan in Rusk County in East Texas, and the detective likely laid claim to the $2,000 reward offered for the black man's capture.[35] There is no record that it was paid. For some unknown reason, Cotton was at large in May, 1879, when the Limestone County Attorney sought a requisition for the fugitive's arrest in Arkansas. This suggests that, among possibilities, Duncan had arrested the wrong man, or Cotton may have escaped. Cotton was still known to be wanted as late as 1884 when Texas authorities were attempting to locate him in Mississippi.[36]

Duncan had continued to maintain a close relationship with his old friends on the police force. Thus, it was no surprise to see him walking along Main Street with officer Ed Cornwell late in the evening of Wednesday, March 24, 1880. Born George Edwin Cornwell in Dallas in 1854, but known as Ed, he had been appointed to the force the previous November after having worked as a special officer and a county jail guard for several years. He would subsequently be a longtime assistant chief of police to Jim Arnold and himself chief of police briefly at the turn of the century. As the two sauntered along, Duncan suddenly began hemorrhaging blood in copious amounts from his mouth and fell to the sidewalk. Cornwell quickly summoned a hack, and Duncan was taken to his father's residence.

Five doctors were called in to examine him, the bleeding continuing and his breathing becoming increasingly more difficult. They concluded that Duncan's condition was a complication from the gunshot wound two years earlier. Determining that coagulated blood was blocking his breathing, the doctors decided to perform a tracheotomy. Early Thursday morning, Doctors Leake and Graham made the incision in his throat. A silver tube was procured and inserted in the hole, the cut being stitched up around it. Although Duncan's breathing improved, the doctors held out little hope that he would survive.

118

The Gunshot

By Saturday, March 27, he was reported doing as well as the doctors could hope for, breathing easily through the tube. The physicians felt that if he continued to improve over the next several days, the tube could be removed from his throat and he would be able to breathe naturally. Already, Duncan was taking food through his mouth. The tough detective was not one to be kept down easily and, by April 5, he was walking in the streets again, although the tube had not yet been removed from his throat. Stopping up the tube, he demonstrated that he could breathe through his mouth. By April 12, doctors had removed the tube from his throat, and it was reported that Duncan had "ceased his artificial atmosphering" and that "his general health is better than it has been for many months."[37]

How long Jack Duncan went without the tube inserted in his throat is unknown. It is known that eventually he had to wear the tube in his throat all of the time, for the rest of his life, in order to breathe. According to his family, since his larynx had been involved, he had to hold his fingers to his throat in order to talk; otherwise, any attempt he made to talk would only come out as garbled noise. A temporary tube was inserted in his throat until a specially ordered three-inch-long curved one from Germany, made of silver, could arrive. A cap for the tube had a thong in it so it could be tied around his neck. Mack Duncan, many years later, would tell of his brother coming in late, in his cups, stumbling around in a dark room and barking his shin on some furniture. The intensity of the sudden strangled, gargling sounds reflected his pain and anger, it probably being a blessing that he didn't put his hand to his throat to clarify his remarks.[38]

The entire Duncan family moved back under a single roof again by the summer of 1880, while Jack was still recovering. Sim's wife, Emma, had died, and he moved back into his parents' home, bringing with him a little girl, Josephine or Josie, 5, whom he and Emma had adopted. The three Duncan daughters, Emma, Anna, and Mary Frances, were still living with their parents, as was Edward Daugherty, a nephew of Kitty's who was living with them and working as a teamster. Mack had formed the George M. Duncan Grocery Company on Elm at Leonard Street, his father helping him out. The family now lived at 1111 Elm Street between Harwood and Cabell Streets.[39]

By the end of the year, for all practical purposes, the rough frontier atmosphere that had characterized early Dallas had more or less subsided. The city had begun to take on more of the cosmopolitan image that it would come to enjoy in the next century. No longer were the city fathers as tolerant of the bawdiness as they had been in the past. Although the habitues of the red-light districts certainly did not disappear, things just weren't as open as they used to be. As an example, late in 1880 the board of aldermen mulled over a new ordinance establishing violations "against public morals and decency." There were questions as to how to enforce the ordinance, and finally the board resolved to suspend enforcement except for "houses in objectional localities." The body adopted one alderman's motion that Marshal Morton "notify Mollie Cross and Lizzie Handley if they do not move in a reasonable time that he would proceed to execute the ordinance."[40] Ultimately, for a number of years until the turn of the century, the city would be successful in herding such houses and saloons into a rigidly defined geographical area that was termed "The Reservation." In this area, prostitution was tolerated, a city ordinance even restricting the police to arresting any prostitute no more than once each month and the fine for that arrest being limited to five dollars. Mollie Cross continued to ply her trade in Dallas until as late as 1883.

Duncan continued his recovery during 1881. By January 25, he had been active enough to again be indicted for carrying a pistol.[41] That summer, on July 13, 1881, Mack Duncan married Isabela Hutton. Isabela, whose father was a Scot and whose mother came from Georgia, had been born in England in August, 1863, coming to the United States in 1879. She and Mack would have five children, only one of whom, their oldest, would survive to adulthood. William H. Duncan was born to them in May, 1882.[42] Mack Duncan served as a volunteer member of a hook and ladder company in East Dallas to help put out fires.[43]

Toward the latter part of 1881, Mack gave up the grocery business and became a conductor for the Texas and Pacific Railroad, he and Isabela moving to a home on Ross Avenue. James Duncan became a real estate agent, working for Sim at his abstract company. Jack, likely because of a dearth of detective business due to his injury, worked as a carpenter, living on Cedar Street.[44] It has been contended that Duncan might have been hired to help establish a ranch in New Mexico during 1881, but, given his physical circumstances at the time, such an arduous task on his part seems highly unlikely.[45]

On the evening of Monday, October 3, 1881, the bookkeeper for the Phoenix Planing Mills, on the east side of Dallas, paid off the company's employees for the week. He put $140 into a pocketbook and laid it momentarily on his desk, intending to put it into the company safe. When he looked for it a few minutes later, however, the pocketbook was gone. The police were notified. When they learned that employee Frank Smith had resigned that same evening, he became their primary suspect. Jack Duncan was hired to help the police find Smith, and the next morning, he took officers to a room at the Long Branch, a house of ill fame in East Dallas. None of the money was turned up by a search, however, and Smith was jailed. Pressing the tube to his throat, Duncan interviewed the prisoner and finally got him to admit that he had "found" some money. Smith offered to take him to one of the prostitutes at the Long Branch to whom he had given it. Smith, accompanied by Duncan and City Marshal Jim Arnold, went to a lumberyard east of the mills where the empty pocketbook was recovered. Two other officers, Charles Clapp and Wood Ramsey, interviewed the prostitute who, after some persuasion, gave them $100 which she said Smith had placed in her keeping.[46]

After a long period of recovery, tube in his throat and difficulty in speaking notwithstanding, Jack Duncan was back in the detective business again.

NOTES

1. *Galveston Daily News*, August 28, 1877.
2. *Dallas Daily Herald*, September 1, 1877.
3. *Austin Daily Democratic Statesman*, August 29, 1877.
4. *Fort Worth Daily Democrat*, August 28, 1877.
5. *Dallas Daily Herald*, August 31, 1877.
6. *Dallas Daily Herald*, September 2, 1877.

7. *Dallas Daily Herald*, September 6, 1877.

8. *Dallas Daily Herald*, September 12, 1877; Wright, "Gunfighter's Southern Vacation," pp. 16 and 17; Parsons, *Capture*, p. 93.

9. *Dallas Daily Herald*, September 12, 1877.

10. Report, September 1, 1877, Adjutant General Records, Texas State Archives.

11. *Austin Daily Democratic Statesman*, September 7, 1877.

12. Telegram, October 14, 1877, Adjutant General Records, Texas State Archives.

13. Texas Ranger Muster Rolls, Texas State Archives.

14. *Dallas Daily Times Herald*, February 19, 1894.

15. *Dallas Daily Herald*, November 28, 1877.

16. *Dallas Daily Herald*, December 5, 1877.

17. *Dallas Daily Herald*, December 7 and 8, 1877; January 11, 1878.

18. Requisition and letter from Duncan, dated December 8, 1877; letter from attorney R. M. Fancher, Groesbeck, Texas, dated December 6, 1877; Executive Records, Texas State Archives (Courtesy Chuck Parsons).

19. Minutes, 14th District Court, Dallas County, Texas, Vol. K, pp. 57 and 65 (*State of Texas v. Jack Duncan*, unknown cause nos.).

20. *Dallas Daily Herald*, February 5, 1878.

21. *Dallas Daily Herald*, May 6, 1875; February 23, 1877; *Dallas Weekly Herald*, October 13, 1877; Minutes, 14th District Court, Dallas County, Texas, Vol. K, pp. 31, 32 and 72 (*State of Texas v. Mollie Cross* and *State of Texas v. Hattie Bates*, unknown cause nos.).

22. *Dallas Daily Herald*, February 12, 23, and 24, 1878; *Dallas Weekly Herald*, February 23, 1878; March 2, 1878.

23. *Dallas Daily Herald*, February 23 and 26, 1878.

24. *Dallas Daily Herald*, March 3, 1878.

25. Minutes, 14th District Court, Dallas County, Texas, Vol. K, p. 178 (*State of Texas v. Hattie Bates*, cause 3809).

26. Minutes, 14th District Court, Dallas County, Texas, Vol. K, p. 179 (*State of Texas v. Jack Duncan*, unknown cause no.).

27. *Dallas Daily Herald*, February 28, 1878; see also Wayne Gard, *Sam Bass* (Lincoln, Nebraska: University of Nebraska Press, 1936).

28. *Dallas Daily Herald*, March 2, 1878.

29. *Dallas Daily Herald*, April 23 and 24, 1878.

30. Minutes, 14th District Court, Dallas County, Texas, Vol. K, p. 397 (*State of Texas v. Mack Duncan*, cause no. 3842).

31. Minutes, 14th District Court, Dallas County, Texas, Vol. K, pp. 410 and 411 (*State of Texas v. Mollie Cross* and *State of Texas v. Hattie Bates*, unknown cause nos.).

Bounty Hunter

32. Dallas City Directory, 1878-1879; Tax Rolls, Dallas County, Texas, 1879; Minutes, Board of Aldermen, City of Dallas, Texas, April 2, 1878.

33. Minutes, 14th District Court, Dallas County, Texas, Vol. L, p. 34 (*State of Texas v. Jack Duncan*, unknown cause no.).

34. Minutes, 14th District Court, Dallas County, Texas, Vol. L, pp. 228 and 229 (*State of Texas v. Hattie Bates*, cause no. 3809).

35. *Brenham Weekly Banner*, January 31, 1879 (Courtesy of Chuck Parsons).

36. Requisition and letter from James Kimbell, dated May 30, 1879; requisition order from State of Mississippi dated May 9, 1884; Executive Records, Texas State Archives (Courtesy Chuck Parsons).

37. *Dallas Daily Herald*, March 24 and 27, 1880; April 6 and 12, 1880.

38. Interview with Mrs. Frances Beebe (granddaughter of Jack Duncan), Houston, Texas, March 5, 1983; Interview with Mrs. Dorothy Young (granddaughter of George M. Duncan), Round Rock, Texas, November 18, 1982; Interview with William B. Duncan (grandson of George M. Duncan), North Richland Hills, Texas, November 26, 1982.

39. Tenth U. S. Census, 1880, Dallas County, Texas; Dallas City Directory, 1880-1881.

40. Minutes, Board of Aldermen, City of Dallas, Texas, December 7, 1880.

41. Minutes, 14th District Court, Dallas County, Texas, Vol. N, p. 16 (*State of Texas v. Jack Duncan*, cause no. 46666).

42. Marriage Records, Dallas County, Texas, Vol. G, p. 188; Twelfth U. S. Census, 1900, Dallas County, Texas.

43. *Memorial and Biographical History of Dallas County, Texas* (Chicago: The Lewis Publishing Co., 1892), p. 288.

44. Dallas City Directory, 1881-1882.

45. Ed Bartholomew, *Wyatt Earp, the Man and the Myth* (Toyahvale, Texas: Frontier Book Co., 1964), pp. 170 and 171. The conclusion that Jack Duncan was hired by leading Texas cattlemen to help locate and establish the San Simon Cattle Company at the San Simon Cienega, and then served as range boss, was based on a magazine article, Holmes Maddox, "The San Simon Cattle Company," *Cattleman* (February, 1948), p. 74. The article mentioned a "John Duncan," without any further identification, as being hired for that purpose. Such a job seems a little out of character for Jack Duncan, especially given his physical condition at the time. Other writers about the San Cienega make no mention of Duncan. Letter to author from Lawrence B. Merchant, *The San Simon* (Carlsbad, New Mexico: Nichols Printing, Inc., 1975).

46. *Dallas Daily Herald*, October 5, 1881.

124

Chapter 6

Manhunter

Some forty miles south of Dallas, in Navarro County, the Houston and Texas Central ran through the small farming community of Rice. About six miles north of there, across the Ellis County line, J. W. Broxon, Sr. had labored many long hours on his farm to provide for his family. A God-fearing man, Broxon led family prayers every night, and he expected his sons, Alex and Stony, to be there. Living with the Broxons early in 1882 were young Frank Clanton and Talley Guynes, who shared a room.

Stony Broxon, Clanton, and Guynes, who was suffering from a sore foot, visited Rice on Saturday, February 18, 1882, for a brief respite from their chores on the farm. They visited the building in the little town that served as both store and post office. J. W. Norris, merchant and postmaster, lived with his wife in a house set apart about ten steps from the small store. The three youths saw that Norris did a fair amount of business for a small-town merchant, and the next day, back at the Broxon farm, sharing fantasies of what it would be like to live the lives of outlaws and freebooters, considered the consequences of robbing the store. Guynes calculated that "a fellow could make a pretty lucky haul on Norris now," but when Stony Broxon suggested that the three of them were enough to do the job, Guynes begged off, allowing as he had a sore foot and that Norris was his friend and would probably know him anyway. Clanton and Broxton decided that they could do it themselves. On Monday evening, February 20, each armed with a pistol, the two left the farm separately for Rice, Broxon on horseback and Clanton walking. Clanton told Mr. Broxon, Sr. that he was going to visit the Fanning Place, which was in the direction of Rice, while Stony said he was going to pay a call to the Shegog place.

It had rained all day that Monday, but after dark it stopped, and the air was crisp and cool under a new moon. At about eight o'clock, Norris came into his house after closing the store and told his wife that, since it was chilly, he was going to go back out and fetch some kindling. Outside, in the dark, he encountered Broxon and Clanton, who told him they would like to buy some tobacco. The two would-be bandits had met at nearby Grape Creek, where Broxon hitched his horse, and walked together into town. Norris briefly returned to his house to get some matches to light a lamp, then returned and unlocked the store, admitting the two boys. As the postmaster lit the lamp, he made a noise which to Clanton sounded like the cocking of a pistol. Alarmed, Clanton pointed his pistol and ordered Norris to throw up his hands, but Norris refused. Clanton, panicking, shouted at him a second time, then fired his .22-caliber pistol at the storekeeper. At the same time, Broxon also panicked and ran into Clanton and also fired, shooting the lamp out. The two ran from the darkened store into the moonlit night, empty-handed.

Clutching his chest, Norris staggered out of the store and back into his residence, telling his alarmed wife, "I am shot." She helped him to bed, then, at his suggestion, went for their cook, Jane Joiner. The pistol shots had not alarmed Mrs. Norris since gunfire was frequently heard in that area. When she and the cook returned, they helped Norris to rise, unsteadily and staggering, but, when he began to fall, they helped him to the floor. Mrs. Norris sent the cook for Doctor Melton, their nearest neighbor, and asked her husband who did the shooting. "He

*James H. Maddox at
the time he was chief of
the Fort Worth
Police Department.
(Author's Collection).*

told me to hold up my hands, and shot me," he replied, then said nothing more and died later that evening.

In the meantime, Broxon returned to his horse and hastily lit out for his father's farm. He and Clanton had planned to meet at a nearby railroad if they got separated, but Broxon did not show up. Clanton, on foot, lost his way and, by dawn, ended up at the Wright place where he sometimes worked. Later, he also returned to the Broxon farm. For the rest of the week, the two stayed huddled together, occasionally practicing with their pistols, trying to determine their next move. Broxon finally left the farm, the plan being for Clanton and Guynes to meet him in Weatherford, in Parker County, from where they would then go into the highway robbery business like Sam Bass and the James Boys. On Friday evening, February 24, 1882, Clanton and Guynes went into Rice and spent the night, taking the train the next morning for Weatherford. While on the train, Clanton told Guynes the details of the murder, confessing his part.[1]

The brutal, senseless murder of the peaceable Norris shocked the area. The governor offered a $250 reward for the culprits, and Mrs. Norris and Norris's brother offered an additional $1,000. The family contacted Jack Duncan in Dallas and hired him to track the killers down. He went down to Rice and, after a few days of questioning people in the area, determined that Frank Clanton and Talley Guynes were likely suspects. He learned that they were known to have a small-caliber pistol, like that used to slay Norris, and that, in addition to being in the vicinity of the killing, had made some contradictory statements concerning their activities. The fact that they had suddenly and unexplainedly left together several days after the murder only strengthened his suspicions.

Duncan mailed out postcards to law enforcement officials around the state which named only Frank Clanton as wanted, giving his physical description and offering a $50 reward for him, but without saying what he was wanted for.[2] The reason for this omission was that, should anyone locate and arrest Clanton, he would likely be unaware that he was wanted for the Norris murder and be less inclined to attempt to claim the $1,500 reward for himself.

One of the postcards from Duncan ended up in the hands of Tarrant County Sheriff James H. Maddox. Keeping his eyes peeled, Maddox and fellow deputy Garretson were at the freight depot of the Missouri and Pacific Railway in Fort Worth on Friday, March 3. Maddox saw two men walking around one side of the depot, instantly noting that one of them fit the description on the postcard. The young man suspiciously pulled his hat down over his eyes when he spotted the two lawmen.
Maddox arrested both men immediately and took a pistol from each of them, Clanton carrying a small-caliber pistol. Maddox asked him if he was not Frank Clanton, and the prisoner responded that he was. Maddox, who was born in Louisiana during the Civil War, had come to Texas with his family in the early 1870's and had worked for a while on his father's farm in Tarrant County. He would serve as a deputy sheriff for fourteen years, three terms of which were to be under the administration

Cor. of Elm and Harwood Sts., 803 Main St., 804 Elm St., Corner and Mc

Protective ꞊ Detective Association

OF TEXAS.

Chartered by the State of Texas. Trade Mark, Letter C on left jaw of live stock.
An Institution for Branding and Registering Live Stock as a protection against thieves. Of stock registered and branded with this association only about one-seventeenth are stolen, and of these ninety-five per cent. are recovered, as the books show. **Headquarters at Dallas, Tex.**
Branch offices, Atoka, I. T.; Ft. Smith, Ark.; Wichita, Kan., and Denver, Colo.
AGENTS WANTED. Apply to Head Office.
Parties having Lost Stock not in the C Brand, should not neglect to send a description of them, as we are finding hundreds of them that had been given up. Remember we do not charge anything unless we find your stock.
For further information address

Protective and Detective Association,
DALLAS, TEXAS.

Gavin Walker, FORT WORTH, TEXAS, has First Mortgages fo bearing 7 and 8 per Cent. Interest on Improved and FARM PROPERTY, on a 40 per cent. Value

An 1890 advertisement for the Protective and Detective Association of Texas, founded in the early 1880's by Jack Duncan and his father. (Author's Collection).

of his brother, W. T. Maddox. Later, he would become city marshal and chief of police in Fort Worth.[3] For now, however, he was a low paid deputy, and it did not take much guesswork on his part to associate Clanton with the well-publicized Norris murder in Rice and the reward being offered. After sending a telegram to Duncan that he had arrested Clanton, Maddox, accompanied by Deputy Sheriff H. P. West, took Clanton and Guynes to Corsicana where they were lodged in the Navarro County jail.[4]

Maddox laid claim to the $1,500 reward after depositing Clanton and Guynes with Navarro County, much to Duncan's chagrin. Duncan, of course, was well aware that the rewards would be paid only upon conviction and he had the necessary evidence for that. There was no problem, however, for when

129

Bounty Hunter

Maddox arrived in Corsicana and learned that Duncan had been employed to "work up" the case, as well as the extent of the detective's investigative efforts, he renounced any claims to the reward. Those overseeing administration of the reward, grateful for Maddox's alertness, gave him $100 to cover his expenses, and it was agreed that Duncan would get the remainder.[5]

Both Clanton and Stony Broxon were indicted by the Navarro County grand jury on July 10, 1882. Clanton went on trial in Corsicana on August 3 and, primarily based on Guynes's testimony, the jury found him guilty of first degree murder, fixing his punishment at life imprisonment in the state penitentiary. On appeal, his conviction was affirmed.[6] Stony Broxon, on the other hand, was never apprehended, and his fate is unknown.

Although the date that it was initially organized is unknown, Jack Duncan was now associated with the Protective and Detective Association of Texas, formed by him and his father. Organized at least by early 1882, it had originally maintained an office over a bookstore in the Gouffe Building in Dallas, then moved to rooms over Delmonico's Restaurant at 609 Main Street. According to an advertisement:

> . . . It is now doing business all over Texas and throughout the Indian Territory, and its agents are branding hundreds of horses daily. No animal branded with the letter C on the left jaw can get away from the owner, no matter whether it strays off or is stolen. The Association never fails to recover an estrayed or stolen animal in its brand, the letter C on the left jaw.[7]

The Dallas City Directory for 1883-1884 listed Duncan as a detective with the Association, his father, James, serving as president.

Merely because Belle Starr nee Reed and the Younger Brothers had moved on, Dallas was still not bereft of notorious characters who drifted in and out of town. One such individual who visited Dallas about this time called himself Dave

*Mysterious Dave Mathers
who was known
in Dallas in 1882 as
Dave Matthews.
(Courtesy of
the Kansas State
Historical
Society
Topeka).*

Matthews, but was better known as Mysterious Dave Mather, a gambler and gunfighter who had on occasion stood on both sides of the law. He was a friend of the well-known Wyatt Earp, as well as Doc Holliday. Wandering all over the Southwest, he had most recently left a job as assistant city marshal in El Paso, ending up in Dallas by January, 1882. Mather, or Matthews, became closely involved with Georgia Morgan, the black madam of the Long Branch sporting house. At some point, Mysterious Dave pawned a dress, a watch, and two diamond rings belonging to Georgia and left for Fort Worth. Infuriated, Georgia took her pistol and went after him, only to be arrested and fined for disturbing the peace.

Mysterious Dave tried to sneak away, but Fort Worth officers took him off the train, and, the next day, he was delivered to Dallas County officials to face the charges of theft brought

Bounty Hunter

by Georgia.[8] By March 14, 1882, Mysterious Dave was in the Dallas County jail awaiting the action of the grand jury. On March 20, already well known as a "noted murderer and desperado of the southwest," he was indicted on four counts of theft. He went to trial on Thursday, April 13, for stealing one of Georgia's brand new $100 silk dresses and pawning it. A still bitter and angry Georgia took the stand but, under cross examination, had to admit that she had told Mysterious Dave that he could pawn anything she had. With that, he was acquitted by the jury and the other three theft charges against him were dismissed on April 19.[9]

Mather wasn't the only notorious character that the equally notorious Georgia Morgan took up with. As early as January, 1879, John Heath had come to the attention of Dallas lawmen for stealing a yearling and for forgery. In July of that year, he was again indicted with a man named D. C. Moore for another theft.[10] Heath jumped bond and fled the state, only to be returned to Dallas in chains in April, 1880, after being arrested in Hot Springs, Arkansas.[11] In June, 1881, he was indicted for both robbery and adultery, at the same time that both Georgia and Mollie Cross were also indicted for their specialties.[12] That same year, several local prostitutes, such as "Annie" and "Laurie," were arrested for vagrancy, each sporting the last name of Heath. Perhaps John was a little fickle.

Originally from Kaufman County, southeast of Dallas, Heath had been married, but his wife left him after he became involved in horse and cattle stealing in that county. Somehow, John Heath managed to squirm his way out of most of his legal problems. By early 1882, he was well known to the police. As one newspaper wrote of him:

> Barnum had his ancient woman, Joyce Heath, about whom volumes were written, but Joyce Heath was a humbug. Texas has John Heath, but John is not a humbug. He is still a live, shrewd, quick-witted young man who can get into more trouble and get out of it slicker than any other man of equal years in all the state.

He has been charged with so many violations of the law, been arrested, been imprisoned, bonded, tried, acquitted, etc., etc., that he has achieved the reputation of being either the slyest, smartest rogue extant or the worst used most unfortunate man living.[13]

Sometime in the middle of March, 1882, Mrs. A. A. Johnson was awakened in her Dallas residence by a breeze blowing in from a door that wasn't supposed to be open. By the light of a lamp burning in her bedroom, she got a good look at a burglar rifling through her possessions. Several hours later, Jack Duncan interviewed her and, through her description, recognized that it fit the well-known John Heath. He was not arrested right away, however, because City Marshal Jim Arnold and his officers were investigating several such burglaries and wanted to gather more evidence.[14] Subsequently, based on Duncan's investigation, on March 20, Heath was indicted for the burglary, the same date that Mysterious Dave was indicted for his problems with Georgia. Released on a $100 bond on April 17,[15] Heath was soon in trouble again when he and Georgia were together indicted in June for keeping a disorderly house.[16] However, true to his luck, the Johnson burglary charge was dismissed against him in November, 1882.[17]

There is no record of any more arrests of Heath in Dallas after 1882. On December 8, 1883, cattle theft, forgery, and robbery charges still pending against him in Dallas were dismissed, and that date proved to be an eerie coincidence. After leaving Dallas, Heath subsequently ended up in the Arizona Territory as a saloon keeper. He associated with a band of cutthroats that was terrorizing various mining camps and towns in the southeastern part of the area. On December 8, 1883—the same date that charges were dismissed against him in Dallas— during the robbery of a mining company store in Bisbee, the gang went berserk and indiscriminately killed three persons, including a deputy sheriff and a woman who ran a boarding house, as well as wounding two others. Although Heath did not actually participate in the shooting, he had waited for the gang outside of town and shared in the loot. He then stayed in town after the gang left and even rode in the posse that trailed them, finally leaving the posse and riding on in to Tombstone. As soon as the posse learned which gang they were after, aware of Heath's association with the outlaws, it returned to Tombstone, and he was promptly arrested. Five other members of the gang were apprehended, and all six were indicted.

The other five outlaws were sentenced to be hung, but Heath was sentenced by a jury to life imprisonment. Angered at the leniency of the sentence for such a heinous crime, the next morning, February 22, 1884, a mob composed of about thirty Bisbee and Tombstone citizens stormed the jail, dragged Heath out, and strung him up to a telegraph pole. Not wishing to name the lynchers, a coroner's jury found that John Heath "came to his death from emphysema of the lungs, which might have been, and probably was, caused by strangulation, self-inflicted or otherwise . . . ."[18] John Heath's luck had finally run out.

Jack Duncan had another successful pursuit which, like that involving the Norris murder, involved Navarro County. Jesse J. Rascoe, the son of Laban and Francis Rascoe, had been born in Rusk, Texas, July 10, 1848. By the end of the Civil War, the Rascoe family was living near Corsicana. As with John Wesley Hardin, who had problems with the occupying forces of Reconstruction, it is said that young Jesse Rascoe also had his share of confrontations, such as the time a Union soldier pushed his mother off a walk, causing her to break an ankle. According to family stories, he was supposed to have killed a number of black soldiers.[19] Whether this is true or not, Rascoe did become a rather well-known "bad man" around Navarro County. In one altercation in Corsicana in August, 1874, he killed one black man and stabbed another in the arm before making his escape.[20] He had a brother, William Perry Rascoe, who had been a Texas Ranger with the Frontier Battalion for a few years before becoming a merchant in Coleman, Texas. The family has said that William, on at least one occasion, prevented his fellow

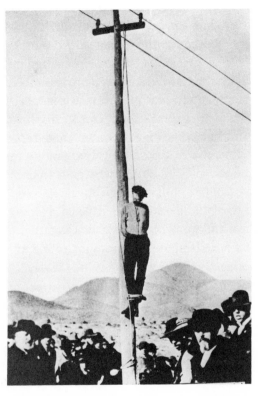

John Heath, the scourge of Dallas County, whose luck ran out in 1884. (Courtesy of the Arizona Department of Library, Archives, and Public Records, Phoenix).

Rangers from going after Jesse and, on another occasion, was supposed to have helped Jesse escape by sewing a saw in a pair of new boots he had delivered to Jesse in jail.[21]

Sometime in 1877, Rascoe and a young man named Harry Lackey had an encounter of some sort, during which Lackey took a pistol away from Rascoe and had him prosecuted. Rascoe was subsequently released because certain witnesses could not be located, perhaps because they were afraid to testify against him, and he then swore he would kill Lackey. On the evening of Saturday, December 29, 1877, Rascoe found Lackey in Smith's saloon on Beaton Street in Corsicana. Lackey was at the bar, his head resting on one hand, when Rascoe entered the rear door. Despite the presence of a city policeman and a deputy sheriff in the room, Rascoe drew his pistol when he spied the man he despised.

"Lackey, you're cock of the walk here!" the badman hollered as he pulled the trigger. The slug tunneled through Lackey's right arm into his right side, and he fell to the floor mortally wounded. Rascoe turned and ran out the back door. William G. Jackson, a pistol prominently displayed in his belt, drunkenly stood up to cover Rascoe's escape, telling everyone in the room, "If anybody wants anything, I'm the man." The two lawmen in the room brushed past Jackson and, outside the saloon, got off five or six shots at the fleeing Rascoe without any effect. The next day, Jackson was arrested and lodged in jail, and a posse, headed up by Captain Sparks of the Texas Rangers, started in pursuit. Rascoe managed to escape,[22] although there is some indication that he might have been later arrested and then escaped. Although Jackson was subsequently brought to trial in February, 1880, pleading self-defense and drunkenness, Rascoe was then at large. The disposition of the case against Jackson is unknown.

In early 1882, rumors began to spread around Dallas that Frank Jackson, the only member of Sam Bass's gang of train robbers still at large, had been located. Jackson, on whom a number of rewards had been outstanding since the gang had been shot up in Round Rock, Texas, in July, 1878, had caught the public's imagination by the manner in which he had braved heavy gunfire from Texas Rangers to pull up a badly wounded Sam Bass onto his horse with him and take him out of town. At Bass's urging, however, Jackson left his dying leader under a tree to be found by lawmen, then rode off into obscurity. In February, 1882, H. J. Franklin, a city marshal at Las Vegas, New Mexico, supposedly sent word to parties in Dallas that Jackson was living there, inquiring if the rewards for the outlaw were still outstanding. Others in Dallas contended that Jackson was at Tombstone, Arizona, and it was rumored that parties had left to apprehend him. One of the parties was Jack Duncan, no doubt motivated by a reported $2,500 reward still offered for Jackson's arrest. In addition, the detective took with him a warrant for the arrest of Jesse Rascoe, who was also believed to be in the Tombstone—Las Vegas—Prescott area.[23]

Rascoe had already run into some serious trouble. On March 5, 1882, he was in Charleston, Arizona Territory, waiting for some wages due him. He had stepped out of a local saloon and, for some unknown reason, the bartender followed him and blasted him with a shotgun as he mounted his horse. Rascoe's right arm had to be amputated at the elbow and, for a while, he was not expected to live.[24] Upon his arrival in the Tombstone area, Duncan no doubt learned of this incident as well as where Rascoe was recuperating. Rascoe had apparently heard that officers might be after him and left the hospital at Tombstone, returning to the ranch where he was staying on the San Simon River.

Duncan hired a teamster named Yearinger, with his wagon and team, to take him to Rascoe's place. Early on the morning of April 3, 1882, Duncan and Yearinger approached the ranch and confronted Rascoe. One account stated that the wagon tongue broke, causing Rascoe to come out, pistol in hand, to find out what was going on. After some innocent discussion about the wagon, lulling Rascoe off his guard, no doubt intrigued about this man who had to put his fingers to his throat in order to talk, Duncan and Yearinger suddenly grabbed him. They manacled their prisoner and, after leaving the impression with others at the ranch that he was to be taken to Tombstone, headed for the nearest station of the Southern Pacific and caught a train for El Paso before Rascoe could be rescued.[25] Rascoe would later assert that this account was incorrect and that he had been enticed away from the ranch under the impression that he was wanted as a witness in Tombstone, then arrested and taken to the nearest railroad station.[26]

Although the man returned to Dallas by other officers who claimed to be Frank Jackson turned out to be a hoax, Duncan, who himself had delayed departure from New Mexico in order to try to apprehend the man alleged to be Jackson, returned to Dallas on April 6 with his prisoner. Rascoe was turned over to Navarro County deputies Cubley and Edens for return to Corsicana. Once back in jail, still bothered by his wound, he wrote a letter to the local newspaper that publicly thanked Duncan "for favors shown while under his charge."[27]

Rascoe went to trial for Lackey's murder in August, 1882, and was acquitted. Perhaps this trial, plus the loss of his arm, gave Rascoe some cause to reflect on his life up to that time. After his release, he returned to New Mexico where he became a stage driver at Eddy, which is now Carlsbad, and at Roswell. He was a constable in Eddy by 1890, and his land west of town was donated as a site for a race track during Fourth of July festivities. In a bizarre coincidence, Rascoe went to El Paso in July, 1895, to identify the remains of Martin Morose, an outlaw wanted in Eddy who had been killed on June 21 in a gunfight as he came onto the American side of the Mexican Central Railway bridge. Deputy U. S. Marshals George Scarborough and Jeff Milton and Texas Ranger Frank McMahon were all acquitted on charges that they murdered him. Four strangers had to be recruited by the undertaker to bury Morose's body. The only mourners at the grave were his prostitute wife and her new lover, John Wesley Hardin, now out of prison and practicing as a lawyer.[29] Perhaps Rascoe and Hardin met, two men with the unique common bond of having been tracked down and brought back to Texas justice by the same man years before.

Rascoe would earn a reputation as an outstanding lawman, despite the absence of one arm, and would become chief of police and a respected pioneer in Roswell.[30] There would be another tragedy in his life, however, when his daughter, Katherine Rascoe Fletcher Halsey, was sentenced to hang, along with two others, for the 1924 ambush slaying of her husband. Her conviction was subsequently reversed.[31]

With Rascoe in jail, Duncan resumed his investigations in Dallas. He received word on August 13, 1882, that a man nam-

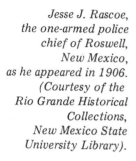

*Jesse J. Rascoe,
the one-armed police
chief of Roswell,
New Mexico,
as he appeared in 1906.
(Courtesy of the
Rio Grande Historical
Collections,
New Mexico State
University Library).*

ed Aaron Strausburger, who was wanted at the small town of Harrold in Wilbarger County for assault to murder, was at Charlie Struck's saloon at the corner of Jackson and Austin Streets. Duncan had no idea what Strausburger looked like, but went to the saloon anyway where he found about a dozen men in a room adjacent to the bar drinking beer and playing dominoes. Pretending to be interested in the games, he studied the crowd but could not determine who might be his man. Starting to walk from the room into the saloon part, Duncan stopped and pretended that he recognized someone in the crowd and called out, "Hello, Strausburger, ol boy! Come take something!" Rising from the group of men, Strausburger, having trouble recalling where and when he had met this friend, joined him for a glass of beer. Afterwards, they walked together up the street, Duncan reminding him of how they had met a year before. When the two reached Main Street, Duncan suddenly placed his man under arrest and escorted the dumbfounded Strausburger to the county jail.[32] Ingenuity had paid off again.

139

Bounty Hunter

Late on the evening of March 12, 1883, at Ferris in Ellis County, south of Dallas, burglars entered the store of N. J. Doty, which also served as a post office for the small station on the Houston and Texas Central Railroad. Attempting to break into the post office safe, the intruders placed quilts around it to muffle the noise of explosives. However, they were only able to blow an outer door to pieces and could not gain access to the main vault of the safe. Satisfying themselves with stealing a few pocketbooks from a showcase and about $40 in stamps, the criminals fled. On discovering the attempted burglary the next morning, Doty telegraphed Jack Duncan and employed him to "work up the case." A $100 reward was offered for capture of the culprits.

Duncan rode down to Ferris and inspected the safe. In addition to asking around about any suspicious characters who might have been seen in the area, he cut out a piece of the quilt used to wrap the safe. He returned to Dallas where, after making some inquiries, he learned that some quilts had been reported stolen from a boarding house in East Dallas. Duncan contacted Mr. Franck, the landlord, who quickly identified the scrap of quilting Duncan had as having come from one of his stolen quilts. Franck gave the detective some idea as to whom he suspected in the theft. Within a very short period of time, Duncan arrested two "hard-looking" parties, Pat Nolan and Charley O' Donnell. When a search turned up several pocketbooks and a large package of blasting powder, the two prisoners would only say that they found the powder in a boxcar and that the pocketbooks were given to them by a friend. Duncan loaded the two onto the 5:00 p.m. train and took them to Ferris for identification, the local newspaper commenting that "an extraordinary swift stroke of detective business has been done."[33]

A habeas corpus hearing was held on March 27, 1883, and bond was set at $500 for both prisoners. Upon being admitted to bail, however, they were immediately re-arrested by federal authorities.[34] Postmaster Doty appeared before the U. S. Commissioner in Dallas to file a complaint against Nolan and O' Donnell on December 8, 1883, Duncan testifying at the hearing. The U. S. Attorney filed an information against the two burglars on January 24, 1884.[35] While the outcome of any of. the charges against them is unknown, Nolan did go on trial at Waxahachie in February 1884.[36] Duncan's reputation for getting his man was certainly bolstered by this case.

Major J. R. Wasson had first entered the United States Army in 1864 during the Civil War. After the conflict, he had attended West Point and was appointed a second lieutenant in the cavalry. Leaving the army for a few years, he was then reappointed in 1876 as a major and an army paymaster. On April 30, 1883, Wasson was aboard a Texas and Pacific train carrying a valise in which there was a package wrapped in brown paper, tied with official pink tape, and sealed with an oval seal. The package contained $24,000 in twenty, ten, and five-dollar bills, the payroll for army troops stationed at Toyah, Fort Davis, and Concho in West Texas. Suddenly, there was no money, and Major Wasson claimed that he had been robbed while on the train.

When the news of the robbery broke, there was considerable skepticism, several persons claiming they had seen Wasson intoxicated in a Fort Worth bawdy house, while other prominent citizens said that he was above reproach. The railroad company put detectives onto the case and Texas Rangers, led by Captain Sam McMurray, searched for the suspects described by Wasson. The major himself hired Jack Duncan to track down the robbers, and the detective left Dallas on Sunday, May 6, 1883, to begin his investigation. The rifled valise, with no money, was found by a Texas and Pacific freight conductor between Baird and Abilene, containing only Wasson's toilet articles, collars and some letters.

Duncan's investigation was short-lived, however. An army audit quickly turned up shortages in Wasson's accounts, leading to his confession that, indeed, he had staged the fraudulent robbery in order to make up those shortages. Wasson led Army authorities to where the remainder of the money was hidden, and he was court-martialed. Duncan, miffed at this turn of events, declined to be interviewed, only too happy to forget the whole thing.[37]

The year 1883 ended for Jack Duncan on a sour note, although the circumstances are unknown. On December 19, he was indicted by the Dallas County grand jury for swindling and for theft of money over $20. He was released on December 31 on a $500 bond on each count, his brother, Sim, and attorney R. E. Cowart acting as sureties.[38] The nature of these charges cannot be determined since case papers for this period were destroyed in one of several Dallas courthouse fires. There are no newspaper accounts of his arrest, and one can only surmise as to what induced these charges, which would remain pending for almost six years.

The new year didn't start any better for Duncan either. Living in the residence of his parents,[39] who probably had long before given up trying to alter his life style, he was again indicted on January 6, 1884, this time for playing cards in a public place. The case, a misdemeanor, was transferred to the court of Justice of the Peace W. M. Edwards.[40]

However, getting caught gambling was nothing compared to what happened next. In Austin, Frank Mooney worked as a bartender in the Sample Room saloon, he and his wife having boarded for several months at the Southern Hotel managed by J. C. McIntyre. Toward the middle of January, Mooney was seen in the company of two strangers in town, a middle-aged, grey-bearded man and a younger man who gave the name of Lewis. One day, while McIntyre was relaxing in the saloon, Mooney approached him about the chance to make some quick money. If McIntyre could put up two or three thousand dollars, he could make ten thousand right away, Mooney asserted. McIntyre told him that if there was that much in it, he

Timothy Isiah Courtright, better known as Longhair Jim Courtright. (Courtesy of the Amon Carter Museum and Fort Worth Public Library).

might take it up. Shortly thereafter, Mooney introduced him to Lewis, who offered McIntyre the opportunity to buy a gold brick which he and his partner were willing to sell far below value in order to get some ready cash for financial problems that had cropped up. The details of the transaction were discussed and McIntyre was interested; however, before he would go any farther, he knew that "gold bricks" were often involved in swindles, and insisted that the brick be verified as the genuine article. Three borings were made and the dust taken to a local jeweler, Mr. Bahn, who pronounced the dust as 18 carat and legitimate. On that word, on Saturday, January 19, 1884, McIntyre paid Lewis and the bearded man $2,975 in cash, which included three $100 bills, promising to pay $2,000 more to them when he sold the brick. The two men asked that the transaction be kept quiet as they did not want it known that they had so much money in their possession. The deal struck, the two strangers left town quickly and, on Sunday, Frank Mooney went to Fort Worth, joined the next day by his wife. Some said they saw him spending several $100 bills.

On Tuesday, January 22, based on information that he had picked up somewhere, Duncan went to Fort Worth and, with the assistance of former Fort Worth city marshal Timothy Isaiah Courtright, now temporarily employed as a policeman, arrested Mooney. Courtright was better known among his contemporaries as a dangerous gunfighter and had been given the sobriquet, Longhair Jim Courtright.[41] Duncan questioned Mooney closely, then released him. Courtright, however, rearrested Mooney and put him in the Tarrant County jail.

Duncan promptly sent a telegraph to the Austin authorities:

> Chief of Police, Austin:
> Have arrested Frank Mooney for selling gold brick to proprietor of Southern Hotel. If wanted, answer.
>
> Jack Duncan

Austin City Marshal H. C. Lee contacted McIntyre to see if he could shed some light on the matter. Thunderstruck, since he had told no one of his purchase, McIntyre immediately took more filings from his brick back to Jeweler Bahn. They were pure brass. McIntyre, in spite of all his precautions, had been taken in by one of the oldest swindles of that time. Marshal Lee sent a telegram to Duncan asking him to hold Mooney until the proper papers were sent. Duncan turned the telegram over to the Fort Worth officers in order to justify holding Mooney until Travis County officers came for him. He tore off one corner of the telegram on which was written "$500 reward" in a different ink than that used to write the text of the telegram. Where Duncan had folded the telegram, prior to giving it to the Fort Worth officers, "$500 reward" was reproduced backwards on the opposite corner.

144

Duncan had already returned to Dallas by Thursday, January 24, when McIntyre, accompanied by Travis County Sheriff Hornsby, came to Fort Worth. Everyone concerned, especially McIntyre, was mystified as to how Duncan had learned of the gold brick swindle. Mooney no longer had any money, as he did when he first arrived in Fort Worth, and officers did not believe Mrs. Mooney's claim that she had loaned her husband some money. A search warrant was acquired to look through her trunk, but no money was found there either. Even more mysterious to McIntyre was the matter of the reversed "$500 reward" impression on the telegram given to local officers by Duncan. The swindle victim had not offered any reward. The notation, it was soon discovered, was not on the duplicate copy of the telegram on file at the Fort Worth telegraph office.

With McIntyre contending that the telegram produced by Duncan involved forgery and that Duncan must have been a party to the swindle, Tarrant County Sheriff Maddox promptly sent a telegram to Dallas City Marshal Jim Arnold to "arrest and hold Jack Duncan," and that officers would be on the first train to Dallas. Arnold complied and had Duncan picked up. However, since no charge had been specified and no one showed up from Fort Worth, Arnold released him on his own recognizance. That same Thursday evening, Duncan caught a train for Fort Worth to discuss the matter with Maddox. He was placed under arrest, but his preliminary trial was postponed.[42] Apparently, he was finally able to satisfactorily explain how he learned of the swindle and the matter of the notation on the telegram, since there is no record that any further action was taken against him. It is likely that Duncan gained information about the two sharpers as a result of his many contacts in the underworld of Dallas and Fort Worth. Such information is the lifeblood of a detective's success. As to the notation on the telegram, it may have been that, given the loss involved and the number of perpetrators involved, the $500 was an estimate of what kind of reward, should one be offered, was appropriate.

Mooney, in the meantime, was returned to Travis County where, after a preliminary hearing, he was admitted to $1,500 bail.[43] Certainly, 1884 had gotten off to a rocky start for Duncan.

NOTES

1. *Frank Clanton v. The State of Texas*, 13 Tex. App. 139 (1882); *Fort Worth Daily Democrat-Advance*, February 22 and 23, 1882.

2. *Dallas Weekly Herald*, March 9, 1882; *Dallas Daily Herald*, March 11, 1882.

3. *A Twentieth Century History and Biographical Record of North and West Texas*, Vol. II, Capt. B. B. Paddock, ed. (New York: The Lewis Publishing Co., 1906), pp. 57 and 58.

4. *Dallas Daily Herald*, March 10, 1882; *Waco Daily Examiner*, March 5, 1882; *Fort Worth Daily Democrat-Advance*, March 8-10, 1882.

5. *Dallas Daily Herald*, March 9, 1882; *Dallas Daily Herald*, March 11, 1882; *Fort Worth Daily Democrat-Advance*, March 11, 1882.

6. Case Records, 13th District Court, Navarro County, Texas (*State of Texas v. Frank Clanton and Stony Broxon*, cause no. 2621).

7. *Dallas Daily Herald*, March 30, 1882.

8. Colin Rickards, *Mysterious Dave Mather* (Santa Fe, New Mexico: The Blue Feather Press, 1968), p. 17.

9. *Dallas Daily Herald*, March 14, 1882; April 14, 1882; *Fort Worth Daily Democrat-Advance*, March 21, 1882; Minutes, 14th District Court, Dallas County, Texas, Vol. N, p. 618; Vol. O, pp. 70, 81 and 82 (*State of Texas v. Dave Mathews*, cause nos. 5635, 5636, 5637, and 5638).

10. Minutes, 14th District Court, Dallas County, Texas, Vol. L, pp. 42 and 319 (*State of Texas v. John Heath*, cause nos. 3935, 3936, and 3937).

11. *Dallas Daily Herald*, April 7, 1880.

12. Minutes, 14th District Court, Dallas County, Texas, Vol. N, pp. 243 and 268 (*State of Texas v. John Heath*, cause nos. 5098 and 5110).

13. *Dallas Daily Herald*, March 21, 1882; April 24, 1880.

14. *Dallas Daily Herald*, March 21, 1882.

15. Minutes, 14th District Court, Dallas County, Texas, Vol. N, p. 628; Vol. O, p. 76 (*State of Texas v. John Heath*, cause no 5624); *Dallas Daily Herald*, April 18, 1882.

16. Minutes, 14th District Court, Dallas County, Texas, Vol. O, p. 218 (*State of Texas v. John Heath and Georgia Morgan*, cause no. 5883).

17. Minutes, 14th District Court, Dallas County, Texas, Vol. O, p. 400 (*State of Texas v. John Heath*, cause no. 5624).

18. William M. Breakenridge, *Helldorado* (New York: Houghton Mifflin Co., 1928); pp. 194-197; Gard, *Frontier Justice*, pp. 205 and 206; Fred Dodge, *Under Cover for Wells Fargo* (Boston: Houghton Mifflin Company, 1969), pp. 44-55; Walter Noble Burns, *Tombstone* (New York: Penguin Books, Inc., 1942), pp. 255-262; Odie B. Faulk, *Tombstone, Myth and Reality* (New York: Oxford University Press, 1972), pp. 157-159.

19. Robert Nelson Smith, Jr., *Storey-Price-Rascoe-Smith Families*, unpublished manuscript (Harlingen, Texas: Robert Nelson Smith, Jr., 1959), pp. 45 and 46.

20. *Dallas Daily Herald*, August 14, 1874.

21. Smith, *Rascoe Family*, pp. 45 and 46.

22. *Dallas Daily Herald*, January 1, 1878; *Galveston Daily News*, January 1, 1878; *Corsicana Index*, as quoted in *Waco* (Texas) *Examiner and Patron*, January 11, 1878; Case Records, 13th District Court, Navarro County, Texas (*State of Texas v. Jesse Rascoe and William G. Jackson*, cause no. 2018).

23. *Dallas Daily Herald*, March 29, 1882; *Waco* (Texas) *Examiner*, March 29, 1882.

24. *Tucson* (Arizona) *Daily Star*, March 8, 1882; *Waco* (Texas) *Daily Examiner*, April 7, 1882; Bartholomew, *Wyatt Earp*, p. 301; Letter to author from Ed Bartholomew, Fort Davis, Texas, September 21, 1982.

25. *Dallas Daily Herald*, April 6, 1882.

26. *Dallas Daily Herald*, April 11, 1882; *Las Vegas* (New Mexico) *Daily Optic*, April 8, 1882, which referred to Duncan using a "sharp trick" to arrest Rascoe.

27. *Waco* (Texas) *Daily Examiner*, April 5 and 7, 1882; *Dallas Daily Herald*, April 6 and 11, 1882.

28. Case Records, 13th District Court, Navarro County, Texas, (*State of Texas v. Jesse Rascoe*, cause no. 2018).

29. Letter to author from Ed Bartholomew, Fort Davis, Texas, September 21, 1982; Lee C. Myers, *The Pearl of the Pecos* (Carlsbad, New Mexico: Lee C. Myers, 1974), pp. 12, 13, 30, and 133; Leon Claire Metz, *John Selman, Texas Gunfighter* (New York: Hastings House, Publishers, 1966), pp. 162-167.

30. Cecil Bonney, *Looking Over My Shoulder* (Roswell, New Mexico: Hall-Poorbaugh Press, Inc., 1971), p. 24; Elvis E. Fleming and Minor S. Huffman, ed., *Roundup on the Pecos* (Roswell, New Mexico: Chaves County Historical Society, 1978), p. 79.

31. Eve Ball, "Murder on Credit," *Frontier Times*, 52:2 (February-March, 1978), pp. 35 and 36 *et seq.*

32. *Dallas Daily Herald*, August 15, 1882.

33. *Dallas Daily Herald*, March 14 and 15, 1883; *Waco* (Texas) *Daily Examiner*, March 15, 1883.

34. *Dallas Daily Herald*, March 22 and 29, 1883; Minutes, 14th District Court, Dallas County, Texas, Vol. P, p.7 (*State of Texas v. Charles O'Donnell and Pat Nolan*, cause nos. 164 and 165).

35. Case Records, U. S. District Court, Northern District of Texas (*United States v. Charles O'Donnell and Pat Nolan*, cause no. 163).

36. *Dallas Weekly Herald*, February 22, 1844.

37. *Dallas Daily Herald*, May 5, 6, 8, 9, and 10, 1883.

38. Minutes, 14th District Court, Dallas County, Texas, Vol. P, pp. 480 and 499 (*State of Texas v. Jack Duncan*, cause nos. 7660, 7661).

39. Dallas City Directory, 1883-1884.

40. Minutes, 14th District Court, Dallas County, Texas, Vol. P, p. 518 (*State of Texas v. Jack Duncan*, cause no. 7672).

41. F. Stanley, *Jim Courtright, Two Gun Marshal of Fort Worth* (Denver, Colorado: World Press, Inc., 1957), pp. 143 and 144.

42. *Fort Worth Daily Gazette*, January 25-27, 1884; *Austin Daily Statesman*, January 24, 1884; *Dallas Weekly Herald*, January 31, 1884.

43. *Austin Daily Statesman*, January 29-31, 1884; February 1, 3, and 10, 1884.

Chapter 7

The Conspiracy

Despite an inauspicious start in 1884 for Duncan, there were some successes. In February, it was reported that he had "unearthed a $300 set of burglars' tools, and is on the track of the cracksmen."[1] Other results were being yielded also:

> The Protective and Detective Association of Dallas paid yesterday to Mr. Crozier, attorney for the parties making the capture, $100 reward offered by them for the capture of the gray mare of Mr. I. M. Ray which had on her left jaw their "O" [sic] brand. The money was paid after satisfactory evidence that the animal was the property of Ray and the thieves—the Barker brothers —had been convicted of theft by the district court of Jack County.[2]

However, no court records or newspaper accounts could be located to explain one item briefly mentioned in an Austin newspaper: "Dallas, March 24, 1884 . . . Wm. J. Grant, chairman Republican Committee, and W. I. Duncan, were today placed under $300 bond by U. S. Commissioner Bently, for alleged opening of letters belonging to detective Jack Duncan."[3] One can only speculate as to what was involved.

Mrs. W. H. Flippin, wife of the Dallas city treasurer, who was away on a trip to Europe, was asleep in her upstairs bedroom with a small girl very early on the morning of June 25, 1884. A black man stealthily gained entry but, while rummaging for whatever he could find, caused Mrs. Flippin to awake.

Bounty Hunter

Her fright was so great that she could not scream, but the little girl did. The burglar choked and struck Mrs. Flippin, then fled out a window, climbing down a portico post. That same morning, two doors east of the Flippin residence at Ross and Masten Streets, the home of Dr. J. L. Carter had been burglarized of a gold watch and chain. Just east of Dr. Carter, someone had attempted to raise a window at Mack Duncan's Ross Avenue residence, but his wife, Isabela, heard the noise and, in awakening Mack, frightened off the would-be intruder.

Jack Duncan, accompanied by another detective identified only as Frisby, began an investigation of the assault, which rumor on the street soon turned into an attempted rape. Taking a careful description from Mrs. Flippin, the two investigators turned to their various sources of information, finally concluding that a black, Henry Broswell, closely fit it. Finding that Broswell was not at his home in an area of Dallas known as Freedmantown, the two lay in wait, watching the house closely. At about 10 a.m., he finally showed up, his face covered with scratches. Questioned closely, Broswell claimed that his wife had scratched him. She denied it, however, and he then told them that he had gotten scratched at a party in a local park frequented by Dallas's black citizens.

Word leaked out that a suspect in the Flippin assault was in custody and talk began circulating about lynching him. Duncan and Frisby hustled their prisoner to Dr. Carter's residence, where the doctor identified him as a person he had hired to cut wood for him a week earlier, but could not identify him as a burglar. By this time, the streets of Dallas were filling with crowds clamoring for a necktie party. One crowd of about 400 to 500 men, believing the rumored suspect to be in the custody of the sheriff, surrounded the county jail and demanded that he be turned over to them. A jailer allowed a committee from the crowd to come in and inspect the jail to satisfy themselves that no such suspect was there. Part of the crowd remained around the jail while others scattered throughout the city hunting for

150

the detectives and Broswell. Duncan and Frisby, themselves not satisfied that Broswell was the right man, were careful to keep the frightened man hidden from sight. They took him to a residence where Mrs. Flippin was recuperating to see if she could identify him, but she was still in the process of recovering, and he was not taken before her. They barely got Broswell out of there before a crowd bent on a lynching showed up. Later that day, they were able to present the prisoner before Mrs. Flippin, and she stated positively that he was not the man who had assaulted her.

Prior to releasing Broswell, Duncan and Frisby allowed him to be interviewed by a committee of six prominent citizens so that there would be no question that he was not the man. Although Broswell's conduct had been suspicious, the committee quickly determined that he had likely not done it. Once word got out that the wrong man had been arrested, the excitement in the streets died down and the crowds dispersed. A reward of $500 was offered for the arrest of the party and the investigation by lawmen continued.[4]

Around the first of September, William Allen Taylor, a black man, was arrested in Fort Worth as a suspect in the Flippin incident and turned over to Dallas Sheriff Billy Smith. Based on identification by Mrs. Flippin and boasts made to other prisoners by Taylor himself while in custody, there was little question that he was the right man. Aware of plans being made to lynch Taylor, Smith secretly transported the prisoner to the Waxahachie jail. However, leaders of the lynching movement learned of Taylor's whereabouts and began to make plans to take him from that jail. Smith, whose movements were being watched, decided to move Taylor to Waco. On September 12, 1884, while Smith and Constable George Miller were en route with Taylor from Waxahachie to Midlothian to catch the train for Waco, their buggy was stopped by nine armed men and the lawmen disarmed. Commandeering the buggy, the nine men returned with their three prisoners to Dallas, where, at about

10 p.m., they were greeted on the outskirts of the city by a welcoming committee of about 100 men. In spite of Sheriff Smith's pleas not to act hastily, the crowd quickly hung Taylor from a small bridge. No action was ever taken against anyone in the mob, and the *Dallas Daily Herald* felt called upon to proclaim:

> Whatever sensational reports may get abroad as to the lynching of the Negro Taylor here Friday night, the plain fact remains that if ever recourse to mob law was justifiable or excusable, that case presented the extenuating circumstances . . . It may be as well learned now as hereafter, that all foul rapists will be strung up at once in Dallas by as just and as determined a body of citizens as any town in the country possesses.[5]

Duncan came under considerable criticism for his actions during the Broswell incident. This led him to volunteer his services to Marshal Jim Arnold without regard to any reward, which Arnold accepted. However, as the criticism continued, the reasons for which are unknown, other than the possibility that an innocent man came close to being lynched, Duncan decided to withdraw entirely from the case. He went on to other investigations, such as the arrest in July of a prostitute named Mollie for being the accomplice of a man who broke into a residence and chloroformed his victim, getting away with nine dollars. However, she was subsequently released.[6]

In August, 1884, Duncan had another encounter with the law when he was arrested for fighting, but was subsequently found not guilty in city court.[7] There are no details as to what was involved, but the arrest is an indication that, except for his speech problem, Jack Duncan had fully recovered from his wound.

Blankenship & Blake was a large Dallas dry goods firm which had been experiencing the theft of a large amount of goods, such as hats, silks, collars, suits, etc., during the summer of 1884. Store officials quietly conducted their own investigation and finally concluded that an employee had to be responsible. They fired a young clerk, Johnny James, who had worked for them about three months. The losses stopped immediately. Satisfied that they had found the actual culprit, the store officials hired Jack Duncan to "work up the case," as well as consulted with City Marshal Jim Arnold and officer John Spencer. It didn't take long. Duncan soon learned that James had been stealing the goods and turning them over to George Rorabaugh, a bartender in a saloon at Camp and Lamar Streets, who disposed of them. On August 22, 1884, James and Rorabaugh were arrested, and James very quickly confessed his part. Ranging out through the city, officers began looking for the stolen goods. Rorabaugh, whose true name was George Scott, had been fencing stolen property for some time, and articles taken in other crimes were also recovered. On August 23, when James and Scott were transferred from the calaboose to the county jail, Deputy Sheriff Henry Lewis made a special visit to the bawdy houses run by Lizzie Handley and Annie Wilson where, from various prostitutes, he recovered handkerchiefs, stockings, jewelry, and other clothing that the two thieves had given them.[8]

Scott was indicted on October 23, 1884, on two counts of theft of personal property over $20. He subsequently pleaded guilty to both counts, and a jury assessed punishment of one day's confinement in the county jail on each charge.[9] James' fate is unknown.

By the middle of 1884, James Duncan had been replaced as president of the Protective and Detective Association by Eugene Duncan, a relative. Eugene Duncan had been born in Russellville, Kentucky, in 1849 to James E. and Chloe Harper Duncan. He had come to Texas with his parents during the Civil War and had lived in Dallas since approximately 1880.[10] Jack's cousin, William T. Duncan, who had filed the charges against Hattie Bates, was superintendent of agents for the association. James Duncan became the general manager of the Livestock Protective

Bounty Hunter

Association. Mack Duncan was working as a clerk in his brother Sim's abstract office.

Jack Duncan took time out on Monday, October 20, 1884, to take a wife. Very little is known of the woman he married. Emma Jane Bowles had been born in Kentucky on November 3, 1855, to John G. and Fetna Ann Rogers Bowles. The eldest child, Emma had a sister, Josephine Helena, and three brothers, John Rogers Bowles, Jesse Davis Bowles, and Frank Read Bowles, the latter two brothers also living in Dallas. Emma's father had died the previous November.[11] However, Duncan didn't let domestic bliss slow him down. Although he may have been associated at this time with his father's organization, his next investigation, one of the biggest of his career next to the Hardin capture, was a freelance effort.

One of the major topics of barroom conversation in Lamar County in November, 1884, was the hotly contested sheriff's race. Lamar County is just south of the Red River, and its county seat, Paris, is not quite 100 miles northeast of Dallas. The incumbent sheriff, George Mack Crook, called Mack by most, had been defeated in the August Democratic primary by James H. Black. Undaunted, Crook announced that he would run on the general ballot in November anyway. The two conducted a bitter campaign, and hard feelings grew between them. At one point, Crook was heard to say, "I'll bet $500 that the damned son of a bitch will never be sheriff of Lamar County." Prior to the general election, the two candidates even ran into each other at a store in Black's home town of Blossom Prairie, about ten miles east of Paris, and a fist fight ensued.[12] On the November 4th election day, however, Black prevailed quite easily, 2,927 to Crook's 1,859 votes.[13]

At the time of the primary election in August, one of Crook's prisoners in the Lamar County jail was John Middleton. A young man in his late twenties, he was a cousin of Jim Reed, the outlaw who had been killed near Paris in 1874 and whose widow, formerly Myra Reed of Dallas, was now the notorious

154

Belle Starr living at "Younger's Bend," south of Eufaula on the Canadian River in the Indian Territory. Middleton had been raised by his mother in Logan County, Arkansas, while his father lived near the Red River in Lamar County. A few years earlier, in 1879, while visiting his father, Middleton had lost part of an ear when he and a half-brother were engaging in horseplay while giving each other a haircut with sheep shears.[14]

Middleton had troubles with the law beginning at a very early age with a series of petty crimes in Logan and Scott Counties in Arkansas. He was sentenced to serve one year in the Arkansas penitentiary for stealing some boots, but this didn't slow him down. After his release, he was soon wanted again for burning down the Scott County courthouse in Waldron.[15] Middleton then went into the horse stealing business, using a fordable place at a rock formation in the Red River known as Slate Shoals, in the northeast corner of Lamar County near his father's place, to transport his stolen stock between Texas and the Indian Territory. During the early 1880's, Dave Bowen, one of Middleton's associates, had been shotgunned to death in the area while plying the same vocation.[16] Finally, the law caught up with Middleton again when he was arrested in February, 1884, for carrying a pistol by Lamar County Constable W. D. "Bill" Nelson, who also charged him with three counts of bringing stolen horses into the state.[17]

The conditions in the Lamar County jail were not the best. Sheriff Crook's head jailer, Newt Harris, lived with his wife, Rebecca, in a residence portion of the jail and looked after the prisoners. In jail with Middleton was Tom Christopher, charged with forgery. Christopher had been released on bail with candidate Jim Black as one of his sureties, but Black went off his bond and surrendered Christopher back to jail. Not surprisingly, Middleton took sick with a severe case of diarrhea, a condition that continued for some time. When Middleton didn't improve, the county physician, Doctor Haden, was called in to examine him. The doctor believed that if Middleton was kept in a cell much longer, he would die. Adamant that the prisoner should be moved from his cell to the residence portion of the jail, which deputy Harris also suggested, Haden procured an order to that effect from County Judge Moore, and Middleton was taken to an upstairs room where Harris and his wife could care for him. In the doctor's opinion, Middleton wasn't faking and the prisoner was in no condition to "stand much fatigue."

On the morning of September 23, 1884, as Crook was leaving to go to Sherman to pick up a prisoner, Jim Yates, an office deputy, expressed his concern about Middleton possibly escaping. Angry about the judge's order, Crook asked Yates to speak with Doctor Haden about returning the prisoner to a cell. "I don't want any damned horse thief to get away from me," he remarked. Haden came by the jail that morning to check on Middleton and Yates broached the idea to him. The doctor objected, stating that, if the deputy really thought there was a danger of his escaping, he probably should return him to a cell, but that he didn't think Middleton would survive in that case. Harris left the jail keys with Yates and, without Crook's knowledge, he and the sheriff's brother, Jim Crook, left Yates in charge while they went to the Red River with a prisoner to let him sell his crop. Yates, being conscientious, wanted to stay at the jail that night after his tour of duty ended, but Mrs. Harris objected, and he left. On the evening of September 23, the "gravely ill" John Middleton escaped and fled.

On the next day, when Sheriff Crook stopped over in Bonham on his way back to Paris with a prisoner, Bonham City Marshal Ed Thornton showed him a telegram from Paris announcing Middleton's escape. He told Crook that he had seen a strange man around Bonham who could be Middleton. Angered by the escape, Crook continued on to Paris and announced a reward of fifty dollars for the outlaw's recapture. Crook then returned to Bonham to look for the man Thornton had mentioned but couldn't locate him. Returning to Paris, he led a posse to the farm of Middleton's father near Slate Shoals.

The Conspiracy

Accompanied by Alex Lowther and Charley Johnson, a deputy sheriff who lived on the Red River, Crook thoroughly searched the area, including cotton pens and outhouses, but not the farmhouse itself. They then hid nearby and watched until sunrise, at which time they searched adjacent fields and brush, but with no luck.

When Jim Black won the sheriff's post on November 4, Crook had still not been successful in locating Middleton. However, the escaped horse thief was not far away. Several people saw him in Paris on the evening after the election results had been announced. Lewis Holman, another deputy under Crook, was approached by Newt Harris, who told him that Middleton was at the county jail if he would like to talk to him. Holman accompanied Harris to the jail where, along with Mrs. Harris, he talked with Middleton for awhile. Holman and others had already heard Harris make a veiled threat that he would have John Middleton kill Jim Black because the sheriff-elect had passed him on the street without speaking. "I'll have his damned toes turned up," Harris had told Holman. Now, they sat in the county jail discussing old times with an escaped prisoner. Afterwards, Holman and Harris walked Middleton to his horse tied on the southwest corner of the courthouse. Holman commented to Harris that it looked strange for him, a deputy sheriff, to be so friendly with an escapee and perhaps he ought to arrest Middleton. Harris responded tartly, "If you try it and Middleton don't kill you, I will!" At this point, Holman's eagerness to do his duty subsided. Because of Crook's anger over Middleton's escape, Harris resigned his deputy's post and went to work as a bartender at the White Elephant saloon.

A few nights later, Holman went to the jail to lock up a trusty prisoner and ran into Middleton again in the kitchen. Middleton was hungry and, since nothing had been cooked in the jail, Holman went over to the White Elephant where Harris gave him fifty cents to buy some bread, ham, and fish, which the deputy took to Middleton. While Middleton was eating,

Bounty Hunter

Holman asked him if he intended to kill Black. The outlaw said that he did, telling Holman, "Harris is a good friend to me, and I'll do anything he wants me to do."

Jim Black and J. A. Booth, who was to be the new sheriff's jailer, were given a tour of the county jail on Saturday, November 15, 1884, by Deputy Jim Yates. Black was to have assumed office that Saturday, but there was a formal defect in his official bond, and he delayed taking over until Monday. Crook was in Hot Springs, Arkansas, having gone there two days earlier in response to a telegram from his sick wife. Black asked Yates to remain on as a deputy until he had familiarized himself with the operations.

At about 7 o'clock on Sunday evening, November 16, the sheriff-elect was at home with his wife and children in Blossom Prairie. They lived in a two-room house on the north side of the railroad near the depot. Black was lying on a bed with a sick child, one boot off in preparation for bed.

John Middleton, armed with a pistol and a muzzle-loading double-barrelled shotgun of ancient vintage, rode his horse up into Black's yard and called out, "Hello!" A lamp was burning in a window on the west side of the house and he expected Black to come out the door on that side. Instead, Black put his head out the other door. Middleton asked him if Mr. Black was in. When he responded, "yes," the escaped outlaw cut loose with the shotgun. Middleton's startled horse jumped and he dropped the gun trying to get his running horse to stop. Regaining control of the animal, he returned and retrieved the shotgun. Middleton then rode off, first heading east, then turning north, then west, changing direction continuously in order to throw off any pursuers. However, he became lost and rode into some woods to get out of sight until he could get his bearings. He decided to stay there for a while and hitched his horse to a tree.[18]

Eighteen pellets had struck Black in the chest and he was barely able to walk back inside the house before he fell to the

158

floor and died without saying a word. A neighbor, H. L. Byrn, heard the gunshot and rushed over to the Black house. Accompanied by a man named Cooper, Byrn took a lantern and located the tracks of Middleton's horse. He followed them until the tracks seemed to come together with another set of tracks about 35 yards beyond the gate. Following the trail for about two and a half miles, they then returned to Blossom Prairie for help. Constable Bill Nelson and others joined them, and they set out to follow the trail again. The trail was finally lost in an area of considerable brush and trees. At one point, the posse neared the wooded spot where Middleton was hiding. Seeing Bill Nelson in the lamplight, the man who had put him in jail, Middleton cocked his gun and thought seriously about killing him. However, he knew that he was outgunned and couldn't get away, so he waited silently while they passed.

On Monday morning, a day filled with heavy rains, the news of Black's murder electrified the community. The Paris mayor called a public meeting that afternoon to decide what steps to take to find the assassin. Over 500 people showed up and pledged $1,500 to a special fund. An additional $2,500 was pledged by others in Lamar County. J. C. Hodges, John Millsap, and William Roland were appointed as a committee to oversee the fund and to help authorities in hunting down the killer. A telegram was sent to the governor asking him to offer an additional reward. Millsap and John Gose, both former sheriffs of Lamar County, organized a posse to try once more to follow the trail, although the rains had likely obliterated it. A jury of inquest found that it did not have sufficient evidence to determine fully what happened.[19]

That same morning, a Mrs. Provine, who lived about three miles east of Paris, was going to visit a neighbor about two miles north of her home, taking her daughter with her. The daughter spotted a saddled horse tied to a bush off a road at a wooded area. Thinking the animal may have escaped, they approached it, only to encounter Middleton, whom she did not know, hunkered down at the base of a tree. When they approached, he said, "I couldn't imagine what you were up to." Mrs. Provine and her daughter, then unaware of Black's murder, left and resumed their journey.

Lewis Crook, another brother of Mack Crook, sent him a telegram at Hot Springs that Black had been killed, and the sheriff returned on the next train to Paris on Tuesday. Already, the fact that there had been bad blood between him and Black sparked rumors that Crook had something to do with his murder.

Middleton, in the meantime, had secured the ancient shotgun in a tree at his hiding place and, that evening, went into Paris. In the jail, Lewis Holman, Jim Yates, and Mrs. Harris were eating when the outlaw brazenly walked in. Newt Harris came in shortly afterwards, and they all sat down to supper. When Yates went to lock up a trusty prisoner, Middleton then told the others how Black was killed. After he was finished, he left them and disappeared. Holman met Mack Crook the next day when he returned from Hot Springs and told him what Middleton had said at the jail. Excited by this turn of events, Crook cautioned him that they should not be seen talking together on the street, well aware of the suspicion it might cause.

The committee appointed to investigate the murder hired several detectives, including Jack Duncan, summoning him from Dallas to begin the search. Crook, Harris, Yates, and Holman were now all widely suspected of being involved in the murder, although no concrete connection had been made to Middleton at the time. Quietly, Duncan set to work sifting information for clues. Apparently, he found enough information to support the belief that the sheriff and his deputies, as well as John Middleton, were guilty of the murder.

About four days after appointee Bill Gunn was supposed to succeed Crook as sheriff, shortly after Black's death, Jim Yates, still an office deputy, received an envelope addressed to the sheriff of Lamar County. Inside were two letters sent from

Briartown, which was on the Canadian River south of Muskogee in the Indian Territory. One letter was addressed to Crook and the other to Harris. Yates took them to Harris, since Crook was out of town, noting that they were signed by a man named Cross. The letter to Harris, among other things, asked for money. Hastily, Harris told Yates that he owed the man some money, but then said worriedly, "I'm afraid this thing is going to give us trouble yet." The letter to Crook spelled out the route to Briartown from Caddo, just north of the Red River. The writer, Cross, said that he had lost his horse and would stay there until he heard from Crook.

On February 10, 1885, several months after Crook and his deputies had left office and after much of the excitement over Black's death had subsided, Yates received a letter addressed to him and signed by a John Howard, postmarked from Wamego in Northern Kansas. The letter, referring to Yates as a friend, inquired as to who was sheriff now and if the new sheriff was a friend of Crook's. Howard also asked Yates to tell Newt Harris that he "would send that present soon." The letter also inquired about any rewards being offered. Yates, believing that the letter was from Middleton and, because it referred to the killing of Black, afraid that it would involve him, took the letter to Mack Crook at Schilling's Saloon. Crook owned a part interest in the saloon and he now tended bar there. Crook read the letter and told Yates, "That damned fellow has been writing to this country for some time. They'll get him. He'll give the whole thing away and then I'll have trouble." Yates asked Crook what he should do about the letter. The former sheriff told him to forget it; then, upon reflection, advised him to answer and tell Middleton to leave the country and go to Mexico. Burning the letter, Yates promptly composed and sent this letter:

> Dear Friend:
> I am just in receipt of a letter from you. Was glad to hear from you. Hope you may soon recover from your afflictions, so you may be able to ride again. You may be assured that I am just as

you regard me to be, and am glad you view it in the light as you express yourself. The question of the money you speak of is true, only more so. But I give you no name of the parties; and some persons are working for it and have made some long trips. The party you asked about giving away, he was not the one. He left the country. But I am credibly informed it was one of your relatives. Do not know which one. I can't say the party is uneasy, but there has been a great deal said. As the next time will soon be here I am looking for another siege of investigation. The citizens made up the amount and placed it in the bank (standing). The party you asked about is no friend, as he was a friend to some one else, and the party is blamed by some people to some extent. Do not go among your relatives, as they are closely watched. I can't advise you to ever come back to Texas, although I would like to see you very much, and would say many things I can't write. I use no names for fear of accident. I have not seen any of the boys you were best acquainted with, for some time, as some people are very curious, you know. You must be on alert and keep a close watch, or some gal might get away with you. In our correspondence we must use no names. First letters will be sufficient. I hardly know how to do to keep my own folks from knowing we have any correspondence, as they sometimes open my mail, and I assure you I want all this kept very close; and be sure you destroy this as soon as you get it, and I will do the same. If you should ever want to visit Texas, I want you to write me what time and place, so I may see you, though I can't advise you to do so. I think if I was a young man and had no encumbrance I should like to go to Mexico, although that seems out of the world almost. I believe this is all I can now write. Do not mail your letters where you write from, and use no name unless you want addressed different from this one. Take care of yourself and be a good boy.

Yours forever & etc
From your friend.

February 10, 1885.

Write once in a while so I may keep you posted about all the girls, and may be so they may forget the past. You know. The principal man you asked about is named Bill Gunn.[20]

Shortly after this letter was mailed to Kansas, Yates ran into Crook at Schilling's Saloon. "I've got another letter from that damned fellow," the ex-sheriff told Yates. "I don't know what to do. The fellow is writing back here that all of his friends have gone back on him. I have to get that damned fellow out of the way; if they get him, I'll have trouble!" Crook asked Yates if he thought he could find Middleton, but Yates expressed reservations and told him he didn't really want to get involved. Crook then wondered if his former deputy, Louis Holman, could be trusted. Crook loaned Yates a horse to go to the store outside of town where Holman was working. He instructed Yates to tell Holman that he wanted to see him and to be prepared to be gone about a week to ten days.

Holman went into Paris and met Crook at the saloon. The two walked down to Britt's wagonyard where Crook told him about the letters: "We must do something to stop him from writing!" The next morning, Crook, Harris, and Holman met in a room over the saloon. They discussed the situation and finally decided that Holman would go to Kansas, see Middleton, and urge him to leave the country for Mexico. Crook and Harris felt that Holman's absence wouldn't be as suspicious as if either of them went. Crook gave Holman forty dollars, and Harris forked over seventy. This money, except for enough for Holman to go to Kansas and return home on, was to be given to Middleton if he would agree to leave the country. Harris told Holman that if the outlaw did not agree, he should try to kill him or, if he couldn't do that, at least lure him to some place where Harris could kill him. Whatever happened, they had to stop him from writing those incriminating letters. On February 20, 1885, Holman left Paris, reaching Wamego, west of Topeka, two days later.

In the meantime, on Sunday, February 21, Sheriff Bill Gunn, at Duncan's request, sent for Jim Yates to come to his office. When Yates arrived, he was told that Middleton had been caught and that he had "given the whole thing away." Gunn and Duncan showed him the letter that he had written to "John Howard." Yates immediately broke down and told them all he knew, although he did not think that Crook had any actual part in the murder itself, only the coverup afterwards when he found out about it. Yates vehemently denied knowing about the murder himself. He was then held at the jail, and no one was allowed to see him.

All of the letters sent to the conspirators had been sent under Duncan's supervision, the intent being to alarm them enough to make a guilty move. Harry Miller, a detective in Wamego, had sent the letter signed by John Howard, as well as those sent to Crook and Harris. Harris had answered one letter, implicating himself, but Crook had not answered any letters. On the basis of both this evidence and Yates's statement, Sheriff Gunn and Duncan immediately arrested Crook and Harris. Duncan then caught a train for Wamego, accompanied by Deputy Sheriff Polk Burris.

When Holman arrived in Wamego on February 22, he had left a note for John Howard at the post office telling him that he had arrived and suggesting a meeting. Miller had Holman under surveillance continuously until Duncan could get there. Holman received no reply to his first message, so he left another a day or so later. He waited several more days and, hearing nothing from Middleton, decided to return to Texas after a brief side trip to enjoy the sights at nearby Junction City. Getting his second note back from the post office, not knowing what became of the first note, Holman went to the Wamego depot and bought his ticket for Junction City on Friday, February 27. Duncan and Burris had just alighted from an afternoon westbound train as Holman was beginning to board his train. Two cocked revolvers at Holman's "brainbox" convinced him that he was under arrest and to surrender peaceably.[21]

The examining trial for Crook and Harris, charged with being accomplices in Black's murder, had already commenced in Paris the day before, February 26. Witnesses were called to testify about the bad feelings between Black and Crook, while Yates took the stand to tell what he knew. The courtroom was crowded on each day of the hearing. The arrest of Holman was a bombshell and on March 2, he took the stand, the prosecution having agreed to drop charges against him if he turned state's evidence. Holman did just that. Other testimony indicated that, prior to the shooting of Black, Crook had been seen removing an ancient double-barrelled shotgun from Schilling's Saloon that had been previously deposited there for safekeeping. Duncan testified as to his role in the investigation and how the letters had been sent. Crook and Harris were both subsequently indicted.[22]

Duncan, accompanied by ex-sheriff John Gose, Bill Nelson, and Hugh Tinnin, went to the wooded area east of Paris where Mrs. Provine had seen the man thought to be Middleton. They looked all over for the old gun, but couldn't find it. Duncan found only a piece of cloth which looked as if it had been used as a bandage for a sore. On Sunday, March 22, the shotgun was finally found by others, rusted and still secured in the tree where Middleton left it. It was quickly identified as the gun that had been taken from Schilling's Saloon.[23]

Duncan's work in bringing Crook and Harris to justice was completed. But John Middleton, the actual killer, was still at large. The hunt was still on.

THE
EARLY WEST

NOTES

1. *Fort Worth Gazette*, February 9, 1884.
2. *Dallas Weekly Herald*, March 13, 1884.
3. *Austin Daily Statesman*, March 25, 1884.

Bounty Hunter

4. *Dallas Weekly Herald*, July 3, 1884.

5. *Dallas Weekly Herald*, September 18, 1884.

6. *Dallas Daily Herald*, July 28, 1884.

7. *Dallas Daily Herald*, August 21-23, 1884.

8. *Dallas Daily Herald*, August 22, 23, and 27, 1884.

9. Minutes, 14th District Court, Dallas County, Texas, Vol. Q, p. 470, and Case Papers, 14th District Court (*State of Texas v. George Scott, alias Rorabaugh*, cause nos. 8091 and 8092).

10. *Dallas Morning News*, May 27, 1921; *Dallas Daily Times Herald*, May 27, 1921.

11. Letter to author from Mrs. Joan Courtney (wife of the late Frank Courtney, grandson of Jack Duncan), Dallas, Texas, December 23, 1983; *Dallas Morning News*, March 18, 1900; *Dallas Daily Times Herald*, March 18, 1900.

12. The account of the investigation of the murder of James H. Black is taken from the following sources, in addition to those otherwise indicated:

> *Mack Crook v. The State of Texas*, 27 Tex. 298, 11 S. W. 444 (1899)
>
> *Sherman* (Texas) *Daily Register*, December 15-18, 1886; November 19-25, 1888.
>
> *Paris* (Texas) *Weekly News-Boy*, March 7, 1885.
>
> *Dallas Weekly Herald*, March 5, 1885.
>
> *Dallas Morning News*, December 18, 21, and 22, 1886.

13. Election Return Book, Lamar County, Texas, November 4, 1844, pp. 4 and 5.

14. A. W. Neville, *The Red River Valley: Then and Now* (Paris, Texas: North Texas Publishing Co., 1948), p. 57.

15. *Muskogee* (Indian Territory) *Indian Journal*, May 28, 1885; Shirley, *Belle Starr*, p. 177.

16. Neville, *Red River Valley*, pp. 58 and 59.

17. Docket Book, District Court, Lamar County, Texas, Fall Term 1884, Vol. 4, pp. 244 and 261 (*State of Texas v. John Middleton*, cause nos. 3397, 3398, and 3432).

18. *Clarksville* (Texas) *Northern Standard*, November 21, 1884; *Dallas Daily Herald*, November 18, 1884.

19. *Dallas Daily Herald*, November 18, 1884; *Clarksville* (Texas) *Northern Standard*, November 21, 1884.

20. *Crook v. State of Texas*, 27 Tex. at 211 and 212.

21. *Kansas Agriculturist*, March 6, 1885.

22. See also Criminal Docket Book, District Court, Lamar County, Texas Vol. 4, p. 258 (*State of Texas v. Mack Crook and Nute Harris*, cause no. 3632).

23. *Dallas Daily Herald*, March 25, 1885.

Chapter 8

End of the Search

John Middleton dropped out of sight, and most lawmen felt that he had gone back to the Indian Territory to lay low, well aware there was a price on his head. Duncan could only wait until the outlaw made some move that revealed his whereabouts. In the meantime, he checked with sources in the Territory who were acting as his eyes and ears.

As April, 1885, rolled around, Duncan was making periodic trips northward to keep tabs on Middleton's whereabouts and, at the same time, get some other work done. For example, on Friday morning, April 10, he arrested Ralph Sanderson, a man wanted for murder in Athens, Alabama, as Sanderson was stepping aboard a train bound for St. Louis at a small railroad crossing at Argenta, Arkansas.[1] When he returned to Dallas on April 13, Duncan brought with him a new friend:

> While he was gone Detective Duncan purchased a genuine pure-blooded veteran bloodhound of a famous breed known as "Sleuth." This dog, since his infancy, has been in the service of guards of railroad convicts, and Mr. Duncan paid $100 for him, and, since testing him under the most difficult circumstances, putting streams of water between him and the mock fugitive, he says no money can buy him. It is claimed that this wonderful dog, for he is a remarkable animal, can catch the trail of a criminal, and run it down, even though it be 10 or 12 days old. Sleuth is the ugliest and most docile of animals on ordinary occasions, and never scents a trail unless commanded to do so. On the streets he is a most docile animal, and children can pull his ears or tail without giving him the least bit of offence, yet when put on

Bounty Hunter

the track of a fugitive from justice he is quite a different animal, and all his energy is aroused. City Marshal. Arnold, Sheriff Smith and Mr. Duncan are combining to get up a pack of pure-blooded bloodhounds for the purpose of trailing more thoroughly the criminals who are wanted for serious crimes.

Duncan told the reporter that Sleuth would not hurt his captive, if the captive stopped when the dog got him. If the fugitive should not stop, however, "Sleuth will stay with him to the last."[2]

Duncan also went back to Paris to see if perhaps Middleton might have returned to his old haunts. It was a good guess, although it was Middleton who observed Duncan rather than the other way around. Middleton, perhaps to help his friends or possibly from a mischievous motive, penned a letter taunting Duncan for his efforts and sent it to the *Fort Worth Daily Gazette*, which printed it on April 16:

Paris, Tex., April 11, 1885
To the Editor of the Gazette:
   I will state now, as I have heretofore, that I am innocent of the charges of being an accessory to the murder of Sheriff-elect James H. Black of Lamar Co., and I still say that I escaped from the Paris jail through my own ingenuity, and was not assisted either by Newt Harris or his wife, and I would like Detective Duncan to tell how much money he gave Lewis Holman and Jim Yates to swear to what they did. I am now in Paris and have been for two weeks. I saw Duncan last week when he came up the street. I was standing in Schilling's saloon, and saw him shake hands with Strother and a young man with a light suit of clothes on; I don't know who he was; I never saw him before. Duncan pretends to be anxious to catch me. He is a make-believe, for he knows that if he does that I will tell a different tale from what he wants me to tell. He may think he is going to convict Crook and Harris on circumstantial evidence, but he will not be able to do it as long as my name is John Middleton, for I have collected enough evidence since I have been out to clear me and I am not going to see Crook and Harris punished just because Holman and Yates will swear falsely for the sake of a little money.

End of the Search

Well, Mr. Editor, if you will publish this you will do me a great favor, as I have to go down on the river right away, I can not write any more today.

Yours respectfully,
John Middleton.[3]

No doubt, this cavalier taunting by the outlaw irritated the feisty detective, leading him to redouble his efforts to find him. In Paris, the case against Crook and Harris was progressing. Their attorneys were applying all of the delaying tactics they could muster, although trial was set for May 4. Middleton was charged with murder, and, on April 18, Newt Harris's wife, Rebecca, was also named as an accessory to murder in the first degree. She was arrested on April 20, 1885, but was subsequently released on a bond of $1,500 posted by family and friends.[4]

Duncan also returned to the Indian Territory in April to look for the fugitive killer, this time accompanied by Deputy Sheriff J. H. Millsap. Middleton was now believed to be staying in the vicinity of Younger's Bend, the home of Sam and Belle Starr on the Canadian River. He was rumored to have been using the Starr place as his headquarters for the last several months, from which he was ranging out to steal horses, rob stores, and commit other depredations. It was even rumored that Belle had become his mistress, despite the presence of her husband, Sam.[5]

To guide them through unfamiliar territory, Duncan and Millsap engaged the services of John C. West, a United States Indian policeman. West's family owned a place about six miles from Younger's Bend. It was his complaint and testimony that had sent Sam and Belle to a federal prison in Detroit, Michigan, for nine months in 1883 for horse theft.[6] West, a one-half Cherokee Indian, had become an Indian policeman in July, 1884. He would later be city marshal of Muskogee and sheriff of the Canadian District in the Cherokee Nation.[7] It is possible that Duncan made a foray into the Indian Territory as early as December, 1884, before the arrest of Crook and Harris, to try to track down Middleton, although contemporary accounts of his movements are not clear. It has been asserted that Duncan and Millsap, in December, assisted by West, made their first raid on the Starr place. The State of Texas was offering a $300 reward, and Duncan offered an additional $500 from the fund collected in Paris in November. If such a raid after Middleton was made soon after Black's death, it proved unsuccessful, although it would have likely alerted Middleton to be more careful. If the outlaw did go to the Indian Territory right after Black's death, he did not stay there, for he returned to Paris at least once in April, 1885, as noted.[8]

Accounts of the three officers' raid in April were brief. Middleton was not there, but Belle Starr was, a pistol prominently displayed on her belt. She supposedly cursed her sworn enemy, John West, for leading lawmen to her place. There is no information indicating that Belle and Duncan knew each other from her former days in Dallas. Exercising what was probably good discretion, given Belle's legend, the lawmen took her pistol away from her before she might get the idea of trying to use it, although they returned it to her when they left. She heaped considerable abuse on the three for trying to nab Middleton;[9] however, after they were gone, she likely wasted little time in getting word to the fugitive that this wouldn't be the last time the lawmen visited. Not only were Texas officers after him, but he was also suspected of having led two others in the robbery several weeks earlier of Sam Brown's store in Weleeka in broad daylight. Both clerks and customers had been robbed of several hundred dollars, five watches, a number of pistols, and other property.[10] This meant that U. S. Marshals out of Fort Smith, Arkansas, where the federal district court was located, as well as Indian Police, were also looking for him. The focus of attention on Younger's Bend was now much too heated, and it was time for Middleton to find a new base of operations.

On Sunday, May 3, 1885, Belle and her sixteen-year-old daughter, Pearl, and fourteen-year-old son, Eddie Reed, packed their effects in a wagon pulled by two horses and set out for a visit to friends in Chickalah, in Yell County, Arkansas, and a trip to Dardanelle, just south across the Arkansas River from Russellville. Accompanying them were Sam Starr and young Frank Cook, whom Belle had hired to do odd jobs and to drive the wagon. Concealed within the covered wagon, according to one writer, was John Middleton. Two horses, belonging to Belle and Pearl, were tied to the rear of the wagon. Since the most direct route to Chickalah and Dardanelle was through Fort Smith, it was planned that Middleton would leave the party at some point and, riding Pearl's horse, go around that city to the south in order to avoid the law. They would all rendezvous in Logan County prior to Belle's going on to Chickalah.[11]

Traveling east, the group camped for the night near White-field where Pearl supposedly became angry with Middleton and refused to loan him her horse to ride. While they breakfasted the next morning, a rancher, Fayette Barnette, out looking after his stock, stopped by to visit. They went and got a sorrel mare, without shoes and blind in the right eye. It had a "31" brand on his neck and a half circle, or "rafter A" branded on one shoulder. Middleton paid Barnette $50 for the animal, then saddled it with Pearl's saddle that Belle had bought for her at Eufaula a short time before. He left his shotgun in the wagon, but, although he already had two pistols on his belt, borrowed another pistol from Belle. Bidding the party adieu, Middleton then struck off by himself toward the Poteau River. After Middleton left, Sam Starr and Eddie Reed turned around and went back to Younger's Bend, while Belle and Pearl continued their journey with Frank Cook. The three arrived in Fort Smith, spent the night at a hotel, then went on to Logan County to meet Middleton.[12]

Duncan and Millsap were still searching for the outlaw. Perhaps assuming that the heat around Younger's Bend in the Indian Territory was sufficient to drive him off, they began concentrating their efforts in his old stomping grounds of Logan

County and the surrounding area in Arkansas. Millsap went to Russellville, while Duncan went down to Little Rock to see if perhaps their fugitive was hiding there.

On Thursday, May 7, a riderless horse wearing a saddle and a bridle, with a belt of cartridges and a pistol hung over the pommel, was found straying alone along the banks of the swollen Poteau River, some twenty-five miles southwest of Fort Smith near Poteau Mountain. It was obvious that the horse, a sorrel mare that was blind in the right eye, had crossed the river, leading the finders to believe that its rider had been swept away and perhaps drowned. On Monday, May 11, about 200 yards downriver from where tracks indicated that the horse had entered the rushing water, Henry Tallay of Pocola in the Choctaw Nation found the body.

The corpse was that of a young man with a heavy mustache carrying no identification. He wore two .45-caliber revolvers at his waist and was carrying $21, two pocket knives, a silver watch, and a pocket comb. Badly decomposed, buzzards had mutilated the face even further, making identification that much more difficult. Apparently, the rider had attempted to swim the river at night, but couldn't successfully negotiate the swift current. Tallay placed the body in a crude box and buried it in a shallow grave by the river, taking possession of personal effects and the horse and notifying the authorities.[13]

O. D. Weldon, a reporter for the *Fort Smith Elevator*, wrote a story on the finding of the body, including a detailed description of the horse, and dispatched it to the *St. Louis Globe Democrat*,[14] from which other newspapers around the Southwest picked up the story. Initially, it was believed that the body might be that of one of the outlaws associated with Jim and Pink Lee, leaders of a gang of rustlers who were wanted for the recent murder of posse members in the Chickasaw Nation, just north of Gainesville, Texas.[15]

How Duncan learned that it might be Middleton's body is unclear. The body was found on May 11. The next day, according to one Texas newspaper, a dispatch was received in Paris from Duncan to the effect that Middleton had been arrested.[16] This could have been a reporter's misinterpretation, perhaps, of a message that Middleton was believed to have drowned or thought to have been located.

On May 14, A. G. McCarty, reading the newspaper description of the mare, left his home in the Territory and went to Fort Smith where he complained that the horse had been stolen from him, probably by the drowned man, who he believed was John Middleton. He knew Middleton and was aware that the outlaw had been in his neighborhood, probably stealing the horse on May 6. McCarty then left Fort Smith for Pocola to identify the horse, satisfied from the description that it was his, and retrieved it on May 15.[17]

Duncan and Millsap arrived in Fort Smith on the evening of Friday, May 15. They met the next day with their old guide, John West, now a captain with the Indian Police. On Sunday morning, at 6 a.m., the three, joined by *Elevator* reporter Weldon, set out for the site of the grave in the Choctaw Nation. On arrival, they borrowed some field hoes and raked away the loose dirt covering the shallow grave, then lifted the lid of the crude box containing the body. Despite the ravages of the buzzards and of decomposition, they determined with little question that the body was that of John Middleton. His size, the color of his hair, and a scar on one knee all matched the outlaw's description. There was a string of beads and a rattle around his neck. Cutting a lock of hair from the remains, they recovered the grave. The identification was strengthened by an examination of the effects now in Mr. Tallay's possession. The saddle that had been on the horse was identified as one purchased by Belle in Eufaula. Of the three pistols, one was the same weapon that the officers had taken from Belle in April at Younger's Bend, the other two being Middleton's.[18] The chase after John Middleton was over.

On Monday morning, May 18, Duncan, Millsap, and West

left Fort Smith for Dardanelle, Arkansas. In the nearby mountains, they located the camp of Belle Starr and Frank Cook. Middleton's brother had already learned of John's death and informed Belle before the arrival of the officers. Belle told the lawmen that she had left Middleton on Wednesday, May 6, about five miles from where he drowned, and that he had $400 in the cartridge belt that was hanging from the pommel of the saddle. She did not believe that his death was an accident but that someone had killed him, then thrown him in the river. She told them that she herself had placed the beads around his neck that were found on him. As soon as she saw the pistol that the officers had retrieved from Mr. Tallay, she identified it as hers, and the officers handed it over.[19] A contemporary writer described a scene in which the officers indicated an intention to break open a trunk belonging to Belle in order to search for evidence of her association with Middleton. "Belle grasped a pistol in each hand, and coolly reminded them that if they broke open the trunk their souls would go speeding to the place of torment. The trunk was not opened."[20] Whether or not that dramatic scene occurred, John West had a warrant for Frank Cook and the young man was taken into custody.

At Russellville, on May 19, Duncan telegraphed friends in Dallas of Middleton's death. [21] West, Duncan, and Millsap then took Cook through Fort Smith on their way to Weleeka to see if he could be identified as one of the desperadoes who robbed Sam Brown's store there.[22] After Cook was returned to Fort Smith, Duncan's job was done, and he returned home.

Cook was subsequently charged with the larceny of currency and a pair of boots from Sam Brown. He pleaded guilty on June 2, 1885, and received a one-year sentence to the federal house of correction in Detroit, where Sam and Belle Starr had served time.[23] A charge of horse theft brought by Cook's father-in-law, Albert Carr of Muskogee, was dismissed. After serving some time, he was again before the court on another horse theft charge, committed on May 10, 1885, and upon being found guilty on August 21, 1886, was sentenced to another one-year sentence, this time at the Southern Illinois Penitentiary at Menard.[24]

Because it was believed that Middleton had stolen the sorrel mare from A. G. McCarty, Belle was suspected of having been an accomplice and was indicted in January, 1886, for that theft. She was subsequently acquitted when Fayette Barnette conveniently testified on her behalf that he saw a stranger sell the horse to Middleton.[25] Belle had reportedly accompanied Middleton's brother and father to the Poteau River in June, 1885, where they exhumed his body and reinterred it in a more fitting grave.[26] In the next few years, after other brushes with the law, Belle Starr left her legend behind when she was shot from her horse in an ambush not far from Younger's Bend on February 3, 1889.[27]

In Paris, although Mack Crook and Newt Harris had been scheduled to go on trial on May 4, 1885, and a special venire of 60 men had been ordered, a change of venue to Sherman in Grayson County was granted since feelings were still running high and the likelihood of an impartial jury was questionable. Rebecca Harris was not indicted after her arrest, and charges against her were withdrawn. Likewise, all of the charges against the deceased John Middleton were withdrawn.[28] On May 8, just prior to going north into Arkansas, Jack Duncan had assisted Lamar County deputies in taking the two prisoners to Sherman to await trial. The Grayson County district judge subsequently announced that he would not hear the case until the fall term of the court later in the year.[29]

In June, 1885, after a habeas corpus hearing, Grayson County District Judge Maltbie granted Mack Crook a release on a bond of $12,000.[30] After one continuance in the case, trial was set a year and a half later for December 15, 1886, at which time the trials of the two defendants were severed. Harris went to trial first. The jury in his case deadlocked, and, on Christmas Day after several days of deliberation, the foreman held up the court's charge and told the judge, "These papers will rust and decay before this jury can agree on a verdict."[31] Harris was then released on $8,000 bond.[32] Crook did not come to trial until November 19, 1888. Harris, in the meantime, had died and his case was dismissed. On November 28, the jury found Crook guilty and sentenced him to life imprisonment.[33] On appeal, though, the Texas Court of Appeals reversed the conviction and remanded the case for a new trial because of errors in some of the trial judge's rulings and in the charge to the jury.[34] Although the case was remanded, and the Grayson County court ordered the summoning of 200 prospective jurors for a trial to begin on November 3, 1891,[35] court records do not mention the outcome of Crook's case.

During the spring of 1885, while Duncan was pursuing John Middleton, another incident occurred in which he would later have some slight involvement. Cattle rustlers in the Delaware Bend area of the Red River, north of Gainesville, Texas, had been ravaging herds on both sides of the river, in Texas and the Indian Territory. The gangs committed numerous robberies and assaults on travelers, but repeated ventures into their stronghold by posses had failed to slow their operations. One of the most desperate of the gangs was that led by two brothers, Jim and Pink Lee, who despite the earnest pleas of their mother to walk the straight and narrow path, raided openly in Delaware Bend. Included in their band was another brother, Tom, as well as Ed Stein, a brother-in-law, and Frank Pierce, whose true name was Frank Pierce Roberts. Pierce bootlegged whiskey to Indians in the Chickasaw Nation, getting his illegal supplies from Stein, who operated a small store at Delaware Bend on the Texas side of the river. Because Jim Lee had an Indian wife, he was entitled to own property in the Nation, and he maintained a place about twelve or fifteen miles northwest of the Bend on a tributary of Caddo Creek, about forty miles from Gainesville. With his brother Pink living with him, Jim Lee offered sanctuary and

End of the Search

membership in the gang to outlaws and desperadoes who came to the out-of-the-way place.[36]

A number of Texas ranchers leased grazing pasture from landholders in the Chickasaw Nation. Jim and Andy Roff and another brother maintained a ranch between Caddo Creek and the Arbuckle Mountains, some distance from the Lee place. One day in April, 1885, Jim Roff was in the mountains looking for stock when he observed a group of five or six horsemen rounding up a bunch of cattle. Riding to investigate, he saw the men hurriedly ride off at his approach. The cattle belonged to two neighboring ranchers named Estes and McColgin, as well as others. Roff concealed himself and saw the men return and drive the cattle off. With Estes and McColgin accompanying him, Roff tracked the cattle south across the river and straight to Stein's store. They were met by the Lees, Pierce, and Stein, all heavily armed. Being outgunned, the three cattlemen said that they were looking for some mules and did not mention the cattle, then quickly left. They got in touch with Cooke County Sheriff Hill in Gainesville, and a posse was formed to go after the rustlers.

The plan was for Sheriff Hill and his deputy, Pat Ware, neither of whom was known by gang members, to saunter into Stein's store, then get the drop on the outlaws. The posse would wait on the Territory side of the Red River until they heard from the sheriff. When Hill and Ware rode up to the store, however, Frank Pierce greeted them cradling a Winchester, and, in response to their explanation that they were looking for the road to Dexter, a nearby town, he pointed at the road with the rifle and told them to "hit the road and don't look back." The two lawmen then rode to Dexter.

Across the river, the waiting posse grew restless. In addition to Andy Roff, there were John Washington, three or four Chickasaw Indians, and a few other men. In hopes of finding out what was happening, they sent a man who lived in the area, Jim Shattles, to visit the store, feeling that this wouldn't be suspicious since Shattles occasionally traded at the store. However, on Shattles's arrival, Pierce ordered him into the house and to stay there. When Shattles didn't return, the posse then decided to check the situation out for themselves and rode to the store.

The posse took up positions along the rail fence around the store just as Frank Pierce came out the back door and walked across the lot toward his horse. John Washington called out to him to hold up, and Pierce fired a shot in reply, running for his saddled horse. As the outlaw started across the river, the posse returned fire and, when the horse reached the other side of the river, Pierce fell to the ground shot full of holes. Shattles, relieved to be alive, welcomed his rescuers. The other gang members had left before the posse arrived.

Much of the stolen stock was rounded up by the posse, who returned it to the proper owners. However, the Lees were infuriated at the news of Pierce's death and gathered a gang of men at their ranch.

Deputy U. S. Marshal Jim Guy, also a sergeant in the Indian Police, held warrants for the arrest of Jim and Pink Lee. Another fugitive, a black man Dallas Humby, who had been arrested earlier by Guy and then released to his brother because of illness, had fled and was now also with the Lee gang. Determined to arrest Humby and the Lees together, Guy went to Andy and Jim Roff's place, and they reluctantly agreed to be members of Guy's posse, knowing full well that the bandits would be heavily armed and on their guard. Also joining the posse were cowboy Billy Kirksey, two "regular posse-men," Windy Johnson and Emerson Folsom, who was a Choctaw Indian, Strother Brown, and two men named Sadler and Turner.

Before dawn on May 1, 1885, Sergeant Guy led his posse from Henderson's store on the Washita River on the ten-mile trip to the Lee ranch. At about sunrise, they arrived at the stronghold, a two-room log house, the rooms separated by a breezeway or dog run, with portholes on all sides through which to shoot. The posse's horses could not get across the boggy Cold Branch stream some 200 yards from the house, so the animals were left with Johnson, and the posse walked up to the house. Guy instructed them to withdraw if the Lees refused to surrender. At the northeast corner of the east room, Ed Stein cautiously opened a window shutter and asked them what they wanted. Guy explained their mission and insisted that the Lees surrender, at which time Stein told them to come around to the front where they could discuss it. Guy and Folsom walked around to the front and, as Guy rested his rifle against a tree, a shot rang out, and he fell dead.

There was a momentary silence, giving Folsom time to run for cover. Then a volley of shots poured from the house into a group of the posse assembled on the east side. Jim Roff and Billy Kirksey were killed instantly. Andy Roff, seriously wounded, managed to make his way to a tree where he sat down on the ground at its base and then died. Strother Brown emptied his Winchester at one of the portholes, then ran for a blackjack tree which proved too thin for cover. He joined the remainder of the posse as it scrambled for the protection of a nearby ravine, from which they returned the gunfire but without doing any damage. They then made their way to their horses and escaped, leaving the four bodies behind. One posse member, Turner, was apparently unable to get to a horse and also remained behind, hidden. He would later describe the emergence of the Lee gang from the house. One of the gang members, Bill Bourland, stood over Guy's riddled body and told the others, "We've played hell! We liked to have killed all of 'em! Here's four dead ones and there's five or six more dead down on the branch!" The outlaws then mounted up and headed in the direction of Delaware Bend, telling parties along the way that someone had better get the corpses back at the house or the "hogs would eat 'em up."[37]

News of the bloody tragedy provoked widespread indignation and outrage, leading to the organization of several heavily armed posses to hunt the Lees down. A large posse returned to the Lee ranch to retrieve the bodies and, finding the gang gone, burned the place down. The remaining Roff brothers posted a large reward for the capture of the members of the gang, thus attracting a number of detectives and other officers from elsewhere in Texas to join in the manhunt. Within the next two weeks, a large number of the Lee gang, including Tom Lee, Ed Stein, Bill Davidson, John and Bill Bourland, Tom Culp, Arthur James, and Albert Cole, were all arrested and behind bars. [38]

Jim and Pink Lee remained at large, however, openly roaming the Indian Territory north of Delaware Bend, aided with provisions and information by friends. At one ranch where they "traded" their wornout mounts for fresh ones, they told a ranchhand that they were going to stay in that country and, if anyone wanted them, to come and get them. Sheriff Hill sent a telegram to Dallas asking for bloodhounds but was unable to get them. Periodically, there were reports of the two Lees accosting riders, threatening to kill them, then sending them on with instructions to tell the authorities that they were "still on the warpath."[39]

Jack Duncan was now back in Dallas, closely following press accounts of the pursuit. On June 14, 1885, a burglar attempted to enter the Dallas residence of Mr. W. H. Murdock but was frightened away. When Duncan was notified, he gathered up Sleuth and other bloodhounds and took up the trail of the fleeing burglar. The dogs followed the scent into the Trinity River bottom, three miles south of the city. However, the midnight darkness being a major handicap, Duncan called the dogs off and abandoned the chase.[40] The lure of the reward offered of $2,500 each for the two Lee brothers, to be "paid upon the arrest and delivery of Jim and Pink Lee to the Sheriff of Cooke County, Texas, inside the jail door,"[41] however, now induced the detective to take up their trail.

Taking three of his trained bloodhounds in late June, Duncan joined one of the many parties scouring the Delaware Bend country and Indian Territory for a trace of the Lees. As one newspaper reported, "Jack Duncan of Dallas is with the party and if anybody doubts that it means business, he doesn't know Jack Duncan."[42] Unfortunately, the Lees successfully eluded their pursuers, and Duncan's posse had to return from the field with nothing to show for its efforts. In fact, it would not be until September when Jim and Pink Lee would fall before the guns of Deputy U. S. Marshal Jim Taylor and another lawman who would gain considerable fame for tracking down badmen, Heck Thomas.[43]

No doubt disappointed at not getting a crack at the sizable reward, Duncan returned to Dallas.

NOTES

1.   *Arkansas* (Little Rock) *Gazette,* April 11, 1885.

2.   *Dallas Daily Herald,* April 14, 1885.

3.   *Fort Worth Daily Gazette,* April 16, 1885.

4.   Criminal Docket Book, District Court, Lamar County, Texas, Vol. 4, pp. 259 and 262 (*State of Texas v. Rebecca Harris,* cause no. 3645; *State of Texas v. John Middleton,* cause no. 3633); *Fort Worth Daily Gazette,* April 21, 26, and 27, 1885.

5.   See Shirley, *Belle Starr,* pp. 180-182; Harry Sinclair Drago, *Outlaws on Horseback* (New York: Dodd, Mead & Co., 1964), p. 147; Paul I. Wellman, *A Dynasty of Western Outlaws* (New York: Bonanza Books, 1961), p. 147.

6.   Case Records, U. S. District Court, Western District of Arkansas (*United States v. Sam Starr and Belle Starr,* 1882); Shirley, *Belle Starr,* pp. 152-165.

7.   Roster of Indian Police, 1885-1886, U. S. Bureau of Indian Affairs, U. S. National Archives and Records Service; Shirley, *Belle Starr,* footnote, p. 284.

8.   *Fort Smith* (Arkansas) *Elevator,* May 22, 1885; *Muskogee* (Indian Territory) *Indian Journal,* May 28, 1885; see also Samuel W. Harmon, "Belle Starr, The Female Desperado," reprint of Chapter XXXII from *Hell on the Border* (Fort Smith, Arkansas: Phoenix Publishing Co., 1898), as quoted in Ed Bartholomew, ed., *Some Western Gun Fighters* (Toyahvale, Texas: Frontier Book Co., 1954), p. 35; Shirley, *Belle Starr,* p. 178 (who states that Duncan was accompanied by Deputy Sheriff Polk Burris).

End of the Search

9. *Fort Smith* (Arkansas) *Elevator*, May 22, 1885; *Muskogee* (Indian Territory) *Indian Journal*, May 28, 1885; Burton Rascoe, *Belle Starr, The Bandit Queen* (New York: Random House, 1941), p. 227.

10. *Fort Worth Daily Gazette*, May 23, 1885; *Fort Smith* (Arkansas) *Elevator*, May 1, 1885; June 5, 1885; see also Shirley, *Belle Starr*, pp. 179 and footnote on p. 286.

11. *Fort Smith* (Arkansas) *Elevator*, May 22, 1885; *Muskogee* (Indian Territory) *Indian Journal*, May 28, 1885; Harmon, "Belle Starr," pp. 35 and 36; Shirley, *Belle Starr*, pp. 175 and 182.

12. Harmon, "Belle Starr," pp. 35 and 36; Shirley, *Belle Starr*, pp. 182 and 183; *Fort Smith* (Arkansas) *Elevator*, May 15, 1885; *Fort Worth Daily Gazette*, May 14, 1885.

13. *Fort Smith* (Arkansas) *Elevator*, May 15, 1885.

14. Harmon, "Belle Starr," p. 37.

15. *Fort Worth Daily Gazette*, May 14, 1885.

16. *Fort Worth Daily Gazette*, May 13, 1885.

17. *Fort Smith* (Arkansas) *Elevator*, May 15, 1885; *Fort Worth Daily Gazette*, May 15, 1885.

18. *Fort Worth Daily Gazette*, May 19, 1885; *Muskogee* (Indian Territory) *Indian Journal*, May 28, 1885; *Fort Smith* (Arkansas) *Elevator*, May 22, 1885.

19. *Fort Smith* (Arkansas) *Elevator*, May 22, 1885.

20. Harmon, "Belle Starr," p. 38.

21. *Dallas Daily Herald*, May 20, 1885.

22. *Fort Worth Daily Gazette*, May 23, 1885; *Fort Smith* (Arkansas) *Elevator*, June 5, 1885.

Bounty Hunter

23. Case Records, U. S. District Court, Western District of Arkansas (*United States v. Frank Cook*, cause no. 764, 1885); *Fort Smith* (Arkansas) *Elevator*, July 10, 1885.

24. Case Records, U. S. District Court, Western District of Arkansas (*United States v. Frank Cook*, cause no. 1497, 1886).

25. Shirley, *Belle Starr*, pp. 188-190, 205, and 206.

26. *Fort Smith* (Arkansas) *Elevator*, June 19, 1885.

27. Shirley, *Belle Starr*, pp. 234-236.

28. Criminal Docket Book, District Court, Lamar County, Texas, Vol. 4, pp. 258, 259, 261, and 262 (*State of Texas v. Mack Crook and Nute Harris*, cause no. 3632; *State of Texas v. John Middleton*, cause nos. 3432 and 3433); *Fort Worth Daily Gazette*, May 3 and 8, 1885.

29. *Fort Worth Daily Gazette*, May 9, 10, 13, 14, and 18, 1885.

30. *Dallas Daily Herald*, June 4 and 5, 1885; *Fort Worth Daily Gazette*, June 5, 1885.

31. Minutes, 15th District Court, Grayson County, Texas, Vol. E-1, pp. 34 and 119 (*State of Texas v. Mack Crook and Nute Harris*, cause no. 2723); *Sherman* (Texas) *Daily Register*, December 15, 17, and 18, 1886; *Dallas Morning News*, December 16, 18, 21, and 22, 1886.

32. Minutes, 15th District Court, Grayson County, Texas, Vol. E-1, pp. 124 and 125 (*State of Texas v. Mack Crook and Nute Harris*, cause no. 2723); *Dallas Morning News*, December 31, 1886.

33. Minutes, 15th District Court, Grayson County, Texas, Vol. E-1, pp. 580 and 581 (*State of Texas v. Mack Crook*, cause no. 2723); *Sherman* (Texas) *Daily Register*, November 19, 21-25, 1888.

34. *Crook v. State of Texas*, 27 Tex. 198, 11 S. W. 444 (1889).

35. Minutes, 15th District Court, Grayson County, Texas, Vol. F-1, p. 360 (*State of Texas v. Mack Crook*, cause no. 2723).

36. Joe T. Roff, "Reminiscences of Early Days in the Chickasaw Nation," *Chronicles of Oklahoma*, Vol. XIII (Oklahoma City, Oklahoma: Oklahoma Historical Society, 1935), p. 182; Glenn Shirley, *Heck Thomas, Frontier Marshal* (New York: Chilton Company, 1962), p. 32; *Fort Worth Daily Gazette*, May 2, 1885.

37. Roff, "Reminiscences," pp. 182-186; Shirley, *Heck Thomas*, pp, 31 and 33; *Fort Worth Daily Gazette*, May 3 and 5, 1885; *Dallas Daily Herald*, May 26-28, 1885.

38. *Fort Worth Daily Gazette*, May 6-9, 14, 17, and 18, 1885.

39. *Fort Worth Daily Gazette*, May 12 and 13, 1885; June 2, 1885.

40. *Dallas Daily Herald*, June 16, 1885.

41. *Muskogee* (Indian Territory) *Indian Journal*, May 28, 1885.

42. *Fort Worth Daily Gazette*, June 28 and 29, 1885.

43. Roff, "Reminiscences," pp. 188 and 189; Shirley, *Heck Thomas*, p. 37.

Chapter 9

Gunfire and Bribery

Back in Dallas, the high adventure of tracking down desperate outlaws settled into a more mundane routine of ferreting out small-time thieves and burglars. For example, on February 17, 1885, at about sunset, several men had stopped the small son of Cass County Treasurer Kinkead as he approached the gate of his home in Kildare, not far from the Texas-Louisiana border. The boy was threatened with harm if he did not open the house for them. However, the small boy began screaming, waking his father who was sleeping inside. Kinkead opened the door to see what was wrong. As the men rushed into the house, he tried to run to a neighbor's house but was caught and forced back inside. After taking Kinkead's pocketbook containing cash, the robbers fled without leaving a clue as to their identity.

While there is little information as to how it was done, Jack Duncan solved the case after he was called in. According to a newspaper account on July 25, 1885:

> It was regarded as a crime unfathomable until the well-known and celebrated detective, Jack Duncan, of Dallas, took the matter in hand and caused the arrest of Saul and Tom Taylor, of Linden, charging them with the robbery, and it is generally understood, although they have not had their preliminary examination, that the guilty parties are at last being brought to justice. Much praise is due to Detective Duncan, who, having no clue whatever to start with, was able to hunt up a trail and evidence found to cause the arrest just made. Great surprise is manifested at the arrests, the

parties being of very respectable family and well connected
through out the county.[1]

On September 10, 1885, J. A. Taylor and T. J. Taylor were
indicted by the Cass County grand jury for robbery, assault
with intent to murder, and unlawfully carrying a pistol. Two
days later, J. A. Taylor was found guilty of robbery and assessed a seven-year sentence in the penitentiary.[2] Charges against
T. J. Taylor were all dismissed for lack of evidence; however, a
J. F. Taylor was indicted for robbery on February 3, 1886, but
found not guilty by a jury the following September.[3] All three
Taylors continued a life in Cass County as law enforcement
problems well into the next century.

Duncan was also busy during the month of November,
1885, at the same time that his brother Mack was "down with
the dengue," a malarial-type disease transmitted by mosquitos.
Between noon and one o'clock on the afternoon of Tuesday,
November 10, E. M. Gates, an agent for the Missouri Pacific
Railroad, reported that someone had broken into the company's Lewisville office, just north of Dallas near Denton,
taking $265 from the safe. Denton County Deputy Sheriff
William Sparks investigated but found no clues. Gates told
officers that he had been at dinner when the burglary occurred.
That same night, it was reported that the safe of the railroad
station at Allen, to the east, had been blown open by burglars.

That afternoon, Duncan received a telegram asking him to
catch the 6:20 Missouri Pacific train to Lewisville to investigate,
according to one newspaper, an attempt to wreck and rob a
train by putting ties across the tracks. However, he ended up
investigating the safe burglary. On Friday, the 13th, Duncan
arrested R. H. Lauderdale, a well-liked young man who worked
as a porter at the Lewisville depot. According to a newspaper
account, "Detective Duncan claims to have facts and circumstantial evidence of a convincing character, and feels safe in
his deliberate conclusions." Duncan had also been to Allen to

check out the circumstances of that safe burglary, probably to see if the two crimes were related.

However, there was something about the Lewisville burglary and Lauderdale's insistence that he was innocent that caused Duncan to take another look at the case. Ultimately, Gates, the railroad agent, was arrested by Duncan for the crime on Monday, November 16, and jailed at Denton. Lauderdale went free.[4] Gates was the only person who knew the safe's combination, and Duncan finally determined that was the only way in which the burglary could have been pulled off.

The new year of 1886 began brightly enough for Duncan. On January 1, he returned to Dallas from Plano just north of the city, and reported that he and Plano City Marshal Rowland had arrested Bill Campbell for stealing $320 from a Mr. Lovelace. The money was quickly recovered and Campbell placed in jail.[5] About this time, Duncan was working with an associate, Dallas detective Elmer Loosley. Next to nothing is known about Loosley as there is scant mention of him in contemporary newspapers and directories. However, he soon came to play a very significant part in a major incident in Duncan's life.

Jesse Bonner was a notorious "bad Negro" from Freestone and Navarro Counties. His family had formerly been slaves in Freestone County. By 1886, he had eleven criminal cases pending against him in Freestone County, mostly for carrying a pistol. A warrant was issued for Bonner's arrest on a horse-stealing charge. Freestone County Sheriff H. J. Childs gave the warrant to deputy Marcus Seeley to serve, Seeley having information that Bonner had gone north to work on the cotton farm of a man named Zimmerman, about four miles south of Dallas. Bonner had once been employed on Seeley's farm, and there would be no problem in identification of the wanted man.

On the afternoon of Thursday, January 28, 1886, Seeley came to Dallas to serve the warrant. The member of a longtime Freestone County family, the deputy had been a farmer, a merchant, and was at one time mayor of the small town of

Bounty Hunter

Wortham, just west of Fairfield. As a deputy, he had been forced to kill Frank Polk in January, 1878, for which, however, he was subsequently indicted. According to family stories, Seeley shot Polk with a rifle and, after Polk went down, shot him one more time so that "I don't have to be looking over my shoulder for the rest of my life."[6] Once in Dallas, Seeley looked up Jack Duncan, with whom he had worked on several cases in the past.

Since the warrant had been issued in another county, both Duncan and Seeley felt that a peace officer from Dallas County should help execute it. They first approached John Overand, a deputy constable who had formerly been a Dallas policeman and had been repeatedly suspended because of unbecoming conduct, but he did not have enough time to go with them. Overand would die the following September after being thrown from his horse. Police officer Henry C. Waller, with whom Duncan had worked when he was on the force, was also unable to accompany them on the arrest. Deputy Sheriff Henry Jacoby talked with Duncan and Seeley, but they did not ask his assistance, telling him they thought Sheriff Childs was going to come to Dallas for the arrest. Detective Elmer Loosley agreed to come along, and, after borrowing a shotgun from the Two Brothers saloon, the three set out in a buggy in the cold January night air, bound for the Zimmerman farm.

Details as to what happened next are sketchy, but available accounts indicate that, at about 7 p.m., the three stopped the buggy about a quarter of a mile from the cabin on the farm, next to the cotton field, where Bonner was believed to be staying. Hitching the horse to a fence, they walked across the field, Loosley carrying the shotgun. A dog barked as they made their way, alerting the occupants inside the cabin. Approaching the structure, a two-room, decaying, ramshackle affair, they found the door ajar and walked in without notice, not really expecting any resistance.

As they walked in the door, pandemonium broke out. Bon-

Gunfire and Bribery

*Dallas police officer
Henry C. Walker
in 1885.
(Author's Collection).*

ner, who had been by the stove warming himself, opened fire
with a .45-caliber Colt revolver. Bob Johnson, another black
man, grabbed for a shotgun and let loose a blast which barely
missed Seeley and flew harmlessly out the open door. The long
flame extending from the shotgun barrel impressed itself vividly
on the deputy's mind. A third black man, Bob's brother, Henry,
fired a shot from a pistol. At the first shot, Loosley had backed
out into the front yard of the cabin. Seeley, who was left-hand-
ed, and Duncan both went for their pistols to return the fire.
Bonner leaped at Duncan, seizing the detective's drawn pistol
with his left hand and firing his pistol at Duncan with the other,
but missing as Duncan desperately thwarted his aim. Duncan
tripped and fell to the ground. As Bonner stood over him and
prepared to shoot again, Seeley shot him in the right side. Both
Bob and Henry Johnson scrambled through the thick, acrid
smoke, brushing past Seeley and Duncan, and ran out the door.
On the outside, Loosley, not sure what was going on, cut loose
with the shotgun, wounding Henry Johnson in the knee. The
light inside the cabin, a small lamp on a bench, had been shot

Bounty Hunter

out, leaving the occupants in total darkness. Seeley and Duncan blasted at the darkness as they hurriedly backed out the door, the air rent by the exploding gunfire and the screaming of women and children who were also in the small two-room cabin.

As the two quickly cleared the house and retreated into the yard to join Loosley, they realized that they were out of ammunition. A black man came cautiously outside and, with empty guns trained on him, told the three that Bonner was dead, as well as a little girl. Not sure who was armed or how many there were or even who had been hit, Duncan, Seeley, and Loosley decided that the wisest course would be to retreat from the scene. Quickly returning to the buggy, they then sped to Dallas. Seeley counted four bulletholes in his grey overcoat, but none of the three men had suffered so much as a scratch.

After the shotgun was returned to the Two Brothers, Duncan and Seeley went to see Sheriff Billy Smith to report the incident and surrender to his custody. Apparently, Loosley's participation was not thought important in regard to events inside the cabin. Late that evening, Sheriff Smith went to the tenant cabin to investigate the shooting. He examined Bonner's body and saw a five-year-old girl, Margaret Young, who had been shot in the head and was believed to be dying. Blacks at the scene told the sheriff that Bonner had been innocently pounding corn into hominy, Margaret in his lap, when the two officers burst in hollering and commencing the shooting without any warning or justification. It was claimed that there were no firearms on the premises of any description. When later asked about the child, Duncan was quoted as saying that she was shot by a black man standing on the outside firing into the cabin. Actually, the confusion of the incident left everyone quite unclear as to just what had occurred at the cabin.

On Friday morning, Justice of the Peace Kendall, Doctor R. W. Allen, and a jury of inquest rode down to Zimmerman's farm to view Bonner's body and to look over the scene. Returning to Dallas that afternoon, Judge Kendall began taking evidence from witnesses. Duncan and Seeley, both under guard, were represented at the hearing by attorneys Barnett Gibbs, who was also the Texas lieutenant governor, and T. J. Freeman, Jr. The courtroom was packed with both blacks and whites eager to hear the sensational details.

Bob Johnson testified that Duncan and Seeley broke in, hollering "Hi Yi!," and began shooting, and that there was no gun on the premises. He mentioned that there was a third man outside who shot his brother, Henry. Gibbs, on cross-examination, tried some intimidating tactics but could not get the witness to change his story. Josephine Davis, a young black woman, testified that she was also in the room when the officers came in and began shooting. In support of Johnson's version of the incident, she stated that it was Seeley, wearing a grey overcoat and a white hat, who had done the shooting. Doctor Allen, having examined Bonner's body, testified that he had been shot five times, two of the wounds being fatal ones. As to the little girl who was shot, the outer plate of her skull was broken, although she was still alive.

Having heard the evidence, the jury returned a verdict that Jesse Bonner "came to his death from the effects of a gunshot wound in the hands of one Seeley and two others to the jury unknown." Duncan and Seeley were taken to the county jail to await the action of the grand jury, both of them denying the version of the shooting given by the witnesses. A rumor was now making the rounds that, when the shotgun was returned to the Two Brothers, one of the three remarked that they had done a "bad killing." On the basis of this, Sheriff Smith arrested Elmer Loosley on Friday evening and locked him in a cell separate from that of Duncan and Seeley.[7]

On Saturday, January 30, 1886, Duncan, Seeley, and Loosley were all indicted for murder. A habeas corpus hearing was held on Tuesday, February 9, having been postponed once because of the absence of Lieutenant Governor Gibbs. Witnesses for the three defendants appeared to give evidence that, on the night of the gunfight, all three men had been sober and that they were all men of good character and reputation. Jesse Bonner was painted as a desperate character and a well-known lawbreaker in Freestone County. Dallas Police Chief Jim Arnold, who had gone to the scene of the shooting, testified that one cartridge was found which did not fit the pistols of either Duncan or Seeley. However, Bob Johnson repeated his testimony without variation. Judge Aldredge set Duncan's and Seeley's bonds at $5,000 each and that of Loosley at $2,500. All three made bond and were released from jail, Sim Duncan and others acting as bondsmen for Jack and Loosley.[8]

While the murder charge remained pending against him, there is little information as to what Duncan was doing for the better part of 1886. Elmer Loosley worked with him through the year, staying with Jack's parents, as did Jack and Emma.[9] In November, there were newspaper accounts of Loosley, who worked for "Jack Duncan's Detective Agency," arresting a thief in one case and accompanying officers in a raid on a craps game.[10] For Duncan, no doubt, the detective work continued, although it was soon to be a matter of jumping out of one scrape into another.

S. S. Floyd and Company called itself a cotton brokerage but was what was commonly termed a "bucket shop" operation. Investors ostensibly bought commodities, but the money was used in a risky, speculative manner, amounting to gambling on how well those commodities would fare as to market prices before the company actually made any purchases. The Floyd Company had an office in Dallas, managed by Dudley T. Stewart, and at least one other in Waxahachie, south of Dallas, which was managed by Thomas H. McDuffie. As an agent of Floyd and Company, Tom McDuffie was authorized to receive and send orders, as well as deposit cash receipts in the Citizens National Bank in Waxahachie. He was not empowered to write any drafts on the company.

Gunfire and Bribery

*Texas Lieutenant
Governor
Barnett Gibbs.
(Courtesy of the
Texas State Archives,
Austin).*

McDuffie disappeared on October 7, 1886. Dudley Stewart, on hearing he was gone, went to Waxahachie the next day and quickly discovered that the young agent had forged a draft and absconded with some $2,700 in company funds. Stewart immediately filed charges against McDuffie and wired his office in Dallas to have Jack Duncan meet him when he returned to Dallas.[11] On his return, Stewart met with Duncan and Loosley and hired Duncan to "work up" the case. He asked the detective what fee he would charge. Duncan replied that, whatever the amount, Stewart would be perfectly satisfied with the charges and that the amount would depend on where McDuffie was caught. Duncan then went to work to find his man. In the meantime, a local newspaper briefly reported McDuffie's embezzlement.[12]

Initially, Duncan sent out several telegrams to police chiefs in selected cities, alerting them that McDuffie was wanted. Then, about 100 postcards were printed up with the facts on McDuffie, and these were mailed out to various law enforcement agencies, the cards announcing a $100 reward for the fugitive's arrest and conviction.

Bounty Hunter

Somehow, toward the first of November, Duncan learned that a letter had been sent from Birmingham, Alabama, to Mrs. Alabama Bradley, McDuffie's mother-in-law, a widow who lived on Cottage Lane in Dallas and with whom McDuffie's wife, Sallie, and their two children were now living. Mrs. Bradley lived upstairs over Mrs. E. E. Craig's Dallas Female Seminary and taught music there. She periodically received letters addressed to her from McDuffie, but the letters were actually intended for her daughter. For a number of weeks, there had been a secret correspondence between Sallie McDuffie and her fugitive husband.

Duncan notified Stewart of the letter from Birmingham and the two immediately went to the Dallas post office and talked with Postmaster John H. Cochran. Duncan told Cochran that there was a letter addressed to Mrs. Bradley in the post office and that he believed it was written by McDuffie. Cochran located a letter addressed to Mrs. Bradley and allowed Duncan and Stewart to examine the postmark, which was from Birmingham. The two men compared the handwriting on the envelope with examples of McDuffie's writing but could not discern any marked similarities. Stewart commented that a bank clerk like McDuffie could write in different "hands" and that he was satisfied that the letter had been addressed by McDuffie. He asked Cochran if the postmaster had any right under such circumstances to open the letter, to which Cochran promptly answered no, even though a glance at the letter would quickly establish whether or not it was from the wanted man. Duncan told Cochran that he was working up the case and that there was a $100 reward for any information leading to McDuffie's arrest. Cochran pledged to help in any way that he could, so far as the law would allow him. A week or so later, Duncan checked back with Cochran to see if any additional letters had arrived for Mrs. Bradley, and, although none could be located at that time, the postmaster reiterated his instructions to distributing clerks to let him know if any letters came for her.

Gunfire and Bribery

Duncan was persistent in pursuing this only available avenue to locating McDuffie. He approached substitute carrier J. W. Renney at the post office to inquire about mail for Mrs. Bradley. Renney told the detective, whom he had known for over a year, himself once aspiring to be a detective, that he did not know what carrier handled mail for Cottage Lane. He checked with a superintendent standing nearby and told Duncan that, although he didn't know his name, Carrier No. 11 was responsible for that address. Duncan told Renney he would give $100 to see the postmark.

Carrier No. 11 was John C. Corder. Toward the latter part of November, 1886, about a week after Duncan had contacted Cochran, Corder delivered a letter to Mrs. Bradley that was "roughly torn open at the end except about half an inch at the upper left hand corner." Mrs. Bradley took one look at the envelope and handed it to her daughter, exclaiming, "Sallie, this is a complete give-away! I expect Tommy's arrest any moment!" The letter had been mailed from No. 48 Bond Street in Toronto, Canada, and, in addition to personal comments, contained a request from Tom McDuffie for some money, which his wife sent.

Corder got in touch with Duncan on Monday, November 29, insisting that he knew McDuffie's whereabouts and would tell him for the $100 reward. Duncan took him to the Floyd Company office and had him wait outside while he discussed it with Stewart. According to a later statement by Stewart, city Police Chief Jim Arnold had already told him that McDuffie was believed to be in Toronto and that a telegram had been sent to the police of that city to be on the lookout for him. When Duncan came in and told him about Corder's claim, it was decided that, since it would be a few days before McDuffie could be arrested anyway, they would pay the mailman $25 now and the balance after his information proved correct. Also, by holding off paying the full amount, it would likely guarantee some secrecy on Corder's part and lessen the likelihood that he would prematurely tip off some of McDuffie's friends that the fugitive's whereabouts were known.

Duncan went out and, after about ten or fifteen minutes, returned with Corder. Stewart told Corder that, because they had been "monkeyed about" so much over the McDuffie matter, they would pay him only $25 for now. Corder thought about it, then agreed, giving them the Bond Street address. Corder was given the cash and a due bill for $75, to be paid after McDuffie was in custody.

That same day, Stewart sent a telegram to the police in Toronto, advising them of McDuffie's address and to keep him under watch. He signed Duncan's name to the telegraph. On December 4, after an indictment was returned that morning against McDuffie,[13] Stewart left for Toronto, arriving there on the morning of the seventh. That afternoon, while he watched from a churchyard across the street, Toronto police entered the boarding house on Bond Street and arrested McDuffie. Extradition proceedings were initiated immediately,[14] and although McDuffie fought it, he was soon returned to Texas.

In the meantime, after Corder had handed over McDuffie's address, Duncan, in good spirits, approached substitute carrier Renney that same afternoon and told him he was a damned fool and that he could have made $100 just as well as Corder did. He told Renney that Corder had been "pretty slick" and had held his knowledge of McDuffie's address over them until he got his money and the note.

No doubt, both Duncan and Stewart were exhilarated at the arrest of McDuffie. Postal authorities, however, hearing bits and pieces about the detective's interest in Mrs. Bradley's mail. began to harbor some suspicions about how the necessary information on McDuffie had been obtained. John E. Hollingsworth, chief postal inspector for Texas, came up from Austin and, accompanied by local postal inspector Leroy J. Randall, went to call on Mrs. Bradley, who had not complained about the open letter. She admitted that she had received a letter that

Gunfire and Bribery

John H. Cochran, Dallas pioneer, was Speaker of the Texas Legislature and Postmaster for Dallas. (Courtesy of the Texas/Dallas History and Archives Division, Dallas Public Library).

had been torn open and the letter and envelope were subsequently turned over to them by Sallie McDuffie on February 8, 1887, in Waxahachie. The next day, John Corder was arrested by U. S. Marshal William L. Cabell on a charge of opening the letter to Mrs. Bradley. He was arraigned before the U. S. Commissioner and released on a $300 bond to await a preliminary hearing.[15]

But Corder wasn't the only target of the postal officials. On Friday, February 11, 1887, Inspector Randall filed an affidavit in the court of Commissioner Nat M. Burford alleging that Jack Duncan had bribed Corder to open the letter. On that same day, a warrant was issued for his arrest, and U. S. Deputy Marshal Joe Record, a former Dallas County deputy sheriff, arrested Duncan. The next day Duncan was released on a $100 appearance bond posted by attorney T. J. Freeman, Jr. and Sim Duncan. Stewart was also arrested on a bribery charge.[16]

A preliminary examination was held for Corder in the U. S. Commissioner's court in the middle of February. Hollingsworth testified that Corder admitted getting $100 but had insisted that he showed Duncan nothing but the postmark and address on the envelope and did not open it.[17] On February 23, after hearing all of the testimony, Commissioner Burford set Corder's bond at $500. Inspector Hollingsworth wired Washington, D. C., that the commissioner had decided that the evidence against the postman was "overwhelming."[18]

Duncan's preliminary hearing before Burford lasted from February 23rd to the 25th. In addition to the testimony of Postmaster Cochran, testimony was heard from Mrs. Bradley, Stewart, Sallie McDuffie, and J. W. Renney. On February 25, Burford continued the hearing until the second week in March. The hearing picked up again on March 8, and, the next day, Burford ruled that the evidence warranted holding Duncan and set his bond at $500, which was immediately posted by Sim Duncan and Richard Morgan, Jr.[19]

McDuffie was finally released from the county jail on April 11, 1887, after posting his $500 bond.[20] The following month, on the 18th, Corder was indicted on two counts by a federal grand jury: accepting a bribe to open a letter and opening the letter. Duncan was indicted on one count of bribery. Both were arrested again and gave bond.[21] Stewart had apparently left Dallas by this time and was not indicted.

Although charges of murder, bribery, theft, and swindling hung over his head, Duncan nevertheless continued his quest for lawbreakers despite his bleak prospects. His skill and ability were again severely questioned very quickly. Shortly before midnight on Sunday, October 2, 1887, two men, out of breath from running, notified Dallas police that a white woman had been raped in the city park on Harwood Street. Rushing to the park, police encountered Lon Barlow, a young man from Forney, Texas, and his fiancee, Julia Walker, the daughter of a blacksmith who lived on Jackson Street. The two, who were scheduled to be married in a few days, told the officers that they were sitting in the darkened park talking when they were accosted by two black men, both armed with pistols. After robbing Barlow, one of the men held him back while the other dragged the young lady to a nearby clump of bushes and pistol-whipped and raped her. Julia Walker said she was able to scream two or three times, although her assailant's hand was on her throat. An old crippled man named Jones heard some screams and came near the bushes, calling out to see if anyone needed help. She screamed that she did, and Jones left to summon help, although he did not actually see anyone. At this point, according to the two, the black men ran off.

Several men, alerted to the trouble in the park, ran to the scene finding Barlow and his fiancee alone. Barlow took Julia home, then notified the police of the assault, giving very specific descriptions of the two men. Until early the next morning, police and volunteers combed the area and the Trinity River bottoms, but without success. On Monday, police arrested a thief named Charley Gaines, and, with a muttering crowd closely following, he was taken before the rape victim. She positively stated that he was not one of the men, and he was released. The city was at fever pitch over news of this terrible crime. The *Dallas Daily Herald* commented:

> Dallas never needed a prompt double hanging worse than now; and it is needless to say that if the proper subjects are found, there will be one. The men of Dallas cannot be too severe with such wretches as the fiends of last night's horror.[22]

The police busily rounded up a number of local black men who fit the description and subjected them to "severe cross-examination," but all were released.

Barlow married Julia on the evening of October 4 at her father's residence, right on schedule and despite the tragic event of only forty-eight hours earlier. In the meantime, the police continued their search for the suspects. Charles Reisenweber, a former Chicago policeman, approached Chief Arnold and presented recommendations from the Pinkerton Detective Agency and the Chicago chief of police, offering his services on the case.

Bounty Hunter

He was granted a commission as a special police officer. Earlier in the day, he had encountered a black man who seemed to fit the description of one of the suspects. He went to Julia Walker, now Barlow, who, from the description he gave, said it sounded like the right man. Reisenweber walked about three miles from town to the place where the black suspect had told him he was staying. Arresting the man, whose name was Billy Bell, the officer turned him over to the sheriff's office. Bell was taken immediately before Mr. and Mrs. Barlow, who both identified him as the one who had held Barlow while she was raped.[23] Because of the distinct possibility of a lynch mob, the sheriff fortified the county jail that evening.

A mob of over seventy men gathered outside the county jail on Wednesday evening, October 5, demanding Bell's body. Several members of the crowd even planned to bring a cannon from a local armory and blast their way into the jail. However, several police officers talked to mob leaders and finally convinced them it would be better to wait until the second suspect was caught. At this, the mob dispersed.[24]

Almost from the beginning, law enforcement officers had reserved strong doubts about the Barlows' story. Barlow at one point had even told Joe Record that no rape had occurred. On the night of the incident, neither victim showed any marks or bruises that one might expect from such an experience. Further, there was some variance between the identification of Bell and the descriptions given of the suspects at the time of the "outrage." However, the Barlows stuck to their original story.

Given these doubts, the amazement of the officers must have been quite profound when, a week later on Friday morning, October 14, Jack Duncan announced that he had arrested two black men for the assault and that one of them had confessed. Duncan told reporters that, on Thursday evening, he had arrested Henry Barclay and Austin White and that Barclay had told him that he was the one who held a pistol on Barlow while White raped the young lady. Chief Jim Arnold, based on the information given him by Duncan, had sent along officers Beard and Waller to assist in the arrest, although the chief expressed grave reservations that they were the right men. Barclay and White were held in jail until the Barlows could come to Dallas from Forney to identify them.

Austin White vehemently denied any involvement in the incident, maintaining that he had been at work at the oil mills at the time and that there were witnesses who saw him there. He also said he had little to do with Barclay as he was "not his sort" and that he worked for a living rather than gambled. Fellow workers soon corroborated White's story that he had been on the job at the time of the reported rape. Barclay, too, now denied any involvement, and the *Dallas Daily Herald* gave him an opportunity to clarify the nature of his reported confession:

> He was at home the night of the outrage, "and could prove it." In answer to questions he said he wasn't at the park, and hadn't made any confession more than what a fellow would say when he was forced to. "They had me in a tight place last night and scared me into saying more than I ought to. Mr. Duncan said, 'Now, Henry, we've got you sure this time. You better turn state's evidence and get out of it best you can. The woman has been right over there, has seen you and identified you. Who was the Negro with you that night; we know you didn't do the outrage, but you held up Mr. Barlow; now just tell us who the Negro with you was?' But I kept telling 'em I didn't know anything about it. But when I heard 'em talking about hanging me, I mumbled something, and Mr. Jack said, 'Oh, he's done confessed to holding the pistol on Mr. Barlow; now, Henry, tell me all about it, who was the other?' I spect when I heard 'em talking about hanging me, I said something I oughten to. But I don't know anything at all about it. Don't hardly know Austin White . . . ."[25]

That same evening, the Barlows came to Dallas and viewed the two suspects. Very quickly, they stated that White was not the man and, when they saw Barclay, laughed because he didn't even come close to the description that they had given. White was immediately released while Barclay was retained in jail on a pistol charge.[26] The incident, on top of Duncan's other

Bounty Hunter

troubles, certainly didn't help his credibility as a detective.

Billy Bell was indicted for rape;[27] however, after his trial was postponed numerous times because the Barlows failed to appear, a jury found him not guilty on January 6, 1888. Despite a positive identification by Julia Barlow, Bell was able to establish an effective alibi, and both Joe Record and Jim Arnold testified as to their doubts in the case. On January 9, robbery charges against him were also dismissed.[28]

By the end of 1887, with numerous criminal charges pending against him and his reputation as a detective seriously undermined, Jack Duncan's life appeared to be a shambles and his future most uncertain. For all practical purposes, despite periodic efforts to stay in business, the career of John Wesley Hardin's captor as a detective was finished.

NOTES

1.   *Dallas Daily Herald*, July 25, 1885.

2.   Minutes, District Court, Cass County, Texas, Vol. H, pp. 79, 85-87, and 99 (*State of Texas v. J. A. and T. J. Taylor*, cause nos. 1739, 1742, and 1748).

3.   Minutes, District Court, Cass County, Texas, Vol. H, pp. 148, 211, and 212 (*State of Texas v. J. F. Taylor*, cause no. 1794).

4.   *Dallas Morning News*, November 10-14, 17, and 19, 1885.

5.   *Dallas Morning News*, January 2, 1886.

6.   Interview with J. R. "Sonny" Sessions, Freestone County Sheriff, Fairfield, Texas, July 16, 1982.

7.   *Dallas Morning News*, January 29 and 30, 1886.

8.   Minutes, 14th District Court, Dallas County, Texas, Vol. S, pp. 154, 176-179 (*State of Texas v. Jack Duncan*, cause no. 8609; *State of Texas v. W. M. Seeley*, cause no. 8610; *State of Texas v. Elmer Loosley*, cause no. 8611); *Dallas Morning News*, January 31, 1886; February 10, 1886.

202

9. Dallas City Directory, 1886-1887, p. 208.

10. *Dallas Morning News,* November 15 and 23, 1886; *Dallas Daily Herald,* November 23, 1886.

11. Except where otherwise noted, the details of the McDuffie case and the subsequent prosecution of Duncan and Corder are taken from the following sources:

> Case Records, U. S. District Court, Northern District of Texas (*United States v. Jack Duncan,* cause no. 386, 1887).
> *Dallas Morning News,* February 22-25, 1887.
> *Dallas Daily Herald,* February 21-24 and 26, 1887.

12. *Dallas Morning News,* October 12 and 13, 1886.

13. Minutes, 14th District Court, Dallas County, Texas, Vol. T, p. 54 (*State of Texas v. T. H. McDuffie,* cause no. 11102).

14. *Dallas Morning News,* December 9, 1886; *Dallas Daily Herald,* December 9, 1886.

15. Report of Arrest (*United States v. John C. Corder*) by L. J. Randall and John E. Hollingsworth, February 9, 1887, U. S. Postal Records, U. S. National Archives and Records Service; *Dallas Daily Herald,* February 9, 1887; *Dallas Morning News,* February 10, 1887.

16. *Dallas Morning News,* February 13, 1887; Letter to Chief Postal Inspector William A. West from John Hollingsworth, February 14, 1887, U. S. Postal Records, U. S. National Archives and Records Service.

17. *Dallas Daily Herald,* February 19, 21, and 22, 1887; *Dallas Morning News,* February 22 and 23, 1887.

18. *Dallas Morning News,* February 24, 1887; *Dallas Daily Herald,* February 23, 1887; Telegram to Chief Postal Inspector from John Hollingsworth, February 23, 1887, U. S. Postal Records, U. S. National Archives and Records Service.

19. *Dallas Morning News,* February 24, 25, and 27, 1887; March 9 and 10, 1887; *Dallas Daily Herald,* February 24 and 26, 1887; March 7 and 10, 1887.

20. Minutes, 14th District Court, Dallas County, Texas, Vol. T, p. 467 (*State of Texas v. T. H. McDuffie,* cause no. 11102).

21. *Dallas Daily Herald,* May 20, 1887.

22. *Dallas Morning News,* October 3 and 4, 1887; *Dallas Daily Herald,* October 3 and 4, 1887.

23. *Dallas Daily Herald,* October 5, 1887; *Dallas Morning News,* October 6, 1887.

24. *Dallas Daily Herald,* October 6, 1887.

25. *Dallas Daily Herald,* October 14, 1887; *Dallas Morning News,* October 15, 1887.

26. *Dallas Daily Herald,* October 15, 1887.

27. *Dallas Morning News,* November 5, 1887; December 14, 1887.

28. *Dallas Morning News,* January 6, 7, and 10, 1888.

Chapter 10

End of an Era

The charges against Jack Duncan remained pending throughout 1888, delay caused by one reason or another. For example, in January, the postal bribery trial had to be continued because Dudley Stewart, who now lived in San Francisco, did not respond to a subpoena.[1] Sometime early in 1888, Jack and Emma Duncan had a baby daughter. In May, the baby was reported to be very ill with a fever.[2] Nevertheless, the arrival of the baby must certainly have helped ease some of the stress in Duncan's life at the time.

Although Duncan's bribery case continued to be delayed, letter carrier John Corder came to trial in June. He pleaded not guilty to accepting a bribe and after his trial, the judge instructed the jury to bring in a verdict of not guilty. The prosecution had not proven its case. As to the charge that Corder opened a letter not addressed to himself, the judge ruled there was a faulty indictment and acquitted him. On hearing the news from Inspector Randall that Corder had gone free, John Hollingsworth sent a cover memorandum with Randall's letter to the chief inspector in Washington "with the remark that the action of the judge in this case is about on a par with the actions of all the U. S. judges of late."[3]

During 1888, Jack and his family lived on Ross Avenue and he continued to pursue his work as a detective. His brother Mack was now raising poultry, he and Isabela living with his parents on Jackson Street. Frank Bowles, Jack's brother-in-law, was also living with James and Kitty Duncan and working as a clerk in Sim's abstract office.[4] In June, Isabela, joined by her husband, brought suit to clear title to some property she had inherited from her mother in Dallas.[5]

In September, 1888, some form of contagious fever struck the family of Jack Duncan. He had a severe attack of the fever, but, after a period of convalescence, he recovered.[6] Unfortunately, on Monday, September 17, 1888, the Duncans' baby daughter died. Curiously, one account indicated that the cause of death was dentition, which has to do with the teething process.[7] It may have been that the child died of an undiagnosed disease which manifested itself in some form of gum disorder. A funeral for the baby was held at their residence off Hall Street near the Missouri-Pacific Railroad, and she was buried in Trinity Cemetery.

It was Jack Duncan's turn to be a victim of a crime when a burglar struck his residence on Wednesday night, November 14, 1888. However, in taking a variety of things from the bedroom, the thief left much clothing in the yard and got away with only an empty pocketbook, a bootjack, and a clay pipe.[8] There is no report that Duncan was able to track down the culprit.

On January 3, 1889, the loss of the Duncans' daughter was softened by the birth of a son, John Francis Duncan.[9]

As the time for trial on the bribery charge neared, Jack Duncan was no doubt ready to get out from under the cloud. However, continuances requested by his lawyer repeatedly delayed the trial date. On February 25, 1889, the prosecution in Tom McDuffie's forgery case decided not to continue, and charges were dismissed against him.[10] It must have then seemed to Duncan that the pursuit of McDuffie had been for nothing, except to produce his current troubles. Finally, in May, a new trial date was set. Duncan's attorney moved for another continuance to locate an absent witness, as well as to quash the indictment, but the court overruled both motions. A jury was empaneled and sworn on May 25 and, after a short trial that same day, found Jack Duncan not guilty of bribery.[11] A month later, on June 26, 1889, the county attorney declined to prosecute him on the swindling and theft charges that had been pending since December, 1883. Those charges were dismissed.[12] Some of the cloud over his head had diminished; however, a brief notice in a newspaper on August 27, 1889, indicates that Duncan, despite his acquittal and his new family, had not wholly forsaken the old life: "An absent witness in the case of Jack Duncan charged with carrying a pistol was fined $10."[13]

It is likely that Duncan's detective business had tapered off and he was having to look to other means of earning a living at the beginning of the 1890's. His brother Mack had gone from being a poultry raiser to being a sand dealer in 1890, still living with his parents.[14] What Jack was doing is unknown. Even though he may have still been trying to generate some clients as a detective, the frontier was passing, and the days of the lucrative rewards for desperadoes such as John Wesley Hardin and John Middleton were over, as he was well aware. Further, the murder charge still pending, plus the mistake he made in the City Park "rape" case, must certainly have damaged his credibility. Perhaps the lifestyle that once proved so successful for him in a more primitive Dallas now worked against him.

The murder case against Marcus Seeley was called for trial on October 18, 1889. Seeley failed to appear for trial, and, after the sheriff formally called for him three times at the courthouse door, his $5,000 bond was ordered forfeited. Probably because there were some miscommunications, the forfeiture order was subsequently set aside, and trial was again set for April 16, 1890. On that date, however, the prosecution announced that it would no longer prosecute, and Seeley was discharged.[15]

On April 12, 1890, Duncan was apparently reindicted for the Bonner shooting in Dallas's 14th District Court. On April 28, in the 44th District Court, murder charges against him and Loosley were dismissed. A new habeas corpus hearing was held for both of them, and they were remanded for trial. However, as with Seeley, on September 22, 1890, the county attorney decided not to prosecute any further, and the murder charge was dismissed.[16] Finally, Jack Duncan was rid of all criminal charges.

With the dawning of the "Gay Nineties," significant changes took place in Jack Duncan's life. In December, 1890, a daughter, Jessie Katherine, was born.[17] He was no longer seriously in the detective business. The 1891-1892 Dallas city directory listed a "J. Duncan" as a clerk in Sim Duncan's abstract office. Mack Duncan, who had always had a way with wood, worked as a carpenter and moved his family out of his father's house.[18] On August 15, 1892, another daughter, Anna or Annie Belle, was born to Jack and Emma. At this time, Jack was doing some blacksmith work,[19] although he still tried to keep a hand in some detective work. On September 24, 1892, his father, James Alexander Duncan, passed away at the age of sixty-six and was buried in Trinity Cemetery.[20]

The Trinity River, by which Dallas was settled, was a snag-filled, 715-mile stream which flowed from four forks in North Texas and meandered southward to Trinity Bay at Anahuac on the northern side of Galveston Bay.[21] The leaders of Dallas had long been convinced that water navigation would prove an inexpensive and efficient means of moving both commerce and passengers. There had been periodic attempts over the years to navigate the Trinity as well as to secure funding for surveys and to widen and clear the channel. Concerned about high railroad freight rates, a group of Dallas businessmen, including Sim Duncan, organized the Trinity River Navigation Company in 1891. The intent of the group was to go ahead and, instead of waiting for federal assistance, build dams, construct locks, clean up snags and debris from the river, and build boats for navigation. At the same time, federal assistance would still be actively sought. Public subscriptions were accepted, and, in September, 1892, a board of directors was elected, including Sim Duncan.

Bounty Hunter

In November, 1892, the company launched a snagboat, the *Dallas*, a twelve-foot-wide and sixty-four-foot-long stern wheeler, to begin clearing the river. A large community celebration was set off on May 20, 1893, by the arrival at Dallas of the steamboat *H. A. Harvey, Jr.*, which had navigated the Trinity all the way from Galveston, having begun its voyage on March 14. Citizens proclaimed this as only the beginning of such travel up and down the river.[22]

Jack Duncan was employed by the Trinity River Navigation Company, no doubt through the influence of brother Sim, who was now publicly referred to as "Commodore" Duncan because of his active efforts to promote navigation of the Trinity. By August, 1893, Duncan and his force of laborers aboard the *Dallas* had successfully cleared the river of debris and "burned up rafts" at certain points.[23] He returned to Dallas, and with brother Mack, began construction of a pleasure boat, the *Annie Belle*, a 22-½-foot stern wheeler covered with an awning. It was their intent to take out fishing and excursion parties of up to twenty people in the backwater created by a temporary dam thirteen miles south of the city, cashing in on the new enthusiasm for river travel, a decided novelty for inland Dallas.[24] Although Duncan was still wont to consider himself a detective even now, he also considered himself a contractor.[25]

John Wesley Hardin walked out of the Texas State Penitentiary at Huntsville on Saturday, February 17, 1894, a free man. Imprisoned for over sixteen years, he had at first resisted the prison discipline and routine and been subjected to harsh punishment, even in those times. However, subsequently adjusting to life in prison and becoming a model prisoner, he studied law and now intended to become a practicing attorney in Gonzales. His release sparked renewed interest in Hardin, and the Dallas newspapers recalled his capture and Duncan's role in it, noting that Duncan had since given up detective work and was now "engaged with the Trinity Navigation Company in trying to make the Trinity River navigable." The article noted that he

Lock and Dam site on the Trinity River, south of Dallas, as it appeared in the late 1890's. (Author's Collection).

was in charge "of some of the river improvements ongoing at McComas' Bluff," about twelve miles south of the city.[26]

After the river had been cleaned up for some miles south of Dallas, the navigation company began construction of its first dam at McComas' Bluff, named for Amon McComas of Scyene. Jack Duncan was foreman of a construction crew of some 75 laborers who camped at the site in tents. Duncan lived in a log house which doubled as his office, with a horse stall at one end. He posted his work rules on the door in pencil:

1. That unless on the sick list every man must rise at 6 a.m.
2. That singing, loud talking and dancing must stop at 10 p.m., except Saturday night.
3. That men will be charged for carelessness in losing or breaking tools.

4. That swearing and rowdyism are prohibited.
5. That a discharge is the remedy for any kind of bulldozing.
6. That loss of one day's pay for first offense, two days' pay for second and discharge for third is the penalty for using certain provoking epithets.
7. That all in camp are subject to these rules.[27]

The work continued on the dam project under Duncan's supervision. On August 17, 1895, he reported to the sheriff that he had seen a nude black man on the bank of the river. The man subsequently turned out to be demented and elderly.[28]

On August 19, 1895, John Wesley Hardin was shot from behind and killed in an El Paso saloon by gunman John Selman.[29] This prompted another round of stories about Hardin's capture in 1877, and Duncan basked somewhat in the old glory, granting interviews and reliving that incident in his life. He told one reporter:

> He was the quickest man with a pistol I ever saw, and was a dead shot. He could take one in each hand and swing them around his forefingers and keep one of them going off all the time. If the constable who killed him had been a second later in shooting he would have been the dead man. He threatened my life a number of times, and if we had ever met one of us would have been killed.[30]

In another interview, Duncan reminisced about his career as a detective, boasting somewhat of his better arrests:

> "During Hardin's earlier, or old career of desperadoism," said Mr. Duncan, "times were mighty ugly on the Texas border, and even in the vicinity of Dallas. Hardin was not the only bad man of this state. "There were others" as the new s[l]ang phrase goes. Shooters, and robbers, and killers, and rewards for their capture, were familiar figures and incidents in the '70s and early '80s. A wonderful change has taken place in the last 15 to 20 years. All the old desperadoes of the Texas border of 20 years ago have "passed in their checks." I can't recall just at the moment a single representative left. John Wesley Hardin, after his release from prison, stood much in the light of a relic of that era of desperate

men and desperate crimes. Any idea of how numerous "bad men" were in those days may be gained from the record of my own work as a private detective during eight years. In that period I captured more criminals and collected a larger amount of reward money than any other three private detectives in Texas, as the names and amounts will show."

The old detective then called off the following list of "bad men" that he had captured and the rewards received in each case:

John Wesley Hardin	$ 4,000
Jesse Rascoe	500
Talley Guynes and Frank Clanton	1,000
Mack Crook, Newt Harris, and Lewis Holman	2,800
George Alsop	500
A. M. Estes	100
Jim Cook	250
Jim Criswell	100
Sol and Tom Taylor	500
John James	250
Green Thompson	250
Jess Bonner	100
John Middleton	500
Tom McDuffie	250
Aaron Strausberg	100
Bill Watson	200
Tom Wilson	100
Total Rewards	$12,050

"As there were other detectives making arrests during those days, it will not require a severe test of the imagination for a newcomer to realize how much more civilized times are now than they were then. The old gang of "bad men" are all gone. However, I am glad of it. It was not a pleasant occupation to be hunting them down. The risks of a detective were many and of extreme danger. In fact, he carried his life in his hands from minute to minute, and occasionally the "bad man" snuffed out the light of life of a detective. John Wesley Hardin's every move from the day he was pardoned out of the penitentiary until he was killed was communicated to me by friends who kept me posted on him. Nearly a month ago, when he first went to El Paso, I learned of his threats to come to Dallas and kill me during the State Fair next October. But he would not have more than got on the train at El Paso before I would have known of the fact, and I, of

> course, should have been on guard for my safety. Had he lived
> and come to Dallas there is no telling what might have happened,
> for his tragic end shows that John Wesley Hardin was at heart
> equally as much a "bad man" in 1895 as he was in 1875."[31]

As Duncan speculated about what might have been, his interviews were wired around the country to other newspapers. Stirring up old wounds, his comments prompted a response by former Escambia County, Florida, Sheriff W. H. Hutchinson. In a letter to the *Dallas Morning News* in September, Hutchinson claimed that Duncan's account of Hardin's capture, as paraphrased by a reporter, was "at variance with the actual arrest." He asserted that he and A. J. Perdue, his deputy, had alone made the capture, Hardin kicking him in the abdomen, "from the effects of which up to date I have never recovered," and that he had forced a pistol from Hardin. With the assistance of a third man, Mr. Callahan, the three then tied Hardin up with rope. According to Hutchinson, Jim Mann then became frightened and as he was poised to leap from a window, was shot from outside. At this point, the ex-sheriff stated, Armstrong and Duncan then entered the railroad car, they having remained on the platform until it was all over and safe. He also claimed that he knew all along that it was Hardin who was to be arrested. Hutchinson complained of the "paltry $500" he was given and which he said he gave to those who had assisted him.[32]

Duncan responded to the attack sharply in writing. Giving the details of the arrest, he gave credit to Hutchinson for grabbing Hardin, but said that he came in with Perdue right behind the sheriff. However, he refuted most of Hutchinson's assertions. As to Hutchinson's version of the death of Jim Mann, Duncan wrote: "He tries to make it appear that Armstrong and myself killed Mann. I have never tried to put this killing on any one of our party. I have shouldered my part of it as all of us should do. I know who killed Mann and so does Mr. Hutchinson, but I will make no public accusation." Then Duncan summed up what he felt about Hutchinson's claim:

> I never met two more gentlemanly and braver officers in life than both of them proved to be [Hutchinson and Perdue], but they only played their part, for which Armstrong and I paid them out of our own pockets. Every person had ample time to put in his claims about Hardin during his life. Now that he is dead, it is useless for anyone to publish any stories about the part they played in his arrest. I have given every person who gave me any assistance all the credit due them. If there is any honor in capturing Hardin it is all due me and me alone.[33]

Duncan's former captain, Red Hall, was asked to comment on the debacle and noted wryly:

> I see that Mr. Hutchinson complains that he received only $500 for arresting Hardin. He probably forgets that at that time the script of Texas was at 40 cents discount, so that after deducting expenses and the 40 cents discount, $500 was probably about his share. I am sure he does the other gentlemen connected with the matter an injustice.[34]

And with this, the matter was closed. If Hardin's legend was to continue after his death, Duncan had insured that his part in that legend was properly and permanently preserved, even if John Armstrong's role seemed to be slighted in the whole discussion.

Duncan's occasionally quarrelsome nature continued to assert itself as it so often had before. On the evening of Monday, November 18, 1895, Deputy Constable John Cornwell, a brother of Jack's friend, Ed Cornwell, now a constable, and Policeman Walter M. Roberts arrested Duncan for shooting at Jack Homes, a bartender at a saloon at Pearl and Main Streets. Duncan gave bond on the charge and was released, angrily telling a reporter: "The man, who was a stranger to me, cursed me and pulled a six-shooter on me. I was unarmed, but ran and got my Winchester and shot at him. That is all there is about it." The police were never able to locate Homes.[35] The assault to murder case against him was subsequently dismissed on April 27, 1896,[36] probably because prosecutors could not locate Duncan's intended victim.

Bounty Hunter

As the nineteenth century closed out, Jack Duncan still tried to ply the trade of a detective, but he was almost fifty years old, and it was a young man's game. In 1896, he and his family lived on Cabell Street, while Mack, still working as a carpenter and a builder, was living near their widowed mother on Jackson Street. Sim Duncan's adopted daughter, Josie, had grown up and left his home. She lived on Camp Street, working as an actress at the Camp Street Theater. Camp Street was in the red-light district designated as "The Reservation," to which ribald activities and bawdy night life were aggressively restricted by the police. The upstanding Commodore must have felt a twinge of embarrassment.

In 1897, Mack Duncan changed occupations again, becoming a dealer in second-hand wagons, then becoming a blacksmith in 1898 and 1899. Jack took work as a painter, moving his family to a residence on Commerce Street.[37] However, his lifestyle didn't change, as reflected in an arrest in September, 1898, for assault.[38]

The citizens of Dallas went on a sanitation rampage in 1899. The relationship between filth and disease and the desire to have a cleaner, more desirable city underscored efforts to organize a major clean-up campaign. The City Council approved the use of mounted police officers to help the sanitary inspector in the enforcement of ordinances relating to the depositing of trash.[39] The council adopted a resolution that the chief of police notify his officers to arrest any person sweeping trash into the gutters or alleys.[40] Along with new sanitation ordinances, a new sanitary force was appointed, Jack Duncan being one of three assistant sanitary inspectors working for Chief Inspector Frank Coe. Under their supervision, the force consisted of fifteen teams and twelve men. Duncan's job, and that of the other two inspectors, Thomas Donahue and J. H. Yeargan, was to "vigorously search all premises, back and front, alleys, etc., for filth, decayed matter, etc., and notify the superintendent of the street cleaning forces who will see that it is removed."[41]

214

Dallas policeman Walter M. Roberts, as he appeared in 1899. He was also known as "Brushy." (Author's Collection).

Duncan and the other two inspectors were given their new commissions by the Dallas Police Board on May 1, 1899, and went right to work in the city's main business district.[42] Very soon, wagonloads of garbage were headed for the city's dumping grounds as enthusiasm for the clean-up project began to swell. A slogan was adopted: "Help keep the city clean and be a public benefactor." Dallas now had a population of over 42,000 and sanitation had become a serious problem. On May 8, a Cleaner Dallas League was formed, and the momentum of the sanitation campaign picked up steam, the League subsequently becoming somewhat of a pain in the neck to city officials because of the zeal with which they criticized and urged those officials to greater effort.

Some of the enthusiasm for the project must have certainly spilled over to Jack Duncan, as witnessed by the eloquence of a statement attributed to him in a newspaper account that propagandized the campaign:

"We're after them," said Sanitary Inspector Jack Duncan to a *News* reporter yesterday, "but we will make it still hotter when we get our uniforms. You see, so far we have been attending to the complaints filed. After we have donned our sanitary uniforms the house-to-house campaign will begin. It is our intention to call upon every property owner and tenant in the city. To date there has been an enormous amount of garbage carted out to the dumping grounds. Five or six thousand loads wouldn't touch it. There has been a general cleaning up all over the city; but, on the dead quiet, it was awful when we first started out. In the rear of some of the big swell houses there were cartloads of garbage—regular cesspool places. The Cleaner Dallas League is helping us out in great shape. You see, it is educating the people, and crystallizing public sentiment. It is all the go to keep clean now, and pride is a great thing. You appeal to a man's pride and reach him when his conscience refuses to budge. And then again, it is getting popular. A man ain't in the swim unless he is [in] favor of keeping his premises clean. Even the kids on the streets are joining the Cleaner Dallas Leaguers. Well, let's all push the good work along and give our friends, the doctors and the undertakers, a long vacation this summer."[43]

The assistant sanitary inspectors were outfitted on Tuesday, May 30, 1899, with "neat gray uniforms," although they rejected rows of brass buttons in favor of "modest black buttons" because the former were "too loud." On that same day, they began a house-to-house inspection, and fair warning was given to violators of the city's sanitary ordinances. Duncan asserted: "Friend or foe, black or white, rich or poor, it is all the same here. Our duty is to make the city clean and to keep it clean. I never play favorites!"[44]

As fortune would have it, the first violator of the city's ordinances was tracked down and cited by Inspector Duncan. Charles Carroll, who ran a restaurant in East Dallas, had a complaint filed against him by Duncan for unsanitary conditions at his place, and a warrant was issued for his arrest. Carroll was arrested on May 23 by officers John Cornwell, no longer a deputy constable since brother Ed was now Dallas' chief of police, and Porter B. Cochran, and fined $3 in city court on Saturday, May 27, 1889. But perhaps Duncan's zeal affected his judgement or maybe he had spoken too soon about playing favorites. Immediately after court adjourned, officers Cornwell and Cochran escorted city court Judge Curtis P. Smith to Carroll's restaurant, which he found to be in "fair sanitary shape." The officers told the judge that it was in the same shape as on the day of arrest. On this basis, the good judge determined that Carroll was entitled to a new trial and admission of the officers' testimony on his behalf. When questioned about his decision, Judge Smith was careful to add:

> Of course, my action is not by any means intended to reflect upon the Sanitary Department, for Officer Duncan did his duty in filing this complaint. Then again, it has heretofore been the custom of this court . . . to dismiss a prosecution upon the abatement of any nuisance, however objectionable it may be. Possibly such a custom has been the cause of many people neglecting sanitary matters until after arrest. As the city now has officers who are paid to apprehend those failing to observe the sanitary laws, and as everybody has been put upon notice that such laws will be rigidly enforced, I am constrained to abolish the above custom from now on and hereafter, when the evidence shows beyond a reasonable doubt that any citizen of Dallas has violated the sanitary ordinances, such a one cannot expect that a cleaning up after arrest will exempt him from the penalty. The health of our people is too sacred in my mind to admit of any compromises upon the law, and, if an observance of the law is to be contingent upon being caught, and after being caught the penalty is to be waived in court, such a prinicple would make a farce of our judicial tribunals and a laughing stock of our police officials. However, under the peculiar circumstances surrounding Carroll's case, I granted him a new trial, but such action must not be understood as forming a precedent in future cases.[45]

Despite the judge's reference to "peculiar circumstances," there must have been a jaundiced eye cast at his statement by the community at large, many people taking it to mean exactly what he said it did not: that taking appropriate steps to clean up after being cited would still excuse the penalty. Despite this setback, Duncan continued in the city's service as a sanitary officer.

Bounty Hunter

Duncan was still working for the city on July 1, 1899, when another incident typical of him occurred. At about 6 p.m. that Saturday evening, John Drake, a locksmith, cut loose with a shotgun blast at Duncan at the intersection of Main and Ervay Streets. A Doctor Ewing, who had heard a vehement argument between the two men, rushed out of a drug store and was barely able to push the shotgun barrel to one side as it discharged. The clustered buckshot slammed into a red Cleaner Dallas League trash barrel at the corner. Dallas Mayor Traylor, Sim Duncan, Doctor Ewing, and Policeman Henry Waller, who were all nearby, pooled their efforts to keep the two men apart, and the shotgun was wrested away from Drake. Drake was arrested for assault with intent to murder and lodged in jail. He asserted that Duncan had made improper remarks about his wife. Later he gave bond in the amount of $500 for his appearance. No other details of this incident are known. Duncan, unharmed, simply left for home after Drake had been arrested.[46]

The twentieth century dawned, bringing with it all of the remnants of the previous century, including Jack Duncan. He was one of many pioneers who represented a more turbulent, primitive time, and now the world was passing him by. The first years of the new century found him an obscure, inconspicuous figure in Dallas. Sometime during 1900, he left the employ of the city to work as a clerk at the Union Depot Hotel, he and his family still living on Commerce Street.[47] As if fate wished to demonstrate that the new century was to hold nothing for him, his wife, Emma, endured a short illness, then died at 11 p.m., Saturday, March 17, 1900, at the age of 44. Her funeral was held at the home of Jack's mother, Katherine, on Jackson Street, and she was buried in Trinity Cemetery,[48] near Jack's father.

The details of Duncan's life from this point on are sketchy. He moved in with his brother Mack, taking with him nine-year-old Jessie.[49] Where the other two children were at this time is unknown. It is possible that his son, who was called Frank, was

218

Police Court Judge
Curtis P. Smith
as he appeared
in 1899.
(Author's Collection).

living with Jack's brother-in-law, Frank Bowles. Subsequently, his two daughters, Annie and Jessie, were supposed to have lived with Commodore Sim Duncan's adopted daughter, Josephine, or Aunt Josie as she came to be known, when she married a judge in Weatherford in Parker County.[50] The 1910 census for Dallas County, however, showed Josie still living at home with Sim and his second wife, Denia.

In 1901, Jack Duncan, still boarding with Mack, gave his occupation as an agent. Mack was now dealing in mineral waters as a profession. The following year, Jack was merely a "laborer," while Mack returned to being a blacksmith. In 1903 and 1904, Jack tried the detective business again, and Mack became a carriage maker. Jack still listed himself as a detective in 1905, but Mack was now building boats. Jack's son, Frank, moved in with his father and uncle. Jack's mother was running a boarding house at her residence.

Jack was working as a carpenter in 1906, still living on Jack-

Bounty Hunter

Jack Duncan and brother Mack lived in this house at the site of Lock and Dam No. One on the Trinity River in the early 1900's. This photograph was taken in 1906 and one of the unidentified men could be Jack Duncan. (Courtesy of the Texas/Dallas History and Archives Division, Dallas Public Library).

son Street with Mack and his wife. Frank Duncan was also still living with them, and was a clerk for the Dallas Consolidated Abstract Company, no doubt with the help of Uncle Sim. The following year, Frank moved in with his grandmother, and it is possible that neither Jack nor Mack was now living in the city.[51] At some point about this time, Mack's wife, Isabela, died, although she was alive prior to April, 1906, when prosecution against her for some unknown charge was dropped in a Dallas district court.[52]

Mack Duncan had become a watchman for the U. S. Army Corps of Engineers on January 1, 1906, likely at Lock and Dam No. One on the Trinity River south of Dallas. They had taken over the canalization project from the Trinity River Navigation Company. On April 1, 1907, he became an engineman for the Corps. He continued in this pursuit until March 1, 1909, when he became lockmaster.[53]

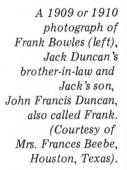

A 1909 or 1910 photograph of Frank Bowles (left), Jack Duncan's brother-in-law and Jack's son, John Francis Duncan, also called Frank. (Courtesy of Mrs. Frances Beebe, Houston, Texas).

At about the same time, Jack was also employed as an overseer for the Corps. The two brothers lived in a two-story white house at the dam site on Lock and Dam Road. Family stories have both of Jack's daughters staying there also, charged with keeping the house cleaned up after the crew that lived there, as well as cooking meals, a chore that both girls disliked intensely.

Now a young man, Frank Duncan married Rowena V. Jackson in Dallas on May 28, 1909.[54] He was a clerk in his uncle Sim's abstract office, as was his other uncle, Frank Bowles.[55] On April 16, 1910, Annie Belle married Dallas electrician Richard H. Farrell, although they would separate after a few years.[56] Jack became a grandfather when a daughter, Frances Virginia, was born to Frank and Rowena on August 17, 1910.[57] One of Jack's presents to baby Frances was a large German doll "just as big as she is." Rowena Duncan came to be greatly impressed with her father-in-law and thought he was a wonderful man.[58]

In December, 1910, Jack Duncan was discharged from his position as an overseer for Corps of Engineers property. It was

Bounty Hunter

John Francis "Frank" Duncan, ca. 1910, he was the son of Jack Duncan. (Courtesy of Mrs. Frances Beebe, Houston, Texas).

contended that negligence on his part had led to the losing of some government property.[59] However, he apparently retained employment on the lock and dam, most likely in a lesser capacity, due probably to the influence Mack could exert with the Corps.

In these early days of the new century, the automobile was a novelty, and few could foresee the indispensable tool it would become. Most automobiles were expensive for the times, costing as much as several thousand dollars. However, one enterprising manufacturer aimed for a vehicle that most could afford. In 1911, the single-cylinder Brush Runabout went on the market for under $500. The "everyman's car," as it was advertised, had a wooden frame, wooden axles, and coil-spring suspension on each wheel.[60] Jack Duncan invested in a Runabout, and it soon allowed him to visit Dallas more frequently, having learned to negotiate the rough roads between the dam and the city.

At about 7:30 p.m., on Thursday, November 16, 1911, as Duncan was guiding his auto over the rough Kaufman road about seven miles south of Dallas, returning home to the dam,

End of an Era

John W. Ryan, Dallas Chief of Police in 1911. (Author's Collection).

the vehicle skidded into a ditch near the store of E. C. Pemberton. The merchant and his son, Hubert, came out and helped Duncan get the car back up on the road again. Thanking them, Duncan started once more on his way, and the Pembertons returned to the store. Approximately 300 yards down the road, Duncan lost control again, and the auto skidded off into a ten-foot ditch, this time overturning and landing on top of him. The high, jutting steering wheel crushed into his chest, and the silver tube flew from his throat as a result of the force. Ten-year-old James Washington, a black boy, discovered the vehicle and ran and told his father. In turn, Mr. Pemberton was notified. He telephoned the Dallas police, having determined that the man pinned beneath the car was dead.

Chief of Police John W. Ryan and his lieutenant of detectives, Henry Tanner, drove out from the city. There were no outward marks of injury on Duncan's body, and those at the scene speculated as to whether his death was caused from internal injuries or whether he was unable to breathe without the tube. Duncan's body was removed from under the wrecked

*Dallas Policeman J. H.
"Henry" Tanner, in
1904. (Author's
Collection).*

Brush and put into Ryan's car, who took it back to Dallas and turned it over to Ed C. Smith, a prominent undertaker.

Funeral services for Duncan were held at 2 p.m. on Saturday, November 18, at Frank's home on Gould Street. Reverend J. Frank Smith read the Twenty-third Psalm and gave a prayer of comfort and hope for the family, especially for Sim and Mack. He briefly reviewed Jack's life, observing that "few men have been blessed with the experience of seeing a wilderness made to blossom as a rose and cities spring up where only cow trails were."

Dead at the age of sixty-one, Jack Duncan was laid to rest in Space 11, Lot 26, Block 24 of Greenwood Cemetery, which had formerly been Trinity Cemetery, next to Emma. Among his pallbearers was Ed Cornwell, with whom he had shared so many adventures years before.[61] The local newspapers briefly mentioned Duncan's role as a Dallas pioneer. One newspaper wrote:

> In the early days of Texas, when desperadoes were numerous and physical courage a common asset, Jack Duncan was conspicuous

for his daring and coolness. As a Texas Ranger he effected many important captures. Probably the most famous was that of John Wesley Hardin, the noted desperado who, for many years, terrorized Texas. With Captain Armstrong, another Ranger, Duncan tracked the man from Texas, across Louisiana, Mississippi, and Alabama into Florida, where they arrested him. The silver tube in his throat was the silent evidence of a wound received at the hands of Texas rustlers in a fierce fight he and other Rangers had with them. He had been wounded several times.[62]

Discreetly, the family conveniently buried the true story of how the silver tube came about, allowing Jack to have his own legend. Another newspaper account, the last ever to be written about him, provided a succinct epitaph for Jack Duncan: "While a peace officer during the early days of Dallas, he is spoken of as having been a courageous man."[63]

NOTES

1. *Dallas Morning News*, January 26, 1888.
2. *Dallas Morning News*, May 12, 1888.
3. Letter to John Hollingsworth from L. J. Randall, June 10, 1888; Memorandum to Chief Postal Inspector from John Hollingsworth, June 12, 1888, U. S. Postal Records, U. S. National Archives and Records Service.
4. Dallas City Directory, 1888-1889.
5. Minutes, 14th District Court, Dallas County, Texas, Vol. V, pp. 560-562 (*Isabella H. Duncan et al v. Charles Howard et al*, cause no. 6692).
6. *Dallas Morning News*, September 14, 1888.
7. *Dallas Morning News*, September 18, 1888.
8. *Dallas Morning News*, November 16, 1888; *Dallas Daily Herald*, November 16, 1888.
9. Birth Records, John Francis Duncan, January 3, 1889, file no. 25373, Dallas, Texas, County Clerk's Office; *Dallas Morning News*, January 4, 1889.
10. Minutes, 14th District Court, Dallas County, Texas, Vol. W, p. 368 (*State of Texas v. T. H. McDuffie*, cause no. 11102).
11. Case Records, U. S. District Court, Northern District of Texas (*United States v. Jack Duncan*, cause no. 386).
12. Minutes, 14th District Court, Dallas County, Texas, Vol. X, p. 200 (*State of Texas v. Jack Duncan*, cause nos. 7660 and 7661).

13. *Dallas Daily Times Herald*, August 27, 1889.

14. Dallas City Directory, 1889-1890.

15. Minutes, 14th District Court, Dallas County, Texas, Vol. X, pp.328, 357, 358, and 439; Vol. Y, pp. 9 and 99 (*State of Texas v. W. M. Seeley*, cause no. 8610).

16. Minutes, 14th District Court, Dallas County, Texas, Vol. Y, pp. 83, 327, 328, and 396 (*State of Texas v. Jack Duncan*, cause no. 15198, which is incorrectly shown on p. 396 as cause no. 15798); Minutes, 44th District Court, Dallas County, Texas, Vol. 1, p. 417 (*State of Texas v. Jack Duncan and Elmer Loosley*, cause no. 8609 and 8611).

17. Twelfth U. S. Census, 1900, Dallas County, Texas.

18. Dallas City Directory, 1891-1892.

19. Birth Records, Annie Bell Duncan, August 15, 1892, file no. 49782, Dallas, Texas, County Clerk's Office.

20. *Dallas Morning News*, September 25, 1892; Letter to author from Raymond Bouska (manager, Greenwood Cemetery Association), Dallas, Texas June 4, 1982.

21. Floyd Durham, *The Trinity River Paradox* (Wichita Falls, Texas: Nortex Press, 1976), p. 6.

22. E. H. Brown, *Trinity River Canalization* (Dallas, Texas: Trinity River Canal Association, 1930), pp. 33-42; Durham, *Trinity River*, pp. 72-82; *Dallas Guide and History*, Texas Writers' Project, unpublished manuscript (Work Projects Administration, 1940), pp. 265-269; Rogers, *Lusty Texans*, pp. 127 and 128.

23. *Dallas Morning News*, August 23, 1893.

24. *Dallas Daily Times Herald*, August 28, 1893; *Dallas Morning News*, September 7, 1893; Brown, *Canalization*, p. 44.

25. Dallas City Directories, 1893-1894, 1894-1895.

26. *Dallas Daily Times Herald*, February 19, 1894.

27. *Dallas Morning News*, March 4, 1894.

28. *Dallas Morning news*, August 18, 1895.

29. Metz, *John Selman*, pp. 174 and 175; Parsons, *The Capture Of John Wesley Hardin*, pp. 86-89.

30. *Dallas Morning News*, August 22, 1895.

31. *Dallas Daily Times Herald*, August 24, 1895.

32. *Dallas Morning News*, September 6, 1895.

33. *Dallas Morning News*, September 11, 1895.

34. *San Antonio Daily Express*, September 12, 1895.

35. *Dallas Daily Times Herald*, April 28, 1896.

36. *Dallas Morning News*, April 28, 1896.

37. Dallas City Directories, 1896-1899.

38. *Dallas Daily Times Herald*, September 26, 1898.

39. *Dallas Morning News*, March 21, 1899.

40. Minutes, Board of Aldermen, Dallas Texas, May 23, 1899.

End of an Era

41. *Dallas Daily Times Herald*, May 1, 1899.

42. Minutes, Board of Aldermen, Dallas, Texas, May 2, 1899; *Dallas Morning News*, May 2, 1899.

43. *Dallas Morning News*, May 28, 1899.

44. *Dallas Morning News*, May 13 and 31, 1899.

45. *Dallas Daily Times Herald*, May 27 and 29, 1899.

46. *Dallas Morning News*, July 2 and 4, 1899; *Dallas Daily Times Herald*, July 2, 1899.

47. Dallas City Directory, 1900.

48. *Dallas Daily Times Herald*, March 18, 1900; *Dallas Morning News*, March 18, 1900.

49. Twelfth U. S. Census, 1900, Dallas County, Texas.

50. Interview with Mrs. Frances Duncan Beebe (granddaughter of Jack Duncan), Houston, Texas, March 5, 1983; Interview with Mrs. Joan Courtney (wife of the late Frank Courtney, grandson of Jack Duncan), Dallas, Texas, August 2, 1982.

51. Dallas City Directories, 1901-1909.

52. Minutes, 44th District Court, Dallas County, Texas, Vol. 20, p. 418 (*State of Texas v. Mrs. G. M. Duncan*, cause no. 1885).

53. Personnel Records of George M. Duncan, National Personnel Records Center, St. Louis, Missouri.

54. Marriage Records, Vol. 6, p. 140, Dallas, Texas, County Clerk's Office.

55. Dallas City Directory, 1910.

56. Marriage Records, Vol. 8, p. 182, Dallas, Texas, County Clerk's Office; *Dallas Morning News*, April 17, 1910; Dallas City Directory, 1916.

57. Birth Records, Frances Virginia Duncan, August 17, 1910, Dallas, Texas, County Clerk's Office.

58. Interview with Mrs. Frances Duncan Beebe (granddaughter of Jack Duncan), Houston, Texas, March 5, 1983. The doll is now in the possession of relatives in Dallas.

59. Index of letter of a Captain Waldron, December 27, 1910, U. S. War Department Records, U. S. National Archives and Records Service.

60. Floyd Clymer, *Treasury of Early American Automobiles* (New York: Bonanza Books, 1950), p. 104.

61. *Dallas Daily Times Herald*, November 17, 1911; *Dallas Morning News*, November 17-19, 1911; Letter to author from Raymond Bouska (manager, Greenwood Cemetery Association), Dallas, Texas, June 4, 1982.

62. *Dallas Daily Times Herald*, November 17, 1911.

63. *Dallas Morning News*, November 17, 1911.

227

Chapter 11

Epilogue

When Jack Duncan died in 1911, with the exception of his father, all of the members of the Duncan family who had come to Texas from Kentucky in the early 1870's were still living, most in Dallas. The next year, however, the family matriarch, Katherine, died at the age of 86 on Sunday, June 2, 1912.[1] Known to all of her friends as Aunt Kitty, she was laid to rest alongside her husband, James, their headstones having no inscription but "Father" and "Mother." Only one grave space separated her from her son, Jack, and his wife, Emma.[2]

The Commodore, Simeon Winfield Scott Duncan, died on October 26, 1916, of Bright's disease.[3] Sim had come to be a very large, portly man, but had only been in ill health during the last few months of his life. His wife, Denia, had died the previous April. The newspapers recalled his role in bringing the railroad to Dallas, as well as calling him the "father of Trinity Navigation."[4] His will left $5,000 to his spinster sister, Mary Frances, but the bulk of his estate went to his adopted Josie. A suit was brought to contest the will by sisters Mary and Emma, the latter now married to W. S. Bell, and by brother Mack and the three children of Jack Duncan. It was claimed that, not only did Sim not have testamentary capacity to legally execute a will, but also Josephine had exercised undue influence on him in order to partially disinherit Mary and totally disinherit the rest of the family. According to the family, it had been tradition for the oldest son to take care of the rest of the family and Sim's will broke with that tradition. The probate suit was dropped in March, 1917, supposedly when Josie agreed to take care of them.[5] In 1922, Josie married Emmanuel A. Meek and moved with him to the west coast.[6]

Of Jack Duncan's sisters, Anna, who had married James A. Kenny, died on January 2, 1935. She left two children, Ida and Harry.[7] Emma Bell also died in 1935 and was buried next to Jack in Greenwood Cemetery.[8]

After Jack died, Mack Duncan continued as lockmaster on the dam until October 31, 1914. When the dam was torn down to be replaced by another one, he was foreman of the construction gang that built it, and then continued as lockmaster until the Trinity River project was abandoned. He also operated a power boat on the Trinity River for the Corps of Engineers until their headquarters was moved out of Dallas. Mack then transferred with the Engineers to Brownsville in South Texas. According to the family, prior to World War I, when punitive expeditions were being sent by the American government into Mexico after Pancho Villa, Mack Duncan was then in Brownsville. He is said to have received a bullet wound in one buttock during a raid by Mexican bandits which subsequently became his "weather prognosticator."

After World War I broke out, Mack Duncan became a Mechanic's Helper for the Quartermaster Corps at Fort Brown in October, 1916. He received a pay raise from $60 to $75 per month in January, 1917, as an Assistant Mechanic in the Motor Transport Branch. Considered a temporary employee, he was transferred in August, 1918, to the Constructing Quartermaster as temporary Post Carpenter for maintenance of the post facilities. In May, 1920, he was admitted to federal civil service status as a carpenter at $120 per month, but his salary was reduced in August to $100 per month. As Post Carpenter at Fort Brown, Mack supervised some sixteen to twenty men. The Post Quartermaster described him as "a master in his line of work."

No real attention had been paid by military authorities to

Bounty Hunter

George McAfee Duncan as an elderly man. "Mack" and his brother, Jack, were living together in 1911. (Courtesy of the Texas/Dallas History and Archives Division, Dallas Public Library).

the fact that Mack had turned 65 on April 1, 1919. Federal civil service law required mandatory termination at that age. In December, 1921, when the Post Quartermaster requested that he be retained in spite of his age, Mack's immediate dismissal was ordered.

Mack was terminated abruptly on January 24, 1922. After the fact, he was officially credited as having been a temporary employee between August 20, 1920, and the date of dismissal. His supervisor, Captain Charles Perfect, sympathized with Mack's plight and brought to the attention of his supervisors the fact that the pay reduction in 1920 had been arbitrary and unwarranted. The American Legion in Brownsville and a local law firm took note of his situation and volunteered their help to straighten out the matter. In a letter to the U. S. Quartermaster General in March, 1922, Mack was described as "quite old" and "certainly in need of the money" he had been shorted. Mack subsequently received $356 and returned to Dallas.[9]

Mack's son, Bill, had been a reporter for the *Dallas Dispatch*. During the chase after Villa, Bill had taken his family to

Simeon Winfield Scott
Duncan, known
as the "Commodore."
(Courtesy of the Texas
Collection, Baylor
University).

Brownsville to cover the story, probably staying with his father. At one point, he helped another noted correspondent, Floyd Gibbons, to get dispatches out of Mexico, but it was later asserted that Gibbons took credit and gained his fame on the basis of work that Bill did. According to the family, Mack's grandson, Bill, Jr., was present as a baby when some Mexican bandits tried to lasso a machine gun, and he had to be hidden under a parapet until after the bandits were killed. After serving in aviation intelligence during the war, Mack's son returned to Dallas and became a longtime police reporter for the *Dallas Daily Times Herald*. Like his Uncle Jack, he had many friends on the police and sheriff's departments. When the notorious outlaws Clyde Barrow and Bonnie Parker were finally tracked down and killed by lawmen in May, 1934, Bill Duncan was able to take his two children, Bill, Jr., and Dorothy, in to see the bodies. He died unexpectedly on August 26, 1937, leaving his father heartbroken.[10]

Mack Duncan had always been a quiet, gentle man, unlike his brother Jack. His family remembers him more as a follower,

Jessie Kathleen Duncan,
born in December, 1890,
was Jack Duncan's
eldest daughter.
(Courtesy of
Mrs. Frances Beebe,
Houston, Texas).

rather than a leader, and as one who had looked to his older brothers for guidance and support. With Jack dead, he had looked to Sim as the eldest to take care of the family but was crushed when Sim died and the estate was left to Josie. With the death of Bill, he couldn't cope any longer and, on Friday morning, August 12, 1938, at the age of 85, died at his home on Llano Street.[11]

The last surviving member of the family who made the trek to Dallas from Kentucky was Mary Frances. At the age of 72, she died on Thursday, September, 26, 1940, and was buried at Greenwood Cemetery between her mother and Emma Bowles Duncan, Jack's wife.[12] She had never married.

Of Jack's children, Jessie Katherine married Frank Halamuda, then was subsequently married to O. W. Courtney. She lived in Dallas with her husband and a son, Frank. Mrs. Courtney died on Thursday, September 27, 1956.[13] Anna Belle, who had married and then divorced Richard Farrell, married Dan M. Bell on June 23, 1920.[14] They had no children, and she died in Dallas on Monday, July 7, 1958, at the age of 65.[15] Jack's son,

Epilogue

Frank, after working for a number of years in the abstract business in Dallas, moved his family to Houston in the early 1920's. He later retired as a vice president of the American Title and Guaranty Company. Frank Duncan died on the afternoon of Saturday, September 17, 1960, leaving his wife, Rowena, and two children, Frances and Jack.[16]

Today, Greenwood Cemetery lies as a quiet, tree-covered oasis in the shadow of towering downtown Dallas, the neighborhood around it a combination of transition blight and bustling renovation. Within its iron fence, the grounds are crowded with the monumental tombstones that were fashionable so many years ago. Sim Duncan rests beneath a large stone that proclaims the sobriquet he was proud of, "Commodore." He is surrounded by members of the Duncan family, whose tombstones are overwhelmed by his.

Approximately one hundred yards away, obscured by bushes and difficult to find, six graves lie side by side, none of them marked with a prominent headstone. James and Kitty Duncan are identified only as "Mother" and "ather," the "F" having been chipped off. The grave of Jack's wife, Emma, is also marked, as is that of Anna Kenny. The other two graves, that of Jack and his sister, Mary, are unmarked, visible only as gaps between the other graves.

Thus, even in death, Jack Duncan remains obscure. The only remaining link there is to the living are the vague references by writers, who credit "Detective Jack Duncan of Dallas" with helping in the capture of John Wesley Hardin. He is a part of another man's legend—an anonymous supporting player —and the legend overshadows his significance as a flesh-and-blood creature who made his own contribution to the story of America's frontier.

THE END

Bounty Hunter

1. *Dallas Daily Times Herald*, June 3, 1912.

2. Letter to author from Raymond Bouska (manager, Greenwood Cemetery Association), Dallas, Texas, June 4, 1982.

3. Death Certificate, Dallas County, Texas, 1916, no. 22821.

4. *Dallas Morning News*, October 27, 1916; *Dallas Daily Times Herald*, October 27, 1916.

5. Probate Records, S. W. S. Duncan, file no. 5042, 1916, Dallas, Texas, County Clerk's Office; Interview with William B. Duncan (grandson of George M. Duncan), North Richland Hills, Texas, November 26, 1982.

6. Marriage Records, Vol. 33, p. 504, Dallas, Texas, County Clerk's Office; Interview with William B. Duncan (grandson of George M. Duncan), North Richland Hills, Texas, November 26, 1982.

7. *Dallas Morning News*, January 3, 1935; *Dallas Journal*, January 3, 1935.

8. Letter to author from Raymond Bouska (manager, Greenwood Cemetery Association), Dallas, Texas, June 4, 1982.

9. Personnel Records of George M. Duncan, National Personnel Records Center, St. Louis, Missouri.

10. *Dallas Daily Times Herald*, August 26 and 27, 1937; Interview with William B. Duncan (grandson of George M. Duncan), North Richland Hills, Texas, November 26, 1982; Interview with Dorothy Young (granddaughter of George M. Duncan), Round Rock, Texas, November 18, 1982.

11. *Dallas Times Herald*, August 12, 1938; *Dallas Morning News*, August 13, 1938; Interview with William B. Duncan (grandson of George M. Duncan), North Richland Hills, Texas, November 26, 1982.

12. *Dallas Morning News*, September 27, 1940; Letter to author from Raymond Bouska (manager, Greenwood Cemetery Association), Dallas, Texas June 4, 1982.

13. *Dallas Times Herald*, September 27 and 28, 1956.

14. Marriage Records, Vol. 29, p. 458, Dallas, Texas, County Clerk's Office.

15. *Dallas Morning News*, July 8, 1958; *Dallas Times Herald*, July 9, 1958.

16. *Houston Post*, September 18, 1960.

Bibliography

BOOKS

Appler, A. C. *The Younger Brothers.* Reprint of 1892 edition. New York: Frederick Fell, Inc., 1955.

Bartholomew, Ed, ed. *Some Western Gun Fighters.* Toyahvale, Texas: Frontier Book Co., 1954.

Bartholomew, Ed. *Wyatt Earp, The Man and the Myth.* Toyahvale, Texas: Frontier Book Co., 1964.

Bonney, Cecil. *Looking Over My Shoulder.* Roswell, New Mexico: Hall-Poorbaugh Press, Inc., 1971.

Breakenridge, William M. *Helldorado.* New York: Houghton Mifflin Co., 1928.

Breihan, Carl W. *Younger Brothers.* San Antonio, Texas: The Naylor Co., 1961.

Bronaugh, W. C. *The Youngers' Fight For Freedom.* Columbia, Missouri: E. W. Stephens Publishing Co., 1906.

Brown, E. H. *Trinity River Canalization.* Dallas, Texas: Trinity River Canal Association, 1930.

Buel, J. W. *The Border Outlaws.* Baltimore, Maryland: I. & M. Ottenheimer, n.d.

Burns, Walter Noble. *Tombstone.* New York: Penguin Books, Inc., 1942.

Clymer, Floyd. *Treasury of Early American Automobiles.* New York: Bonanza Books, 1950.

Collins, Lewis. Revised by Richard H. Collins. *History of Kentucky.* Vol. II. Frankfort, Kentucky: Kentucky Historical Society, 1966.

Confederate Kentucky Volunteers, War 1861-65. Report of the Adjutant General of the State of Kentucky. Frankfort, Kentucky: The State Journal Co., 1915.

Bounty Hunter

Dallas Guide and History. Texas Writers' Project. Unpublished manuscript. Work Projects Administration, 1940.

Davis, William C. *The Orphan Brigade*. Garden City, New York: Doubleday & Company, Inc., 1980.

Dodge, Fred. *Under Cover for Wells Fargo*. Boston: Houghton Mifflin Company, 1969.

Drago, Harry Sinclair. *Outlaws on Horseback*. New York: Dodd, Mead & Co., 1964.

Durham, Floyd. *The Trinity River Paradox*. Wichita Falls, Texas: Nortex Press, 1976.

Faulk, Odie B. *Tombstone, Myth and Reality*. New York: Oxford University Press, 1972.

Fleming, Elvis E. and Minor S. Huffman, ed. *Roundup on the Pecos*. Roswell, New Mexico: Chaves County Historical Society, 1978.

Gard, Wayne. *Frontier Justice*. Norman, Oklahoma: University of Oklahoma Press, 1949.

Gard, Wayne. *Sam Bass*. Lincoln, Nebraska: University of Nebraska Press, 1936.

Gillett, James B. *Six Years With the Texas Rangers*. New Haven, Connecticut: Yale University Press, 1925.

Greene, A. C. *Dallas: The Deciding Years*. Austin, Texas: The Encino Press, 1973.

Hardin, John Wesley. *The Life of John Wesley Hardin*. Reprint edition. Norman, Oklahoma: University of Oklahoma Press, 1961.

Hendricks, George. *The Badmen of the West*. San Antonio, Texas: The Naylor Co., 1970.

Horan, James D. *The Authentic Wild West: The Gunfighters*. New York: Crown Publishers, Inc., 1976.

Jahns, Pat. *The Frontier World of Doc Holliday*. New York: Hastings House, Publisher, 1957.

Jennings, N. A. *A Texas Ranger*. Dallas, Texas: Southwest Press, 1930.

Bibliography

Johnson, Frank W. *A History of Texas and Texans.* Vol. V. New York: The American Historical Society, 1914.

Jones, James Allison and Mary Josephine Jones. *Hardin County, Kentucky, Cemetery Inscriptions.* Vol. II. Owensboro, Kentucky: McDowell Publications, 1980.

Jones, Mary Josephine. *Marriages, Hardin County, Kentucky, 1820-1829.* Hartford, Kentucky: McDowell Publications, 1977.

Makers of Dallas. Dallas, Texas: Dallas Newspaper Artists' Association, 1912.

McClure, Daniel E., Jr. *Two Centuries in Elizabethtown and Hardin County, Kentucky.* Elizabethtown, Kentucky: The Hardin County Historical Society, 1979.

Memorial and Biographical History of Dallas County. Chicago, Illinois: The Lewis Publishing Co., 1892.

Merchant, Lawrence. *The San Simon.* Carlsbad, New Mexico: Nichols Printing, Inc., 1975.

Metz, Leon Claire. *John Selman, Texas Gunfighter.* New York: Hastings House, Publishers, 1966.

Myers, John Myers. *Doc Holliday.* Lincoln, Nebraska: University of Nebraska Press, 1955.

Myers, Lee C. *The Pearl of the Pecos.* Carlsbad, New Mexico: Lee C. Myers, 1974.

Neville, A. W. *The Red River Valley: Then and Now.* Paris, Texas: North Texas Publishing Co., 1948.

Nordyke, Lewis. *Wes Hardin, Texas Gunman.* London: John Long Limited, 1958.

Paddock, Capt. B. B., ed. *A Twentieth Century History and Biographical Record of North and West Texas.* Vol. II. New York: The Lewis Publishing Co., 1906.

Parsons, Chuck. *The Capture of John Wesley Hardin.* College Station, Texas: Creative Publishing Co., 1978.

Payne, Darwin. *Dallas: An Illustrated History.* Woodland Hills, California: Windsor Publications, Inc., 1982.

Pendleton, Albert S., Jr., and Susan McKey Thomas. *In Search of the Hollidays.* Valdosta, Georgia: Little River Press, 1973.

Rascoe, Burton. *Belle Starr, The Bandit Queen.* New York: Random House, 1941.

Raymond, Dora Neill. *Captain Lee Hall of Texas.* Norman, Oklahoma: University of Oklahoma Press, 1940.

Rickards, Colin. *Mysterious Dave Mather.* Santa Fe, New Mexico: The Blue Feather Press, 1968.

Ripley, Thomas. *They Died With Their Boots On.* Reprint edition. New York: Pocket Books, Inc., 1949.

Rogers, John William. *The Lusty Texans of Dallas.* New York: E. P. Dutton and Company, Inc., 1951.

Rosa, Joseph G. *The Gunfighter: Man or Myth?* Norman, Oklahoma: University of Oklahoma Press, 1969.

Shirley, Glenn. *Heck Thomas, Frontier Marshal.* New York: Chilton Company, 1962.

Shirley, Glenn. *Belle Starr and Her Times.* Norman, Oklahoma: University of Oklahoma Press, 1982.

Smith, Robert Nelson, Jr. *Storey-Price-Rascoe-Smith Families.* Unpublished manuscript. Harlingen, Texas: Robert Nelson Smith, Jr., 1959.

Sonnichsen, C. L. *I'll Die Before I Run.* New York: The Devin-Adair Co., 1962.

Stanley, F. *Jim Courtright, Two Gun Marshal of Fort Worth.* Denver, Colorado: World Press, Inc., 1957.

Streeter, Floyd B. *Ben Thompson: Man With a Gun.* New York: Frederick Fell, Inc., Publishers, 1957.

Sutton, Robert C., Jr. *The Sutton-Taylor Feud.* Quanah, Texas: Nortex Press, 1974.

Texas State Gazetteer and Business Directory. Vol. III. Chicago: R. L. Polk & Co., 1890.

Webb, Walter Prescott. *The Texas Rangers.* 2nd ed. Austin, Texas: University of Texas Press, 1965.

Bibliography

Wellman, Paul I. *A Dynasty of Western Outlaws*. New York: Bonanza Books, 1961.

Winstead, Mrs. Thomas Durham. *Chronicles of Hardin County, Kentucky, 1766-1974*. Elizabethtown, Kentucky: Mrs. Thomas Durham Winstead, 1974.

Younger, Cole. *The Story of Cole Younger*. Reprint of 1903 edition. Houston, Texas: Frontier Press of Texas, 1955.

ARTICLES

Ball, Eve. "Murder on Credit," *Frontier Times*, Vol. 52, no. 2 (February-March, 1978), pp. 35-36 *et seq.*

Godbold, Mollie Moore. "Comanche and the Hardin Gang," *Southwestern Historical Quarterly*, Vol. 67 (July, 1963), p. 260.

King, Edward. "The Great South," *Scribner's Monthly Illustrated Magazine*, Vol. 6, no. 3, 1873.

Maddox, Holmes. "The San Simon Cattle Company," *Cattleman*, (February, 1948), p. 74.

Parsons, Chuck. "The Death of Brown Bowen," *Real West*, Vol. 19, no. 148 (November, 1976), pp. 32-34 *et seq.*

Roff, Joe T. "Reminiscences of Early Days in the Chickasaw Nation," *Chronicles of Oklahoma*, Vol. 13. Oklahoma City, Oklahoma: Oklahoma Historical Society, 1935, pp. 182-189.

Taylor, T. U. "New Light on John Wesley Hardin," *Frontier Times*, Vol. 2, no. 11 (August 25, 1925), p. 16.

Wiltsey, Norman B. "40 Times a Killer," *Frontier Times*, Vol. 38, no. 1 (January, 1964), pp. 68-69.

Wright, A. J. "John Wesley Hardin's 'Missing Years'," *Old West*, Vol. 18, no. 1 (Fall, 1981), pp. 6-11; "A Gunfighter's Southern Vacation," *Quarterly of the National Association and Center for Outlaw and Lawmen History*, Vol. 7, no. 3 (Autumn, 1983), pp. 12-16.

NEWSPAPERS

Arkansas (Little Rock) *Gazette,* April 11, 1885.
Atlanta (Georgia) *Daily Constitution,* September 1, 1877.
Austin Daily Democratic Statesman, August-September, 1877.
Austin Daily Statesman, 1884.
Clarksville (Texas) *Northern Standard,* November 21, 1884.
Dallas Daily Commercial, 1874.
Dallas Daily Herald, 1874-1878, 1880-1889.
Dallas Daily Times Herald, 1891-1895, 1899-1900, 1911-1912, 1916, 1921, 1937.
Dallas Herald, 1869, 1871, 1873.
Dallas Journal, January 3, 1935.
Dallas Morning News, 1885-1889, 1892-1900, 1907, 1910-1911, 1916, 1921, 1935, 1940, 1958.
Dallas Times Herald, 1938, 1956, 1958.
Dallas Weekly Herald, 1876-1878, 1882, 1884-1885.
Fort Smith (Arkansas) *Elevator,* May-July, 1885.
Fort Worth Daily Democrat, August 28, 1877.
Fort Worth Daily Democrat-Advance, February-March, 1882.
Fort Worth Daily Gazette, 1884-1885.
Fort Worth Gazette, 1884.
Galveston Daily News, 1877-1878.
Houston Post, September 18, 1960.
Kansas Agriculturist, March 6, 1885.
Las Vegas (New Mexico) *Daily Optic,* April 8, 1882.
Mobile (Alabama) *Daily Register,* September 22, 1877.
Montgomery (Alabama) *Advertiser,* August, 1877.
Muskogee (Indian Territory) *Indian Journal,* May 28, 1885.
Norton's Union Intelligencer (Dallas), 1872.
Paris (Texas) *Weekly News-Boy,* March 7, 1885.
San Antonio Daily Express, September 12, 1895.
Sherman (Texas) *Daily Register,* 1886, 1888.
Tucson (Arizona) *Daily Star,* March 8, 1882.
Waco (Texas) *Daily Examiner,* 1877, 1882-1883.

Bibliography

Waco (Texas) *Examiner and Patron,* January 11, 1878.

PUBLIC RECORDS

Cass County, Texas
 District Court Minutes:
  State of Texas v. J. A. and T. J. Taylor, cause nos. 1739,
   1742, and 1748 (1885).
  State of Texas v. J. F. Taylor, cause no. 1794 (1885).
Dallas County, Texas
 Birth Records, County Clerk's Office.
 Dallas City Directories, 1873-1916.
 Deed Records: Vol. J, N, and R.
 14th District Court Minutes: Vol. D, E, H-2, I, J, K, L, N,
  O, P, Q, S, T, V, W, and Y (see footnotes for specific
  case citations).
 44th District Court Minutes: Vol. 1 and 20.
 Ledger Book, E. M. Kahn & Co., 1877 (Dallas Public
  Library).
 Marriage Records: Vol. G, 6, and 8.
 Minutes, Board of Aldermen, City of Dallas, Texas.
 Tax Rolls, 1859-1879.
Escambia County, Florida
 Circuit Court Papers:
  State of Florida v. Martin H. Sullivan, record no. 1877-
   5945-Ca-01 (1877).
  State of Florida v. William H. Hutchinson, record no.
   1877-5918-Ca-01 (1877).
Grayson County, Texas
 15th District Court Minutes:
  State of Texas v. Mack Crook and Nute Harris, cause no.
   2723 (1885-1891).
Hardin County, Kentucky
 Circuit Court Order Books: Vol. 3, 4, 6, 10, and 11.
 County Court Order Books: Vol. I and L.

Bounty Hunter

Deed Book: Vol. L, N, V, W, X, Y, 1, 2, 3, 5, 7, 8, 9, 10, 11, and 12.

Marriage Register: Vol. B.

Tax Rolls, 1840-1866.

Kentucky State Archives

Executive Journal, 1875-1877, Governor James B. McCreary.

Lamar County, Texas

District Court Docket Book: Vol. 4 (1884).

Election Return Book (1884).

Navarro County, Texas

13th District Court Case Papers:

State of Texas v. Frank Clanton and Stony Broxon, cause no. 2621 (1882).

State of Texas v. Jesse Rascoe and William G. Jackson, cause no. 2018 (1878).

Special Collections, Southwest Texas State University

John Wesley Hardin Collection.

Texas Court of Appeals

John W. Hardin v. The State of Texas, 4 Tex. App. 355 (1878).

Frank Clanton v. The State of Texas, 13 Tex. App. 139 (1882).

Mack Crook v. The State of Texas, 27 Tex. 198, 11 S. W. 444 (1889).

Texas State Library and Archives

Adjutant General Records, May-November, 1877.

Report of State Adjutant General, 1873.

Texas Ranger Muster Rolls.

United States Census Records

Sixth U. S. Census, 1840, Hardin County, Kentucky.

Seventh U. S. Census, 1850, Hardin County, Kentucky.

Eighth U. S. Census, 1860, Hardin County, Kentucky.

Ninth U. S. Census, 1870, Hardin County, Kentucky.

Tenth U. S. Census, 1880, Dallas County, Texas.

Bibliography

Twelfth U. S. Census, 1900, Dallas County, Texas.

Thirteenth U. S. Census, 1910, Dallas County, Texas.

United States National Archives and Records Service

Confederate Army Company Muster Rolls (James A. Duncan).

Index to correspondence, 1910, U. S. Army Corps of Engineers, U. S. War Department Records.

Roster of Indian Police, 1885-1886, U. S. Bureau of Indian Affairs.

U. S. District Court Records, Western District of Arkansas:

U. S. v. Sam Starr and Belle Starr (1882).

U. S. v. Frank Cook, cause no. 764 (1885); cause no. 1497 (1886).

U. S. District Court Records, Northern District of Texas:

U. S. v. Charles O'Donnell and Pat Nolan, cause no. 263 (1883).

U. S. v. Jack Duncan, cause no. 386 (1887).

U. S. Postal Records, 1887-1888, with reference to *U. S. v. John Corder* and *U. S. v. Jack Duncan.*

U. S. National Personel Records Center

Official Personnel Folder, George McAfee Duncan.

INTERVIEWS

Mrs. Frances Duncan Beebe (granddaughter of Jack Duncan), Houston, Texas, March 5, 1983.

Mrs. Joan Courtney (wife of the late Frank Courtney, grandson of Jack Duncan), Dallas, Texas, August 2, 1982.

Mr. William B. Duncan (grandson of George M. Duncan), North Richland Hills, Texas, November 26, 1982.

Sheriff J. R. "Sonny" Sessions, Freestone County, Texas, July 16, 1982.

Mrs. Dorothy Young (granddaughter of George M. Duncan), Round Rock, Texas, November 18, 1982.

243

Bounty Hunter

LETTERS

Ed Bartholomew, to the author, Fort Davis, Texas, September 21, 1982.

Raymond Bouska (manager, Greenwood Cemetery Association), to the author, Dallas, Texas, June 4 and 11, 1982.

Mrs. Joan Courtney (wife of the late Frank Courtney, grandson of Jack Duncan), to the author, Dallas, Texas, December 23, 1983.

Lawrence B. Merchant, to the author, Carlsbad, New Mexico, March 17, 1983.

Chuck Parsons, to the author, South Wayne, Wisconsin, May 20, 1986.

Mrs. Susan McKey Thomas, to the author, Valdosta, Georgia, October 11, 1983.

Index

Index

Index

Index

The Author

Rick Miller

Born Richard Joseph Miller in San Diego, California, on January 20, 1941, the author was raised and educated in Dallas, Texas. After a peacetime tour as an Army paratrooper, Rick joined the Dallas Police Department in 1963, rising to the rank of Lieutenant by the time he left the department in 1975. He served as a Program Coordinator for the Texas Organized Crime Prevention Council, after which he was Chief of Police in the Texas cities of Killeen and Denton.

While a Dallas police officer, Rick received his B. A. in 1970 from the University of Texas at Arlington and a Master's Degree in Public Administration from Southern Methodist University in 1974. He left law enforcement in 1981 to study law, and received his Juris Doctorate from Baylor University in 1983.

Now a practicing attorney, Rick lives in Killeen with his wife, Paula. He's had a number of interests, including skydiving, cartooning, and running, but his most passionate interest is research into the Old West. His previous book, *The Train Robbing Bunch*, was a biography of Louisana bandit Eugene Bunch.

GOV. J. W. THROCKMORTON, Pres't.   S. J. ADAMS, Treasurer.
W. G. VEAL, Vice-President.   S. W. S. DUNCAN, Secretary.

OFFICE OF

TEXAS

Copper Mining & Manufacturing Co.

No. 411 ELM STREET.

Dallas, Texas, Dec 3ᵈ   1877

His Excellency R. B. Hubbard
        Gov. State of Texas
                Austin.
        Dear Governor.

                        Will you
please send me by first mail
a requisition for the body of
Mitch Cotton (colored) alias Bill Williams,
on The Gov. of Louisiana,
The Offence was the killing of
the Sheriff of LimeStone Co. some
five or six years ago. You will find
his name on the fugitive list —
Also please send me a commis-
as agent for the State to arrest
and take Charge of him, — I thin